4/12

D0938451

The Battle Over
Health Care

The Battle Over Health Care

What Obama's Reform Means for America's Future

Rosemary Gibson and
Janardan Prasad Singh

ROWMAN & LITTLEFIELD PUBLISHERS, INC.
Lanham • Boulder • New York • Toronto • Plymouth, UK

Published by Rowman & Littlefield Publishers, Inc.
A wholly owned subsidiary of The Rowman & Littlefield Publishing Group, Inc.
4501 Forbes Boulevard, Suite 200, Lanham, Maryland 20706
http://www.rowmanlittlefield.com

Estover Road, Plymouth PL6 7PY, United Kingdom

Distributed by National Book Network

British Library Cataloguing in Publication Information Available

Library of Congress Cataloging-in-Publication Data

Gibson, Rosemary, 1956-
  The battle over health care : what Obama's reform means for America's future /
Rosemary Gibson & Janardan Prasad Singh.
       p. ; cm.
  Includes bibliographical references and index.
  ISBN 978-1-4422-1449-1 (cloth : alk. paper) — ISBN 978-1-4422-1451-4 (electronic)
  I. Singh, Janardan Prasad, 1960- II. Title.
  [DNLM: 1. Health Care Reform—United States. 2. Delivery of Health Care—
economics—United States. 3. Delivery of Health Care—legislation & jurisprudence—
United States. 4. Health Policy—United States. 5. Insurance, Health—legislation &
jurisprudence—United States. 6. Politics—United States. WA 540 AA1]
  LC classification not assigned
  362.1'04250973—dc23   2011030065

∞™ The paper used in this publication meets the minimum requirements of
American National Standard for Information Sciences—Permanence of Paper
for Printed Library Materials, ANSI/NISO Z39.48-1992.

Printed in the United States of America

Contents

Acknowledgments   vii

Introduction: The Politics of Appeasement   1

Part 1: Deal Makers, Deal Breakers   7

1   Health Insurers: What Did They Get?   9

2   The Drug Deal of the Century   21

3   Hospitals and Doctors: Their Takeaway   29

4   Who Will Pay for Trillion-Dollar Health Care Reform?   43

**Part 2: How Health Care Reform Did Not Reform
     Health Care**   51

5   How the AMA Killed the Family Doctor   53

6   Why Hospitals Don't Stop Harming Patients   63

7   Hospitals: Do This, Not That   77

Part 3: How Health Care Caught the Wall Street Fever   89

8   Too Big to Fail Just Got Bigger   91

9   If Only They Were iPhones   109

Part 4: Until Debt Do Us Part   119

10   Good-bye Busboys   121

11   Promises Made, Promises Broken   131

12   Government by Default   139

Part 5: Privatize the Gains, Privatize the Losses   153

13   The Real Medical Malpractice Fix   155

14   Health Care Fraud: Follow the Money   169

15   Ten Steps to More Affordable Health Care   183

Notes   189

Index   217

About the Authors   223

Acknowledgments

$\mathscr{T}$his book is a culmination of more than thirty years of observing and working in health care at a public-policy think tank, a university, a state legislature, and a philanthropic foundation. It was shaped by the confluence of experiences of colleagues and friends who are doctors, nurses, economists, leaders of health care organizations, and policy makers who strive to make health care better. Most important of all, it was informed by the experiences of people who have been patients. They were our compass, our true north, as we waded through the health care reform legislation and analyzed its impact.

We extend our heartfelt appreciation to leaders around the country who are an integral part of the Consumers Union Safe Patient Project. They are an enormous inspiration to us and a constant reminder of what health care is really all about. We are thankful to colleagues at the American Board of Internal Medicine Foundation who have stimulated a critical dialogue among physician leaders about the wise use of health care resources. The foundation's work reinforces our belief that it is possible to have great health care in America and be good stewards of resources. We are indebted to Dr. Larry Jassie, who patiently reviewed the manuscript and provided immensely valuable insights. We especially want to thank Sarveshwari Singh, who helped us research information about the health care reform law.

We will always be grateful to Marcus Boggs at Rowman & Littlefield for valuing independent thought and writing that serves the public interest. Our thoroughly enjoyable conversations have made the preparation of this book a distinct pleasure. Suzanne Staszak-Silva provided wonderfully wise counsel as she kindly guided us along the way. Melissa McNitt was eminently gracious as the manuscript was transformed into a book.

Finally, we are grateful beyond words to the one who made the writing of this book and everything else possible.

Introduction: The Politics of Appeasement

$\mathcal{W}$e write this introduction as the battle over health care is being waged at a feverish pitch on Capitol Hill in Washington, DC. Members of Congress and President Barack Obama continue to grapple with how to cut federal spending and get the country's fiscal affairs on a sustainable path. Health care is at the crux of the debate. The promises made to the American people to ensure their health care security are beyond the capacity of the federal government to keep. This is not a Democrat or Republican stance. It's simple math, and it was true even before the landmark Patient Protection and Affordable Care Act was signed into law by President Obama on March 23, 2010.

As an unprecedented heat wave gripped the nation in 2011, politics reached a boiling point over raising the federal government's debt ceiling. Congress and the president acted to prevent the unthinkable: a default by the government on its debt. None of the sound and fury was enough to stop Standard & Poor's from reducing the country's credit rating, the same rating agency that failed to do its job and warn investors of the worthless mortgage-backed securities that triggered the Great Recession in 2008. The summer of discontent turned into a winter whose Cold War–like tensions have split Democrats and Republicans battling for control of the White House and Congress in the 2012 elections.

Health care reform was born in the middle of the Great Recession. Its future depends on the outcome of the 2012 elections, the US Supreme Court's stance on the constitutionality of the individual mandate, and the

1

court of public opinion. One thing is certain. The country's ability to pay its bills will determine the fate of health care reform for decades to come.

In this context, we examine the Patient Protection and Affordable Care Act, the most sweeping overhaul of the US health care system. Not since 1965, when Medicare was created, has the country witnessed such a profound shift in how Americans will receive and pay for health care.

It was a moment that was as historic as it was divisive. Since the time of President Franklin Roosevelt, American presidents have tried to protect people from the unexpected cost of illness. Health care debates have always been fraught with discord, and this time was no different. The law is heralded by supporters as a grand achievement. Opponents disdain it.

The law sought to narrow a chasm in American society into which millions of people have fallen. There is nothing worse than to have a serious illness and lie awake at night knowing that treatment is out of reach because it costs too much.

The law reins in unbridled health insurance companies whose egregious practices have become legendary. No longer will the sick forgo the medical care needed to thwart life-threatening disease for want of the ability to pay.

This book does not examine the political tangles of the debate. Nor does it chronicle the implementation of the law. We take a long-term view and ask what health care reform means for America's future. To answer this question, we look at health care not in its own silo but as part of the economic life of the nation.

In part 1, we begin by dissecting how the deals were made between the Obama administration and the health care industry. In a speech at George Mason University in Fairfax, Virginia, a few days before the vote on health care reform, President Obama asked the assembled crowd, "Are we going to let the special interests win once again? Or are we going to make this vote a victory for the American people?" We trace highlights of the deals with each of the key industry players—the health insurance companies, drug makers, hospitals, and doctors. We assess what was won and what was lost when the spoils were divided on the political battlefield where more than 4,500 lobbyists roamed Capitol Hill and about a billion dollars was spent to influence the legislation. The sweeping overhaul did not solve the root cause of the problem with America's health care: the unfettered power of the medical-industrial complex that has made health care unaffordable for the American people and its government. We describe the deal that Americans should have gotten but didn't. The Obama administration played the politics of appeasement, the path of least resistance. The same people who have made health care unaffordable, wasteful, and too often harmful were rewarded with an even larger canvas on which to paint Americans' health care future. In the end, with the stroke of a pen, health care reform merely shifts the risk of bankruptcy of individuals and families to the bankruptcy of the federal government.

In part 2, we chronicle how thirty-two million newly insured Americans will enter a health care system that isn't ready for them. Health care reform did more to reform health insurance than to reform the provision of health care. A single law cannot fix everything at once, and an urgent to-do list remains. We highlight top priorities for this list.

One of those priorities is to make health care safe. We estimate that in the decade ending in 2020, at least 2.25 million Americans will have lost their lives because of medical mistakes, hospital-acquired infections, overuse of cancer-causing CT scans, and surgeries that are unnecessary and inappropriate. The number of lives that will be lost is equivalent to the combined populations of North Dakota, Rhode Island, and Vermont, all gone because of a man-made disaster. Health care reform rewarded those who have failed to ensure the safety of Americans when they are sick and most vulnerable.

In part 3, we trace how the health care reform debate unfolded against the backdrop of the near collapse of the banking and financial system in 2008 and the Great Recession that followed. The political debate was cocooned from the economic reality unfolding around the country as millions of Americans lost their jobs, their health insurance, and their homes. The economic reality made health insurance coverage as urgent as ever.

We highlight uncanny similarities between the health care industry and the banking and finance industry. Both sectors have price bubbles, toxic assets, and the too-big-to-fail syndrome. We chronicle how health care has caught the same Wall Street fever that afflicted the banks. Just as the Wall Street mentality messed with peoples' wealth, we examine how it messes with peoples' health.

In part 4, we show how the country's economic security will be the dominant factor shaping Americans' health security in the years to come. Businesses will face even greater competition from China, which has evolved from sewing socks to making stealth bombers. The competition will be fierce and will determine the kinds of jobs, wages, and benefits that American workers will have. In fact, we predict that the rise of China could have a greater impact on employer-provided health insurance by 2020 than the reform law. We highlight the reasons that lead us to this conclusion.

Because health care spending is a major reason for the federal government's growing federal debt, we pose a tantalizing question. Will untamed health care spending be the spark that eventually triggers a government default and requires the federal government to seek a bailout from the International Monetary Fund? We raise this question not as idle speculation but as a very real and frightening possibility.

In part 5, we show how the health care industry has its own way of privatizing gains and socializing losses. The banking industry elevated this practice to an art form when it made enormous sums from fraudulent lending practices but turned to the taxpayers to bail it out when the house of cards crashed. The health care industry socializes many of its losses while making enormous private gains. If these losses were privatized, enough money exists in the health care system to provide health insurance for all.

No one has a crystal ball to predict the future. It will be shaped by the decisions made by millions of individuals, families, employers, drug and insurance company executives, Wall Street analysts and investors, hospitals, doctors, and nurses who will act in their own self-interests. Yet every system is designed to achieve the results it gets. An examination of the law and the economic and political context in which it unfolds can suggest the future state.

America has a unique way of dealing with thorny problems: it throws money at them. The country can't afford to do that anymore. There is a different path to take. We show how careful pruning of the enormous inefficiency and waste in health care *can* make reform financially sustainable and health care affordable. Howls of protest from moneyed interests will pierce the airwaves and blogosphere to frighten the American people into believing that their benefits will be taken away. The truth is that spending can be pruned responsibly so that not a single person who needs medical care is hurt. In fact, they will be better off. The alternative is crude cutting of federal spending that protects corporate health care interests at the expense of the public's interest. If this happens, the hard-working people of America who play by the rules will be hurt the most. Their health insurance coverage will become a mere shred of what they need to protect themselves from an out-of-control health care marketplace.

Amid the discord between Democrats and Republicans, another certainty prevails. The battle over health care will continue. Proponents of the health care reform law acknowledge its flaws and recognize that improving a complex system cannot happen quickly. Republicans want to keep the battle brewing because it suits their political interests to challenge President Obama's health care reform.

A battle waged without principle never yields victory. Abraham Lincoln once said, "America will never be destroyed from the outside. If we falter and lose our freedoms, it will be because we destroyed ourselves." We wrote this book because we do not want an endeavor as noble as the health and healing of human beings to be part of America's undoing.

We wrote this book for the American people. They are the only special interest we represent. We bring to light facts and perspectives that the media have not had the courage to report. We cut through the rhetoric and political correctness on both sides of the political aisle that have dominated the airwaves. Readers can gain a fresh perspective about what health care will look like in 2020 and beyond.

If you are concerned about your health and your health care, this book is for you. We hope it will help you come to your own conclusions about the changes that are occurring and what they mean for you.

For policy makers in federal and state governments, we hope you will gain a fresh and compelling perspective on the work that lies ahead to fix a broken system and ensure its viability for generations to come.

For doctors, nurses, and health care executives, we hope this book will help you see the bigger picture as you take care of patients, which is what health care is really all about.

Rosemary Gibson
Janardan Prasad Singh
Winter 2012

Part 1

DEAL MAKERS, DEAL BREAKERS

$\mathscr{A}$s the health care reform debate raged on talk radio, the Internet, and television and in town hall meetings around the country in 2009 and 2010, President Obama promised Americans that they could keep their health insurance. Republican opponents warned of government-run health care. For those who were busy in their daily lives going to work and taking care of their families, it was hard to make sense of health care reform and what it would mean.

That same year, the country was reeling from the near collapse of the financial system. On March 5, 2009, Obama held a White House forum to launch his reform effort that included members of Congress and representatives of the health care industry. The next day, the stock market tanked. The Dow Jones Industrial Average plummeted below 6500 points, and trillions of dollars of retirement savings disappeared. Fears swirled that the country was headed for another Great Depression.

A brutal truth had been exposed. Much of the nation's economic growth had been fueled by a housing market whose asset values were propped up by debt of Mount Everest proportions. As bailed-out banks took taxpayers' money and rewarded their top brass with bonuses, millions of Americans who had lost their jobs, their health insurance, and their homes wondered why they weren't being helped.

Against this backdrop, President Obama forged ahead and made health care reform his domestic priority. As Americans were losing health insurance because of the economy, the timing for legislation to provide coverage seemed auspicious. The president wanted a bill on his desk for his signature by the end of 2009. Three months late, after a roller-coaster ride, the deal was done, and he signed the Patient Protection and Affordable Care Act on March 23, 2010.

In the following chapters, we examine how the deals were made with the drug companies, health insurers, hospitals, and doctors. Without their support, a health care reform law would never have been enacted. Politics is give and take. What did they give and what did they take? In the end, did they really give? For Washington lobbyists representing the health care industry, reform had nothing to do with providing care for people who desperately need it. It was about money, lots of it, and how they could get it.

Martin Luther King Jr. once said, "Laws may not change the heart but they can restrain the heartless." He wasn't talking about the health insurers or drug companies, but his words may be apropos for the country's debate on health care reform. Time would tell.

• 1 •

Health Insurers: What Did They Get?

$\mathcal{O}$ne of the biggest achievements of the health care overhaul was a commitment from health insurance companies to stop their most offensive and inhumane practices that angered and frustrated millions of Americans. Why did they agree to stop? After all, they aren't charitable enterprises.

Insurance company abuses were chronicled at a June 16, 2009, congressional hearing chaired by Representative Henry Waxman, a Democrat from California. During the hearing of the Subcommittee on Oversight and Investigations of the House Energy and Commerce Committee, members of Congress heard testimony about how health insurance companies treated many of their policyholders.

The committee had requested information from fifty state insurance commissioners and three health insurance companies that offer individual health insurance policies: Assurant Health, WellPoint, and UnitedHealth Group. With 116,000 pages of documents and interviews with numerous policyholders who had had their coverage terminated or "rescinded" after they became sick, the committee let the world see a glimpse of the abuse.

An Illinois man diagnosed with lymphoma had his health insurance policy terminated because he failed to report a possible aneurysm and gallstones that his physician noted in his chart but did not discuss with him. The company denied him chemotherapy and a life-saving stem cell transplant. After direct intervention from the Illinois Attorney General's Office, his insurance was reinstated and he continued with treatment.

A Texas woman diagnosed with a lump in her breast had her health insurance cut off when the company investigated the patient's medical history and found that she did not disclose that she had been diagnosed previously with unrelated osteoporosis and bone density loss. The company rescinded her policy and refused to pay for medical care for the breast lump.

Americans are already benefiting from the law. Insurers agreed to stop denying coverage to children with preexisting medical conditions. People who are sick have no lifetime limits on benefits. Children can stay on their parents' family plan until age twenty-six. Insurance plans must offer preventive services such as mammograms and colonoscopies without charge. Women can go to obstetricians and gynecologists without a referral from another doctor.

Beginning in 2014, insurers agreed to stop canceling policies when policyholders become ill. They will stop denying insurance to adults with preexisting medical conditions and charging higher rates because of poor health.

Most Americans like these commonsense protections. Seventy-five percent of people say they favor the prohibition against insurance companies denying coverage because of preexisting medical conditions. Two-thirds favor allowing children up to age twenty-six to stay on their parents' policies, and most believe the elimination of lifetime caps on insurance coverage is a good idea.

As the health insurance companies agreed to these concessions, another story was playing out behind the scenes.

GOOD-BYE PUBLIC OPTION

One of the most controversial ideas in the health care reform debate was the public option. Here's how it was supposed to work. Uninsured Americans could choose a new public health insurance plan similar to Medicare. The public plan would be less expensive than private insurance because it would incur no marketing costs, profit margins, or high salaries that are characteristic of private insurance companies.

An outspoken proponent of the public option, former Vermont governor and physician Howard Dean, made the case for it this way: "I don't think we ought to dump $60 billion a year" onto the insurance industry because it would be pouring money into a broken system.

The idea was to give Americans a choice between a public option and private insurance. "If they think the private sector is great, they will stay in the private sector—if they like insurance that can be taken away if they get sick," said Dean. "Or you can try what everyone over sixty-five in this country has had. . . . [Medicare] can't be taken away; it can't be denied to you." With competition from a public option, the insurance companies would have to clean up their act and treat their customers better, he said.

The public option met with fierce resistance. John Boehner, who was House Minority Leader for the Republicans at the time, said the public option was "about as unpopular as a garlic milkshake." Conservatives decried it as a government takeover of health care.

In raucous town hall meetings during the August 2009 congressional recess, members of Congress heard from people opposed to health care reform. The insurance industry orchestrated a plan for thousands of its employees to voice opposition to the public option. Competition with a public option would be a death knell for the insurers because they could not compete successfully with a public plan. The firestorm compelled President Obama to step back from the public option, saying it was "just one sliver" of reform.

To smash up the whole health care reform process, insurance companies funneled millions of dollars to the US Chamber of Commerce for television ads blasting the bills in Congress. Aetna, Cigna, Humana, Kaiser Foundation Health Plans, UnitedHealth Group, and WellPoint reportedly chipped in to pay for the ads.

At the same time, Karen Ignagni, the chief lobbyist for the insurance industry trade group America's Health Insurance Plans (AHIP), wrote a letter published in the *Washington Post* saying, "Let me be clear and direct. Health plans continue to strongly support reform." Yes, they wanted reform, but it had to be on *their* terms.

To salvage a health care overhaul, President Obama unveiled a new plan in February 2010 that left out the public option. Instead, it included a requirement that everyone buy private health insurance, a flashpoint in the health care reform drama.

The idea of a mandate was not new. During the 2008 presidential campaign between Barack Obama and John McCain, Ignagni visited Obama's health advisors and proposed the idea. In return, the industry agreed to stop dropping coverage for people when they were sick and discriminating against those with preexisting medical conditions.

During the 2008 presidential campaign, Obama was not enamored with the idea of a mandate but warmed up to it later. He said, "When I ran in the Democratic primary, I was opposed to the mandate. . . . My theory was . . . people don't have health insurance . . . because they just can't afford it. So I was dragged kicking and screaming to the conclusion that I arrived at, which is that it makes sense to have everybody purchase insurance. . . . This is not a Democratic idea. There are number of Republicans . . . who have supported the idea of an individual mandate."

The health insurance industry saw the writing on the wall. A growing number of middle-class Americans and employers can no longer afford to buy health insurance because it is too expensive. The public option would accelerate the decline of private health insurance in America.

Insurers saw opportunity in health care reform to obtain more market share. They had their sights set on a never-ending federal stimulus that would bolster their bottom line in perpetuity.

THREE WISHES

The health insurance industry had staked out its position early in the 2008 presidential campaign when Barack Obama made health care reform a priority. After the November 2008 election, it issued a public statement with its "must-haves" in a reformed health care system. The industry sought to convince the White House and congressional leaders to subsidize people who purchased private health insurance. This strategy would halt the erosion in private insurance and expand the industry's customer base. It was a shrewd strategy.

According to the industry's script, insurers would agree to stop their most egregious practices. In return, they insisted that everyone be brought into the system and participate in obtaining coverage. The insurers signaled the individual mandate as a "must-have." They realized that many Americans would buy insurance only if they were forced to do so. "Achieving this objective will require specific attention to the mechanisms for making the mandate enforceable," they said in a public statement. In other words, the *health insurers* wanted the government to impose penalties to force people to buy their products.

Insurers were granted their first wish. The Obama administration included the individual mandate to buy private insurance in its February 2010 salvage plan along with penalties for failure to comply. The Republicans excoriated the individual mandate and its Democratic party supporters when, in fact, the mandate was a centerpiece of the health insurance industry's strategy.

The industry wanted more. Insurers proposed that the federal government help small businesses provide coverage for their employees. They wanted tax-code incentives or other types of assistance to encourage small businesses to offer or contribute to coverage. The insurers were specific. Small firms with lower-wage workers should receive taxpayer-funded subsidies.

The industry was granted this second wish. The White House plan included tax credits for small employers with lower-wage workers.

Finally, the industry scored the biggest win of them all. Insurance companies wanted American families who earn less than $88,000 a year to receive taxpayer subsidies to help them buy their products. The White House agreed to the federal subsidies for low- and moderate-income families.

With the stroke of a pen, the insurance industry gained sixteen million new customers beginning in 2014. Most of the new customers will qualify for federal subsidies that will shield them from the financial impact of the individual mandate.

In return, the health insurance industry agreed to stop its worst abuses: preventing sick people from buying insurance, increasing premiums for people who have the misfortune of being sick, charging higher premiums because of a policyholder's gender or occupation, and imposing lifetime and annual coverage caps on benefits. The health care overhaul identifies essential benefits that must be covered by insurance plans and requires a fair grievance and appeal process.

These concessions were a down payment made by health insurers on a very lucrative investment. The "mortgage" on this investment will be paid by Americans through premiums and taxpayer-funded subsidies that will balloon in years to come as health care costs continue to rise out of control.

For consumers, health care reform is like an adjustable-rate mortgage. It begins with attractive, low-cost introductory teasers—the new features that so many people favor such as no limits on lifetime benefits. Eventually, ballooning premiums will be too high for the federal government to subsidize at levels stipulated in the health care reform law.

In the end, the health care reform law richly rewarded health insurance companies in return for a commitment to change their practices. Will they really change?

THE INDIVIDUAL MANDATE: PRINCIPLE, POLITICS, AND POCKETBOOKS

The battle over health care continues. Opponents of the individual mandate want it to go away. For some, it is a matter of principle. For others, it is about politics. For those required to buy insurance, the mandate is a matter of their pocketbook.

Virginia was the first state to fire a shot in the battle over the mandate. In a preemptive strike in early March 2010 before Congress voted on the White House makeover plan, the Virginia House of Delegates voted eighty to seventeen in favor of a new law saying that no resident of the commonwealth should be required to obtain or maintain individual health insurance coverage.

The bill's sponsor, Republican Robert G. Marshall, quipped to a reporter, "Mobsters used to offer 'protection' to business owners, so when Congress says that if individuals don't become customers of businesses that contribute to them, to me that crosses the line. . . . For me, it is hard to distinguish what is going on in Washington, D.C., from criminal activity." Republican Governor Bob McDonnell signed the bill into law.

In special ballot initiatives during the midterm elections in November 2010, Arizona and Oklahoma residents voted against the individual mandate. Colorado voted in favor of it. These results came on the heels of a Missouri vote in August in which 70 percent of voters disapproved of the individual mandate.

In the fall of 2010, the battleground shifted to the federal district courts, where state governments, conservative stalwarts, businesses, and others filed separate legal challenges to the reform law, and many were about the individual mandate.

Five decisions were handed down by federal district courts from October 2010 through February 2011. They are proof that health care reform is as partisan as it can be.

Federal judges appointed by Democratic presidents upheld the individual mandate. US District Court Judge George Steeh in Michigan, appointed by President Bill Clinton, ruled that the individual mandate is constitutional. Steeh wrote in his opinion that it acknowledges the reality that most people will get sick someday and will need a means to pay for it.

> The health care market is unlike other markets. No one can guarantee his or her health, or ensure that he or she will never participate in the health care market. . . . The question is how participants in the health care market pay for medical expenses—through insurance, or through an attempt to pay out of pocket with a backstop of uncompensated care funded by third parties. This phenomenon of cost-shifting is what makes the health care market unique. . . . Plaintiffs are making an economic decision to try to pay for health care services later, out of pocket, rather than now through the purchase of insurance, collectively shifting billions of dollars, $43 billion in 2008, onto other market participants.

Shortly after Judge Steeh's ruling, a federal judge in Lynchburg, Virginia, also rejected a legal challenge to the mandate. US District Court Judge Norman Moon, another Clinton appointee, penned an opinion that resonated with a similar theme:

> I hold that there is a rational basis for Congress to conclude that individuals' decisions about how and when to pay for health care are activities that in the aggregate substantially affect the interstate health care market. . . . Nearly everyone will require health care services at some point in their lifetimes, and it is not always possible to predict when one will be afflicted by illness or injury and require care.

In February 2011, Judge Gladys Kessler of the US District Court in Washington, DC, dismissed a lawsuit against the individual mandate brought by three people who said that they did not intend to use medical services for the rest of their lives for religious reasons and two others who said they use holistic healing practices that health insurance does not cover. Judge Kessler rejected their arguments saying that Congress can regulate health insurance under the Constitution's commerce clause, and that individuals can pay the penalty prescribed in the law if they decide not to purchase insurance.

Two federal judges appointed by Republicans had their turn and ruled against the mandate. US District Court Judge Henry E. Hudson in Richmond, Virginia, was the first federal judge to strike down the individual mandate and rule that Congress exceeded its powers by requiring individuals to have health insurance or pay a penalty to the federal government. An appointee of President George W. Bush, Judge Hudson declared that the provision overstepped the bounds of authority granted in the Constitution: "Neither the Supreme Court nor any federal circuit court of appeals has extended Commerce Clause powers to compel an individual to involuntarily enter the stream of commerce by purchasing a commodity in the private market. . . . At its core, the dispute is not simply about regulating the business of insurance—or crafting a scheme of universal health insurance coverage—it's about an individual's right to choose to participate."

Judge Hudson also disagreed with the Obama Administration's argument that federal tax law allows the government to require individuals to pay a penalty if they fail to purchase insurance, stating that the penalty is not intended to raise revenue.

US District Court Judge Roger Vinson from Pensacola, Florida, who was appointed to the bench by President Ronald Reagan, said that if Americans can be forced to have health insurance because everyone needs health care, that logic can be used to force people to buy groceries or clothes.

"A lot of people, myself included for years, have no health insurance," Judge Vinson said during the hearing on the case that was brought by twenty-six states and other challengers. Vinson recalled his years as a law student when he paid cash to the doctor who delivered his first child. "It amounted to about $100 a pound," he said, laughing.

In his ruling, Vinson wrote that Congress exceeded the bounds of its authority with the requirement to buy insurance. Because the individual mandate is unconstitutional, and not severable, the entire act must be declared void, Vinson said.

In June 2011, a three-judge panel of the US Court of Appeals in Cincinnati ruled that the individual mandate is constitutional. Justice Jeffrey Sutton, an appointee of President George W. Bush and a former law clerk for conservative US Supreme Court Justice Antonin Scalia, joined a Democrat-appointed judge on the ruling. Sutton was the first Republican-nominated judge in the country to rule in support of the law.

The dispute over the mandate is headed for the US Supreme Court, where partisan politics will play out just as they have done in lower court decisions. Five of the justices were appointed by Republicans and four by Democrats.

In the battle between George W. Bush and Al Gore in the 2000 presidential election, a 5–4 Supreme Court vote along partisan lines determined who would become president. Another pivotal swing vote will likely determine whether Americans can be required by their government to buy health insurance.

The swing voter to watch is Justice Anthony Kennedy. His stance has been pivotal in contentious cases. Appointed by President Ronald Reagan, he has supported conservative majorities but has sided with liberal justices on cases involving free speech and religious freedom.

If the Supreme Court votes against the mandate, supporters are exploring alternatives. One idea is to use carrots rather than sticks to encourage people to buy insurance, an approach that Medicare uses. When Americans become sixty-five and postpone signing up and paying for Medicare's physician and drug coverage, but decide to buy it a few years later, they pay a 10 percent penalty for each year they waited.

When all is said and done, it is ironic that the future of health care reform could be decided on the interpretation of a clause in the Constitution about interstate commerce. Healing is rooted in science and medicine. Its purpose is to ameliorate suffering from disease and ill health. Healing is not derived from commerce. Yet that is what health care in America has become, so far removed from the science and art it was meant to be.

STILL AT THE MERCY OF HEALTH INSURERS

Less than six months after the ink was dry on the reform law, insurers announced premium rate hikes as high as 20 percent for 2011. In letters to their policyholders, some companies blamed the increases on the new law.

The Obama administration fired back with a letter from Secretary of the US Department of Health and Human Services Kathleen Sebelius to Karen Ignagni, the president of the insurers' lobbying group. In an unusually sharp letter, Secretary Sebelius said that insurance companies could not blame their high rate increases on the new health care overhaul and that, at most, 1 to 2 percent of any increase could be attributed to it.

"There will be zero tolerance for this type of misinformation and unjustified rate increases," she wrote. "Simply stated, we will not stand idly by as insurers blame their premium hikes and increased profits on the requirement that they provide consumers with basic protections."

The Obama administration came out forcefully against proposed premium hikes in California, Connecticut, Maine, and Massachusetts, among other states. Secretary Sebelius said the administration will keep track of insurers whose premium increases are unreasonably high.

Under the reform law, the federal government cannot stop rate hikes. It can only require insurers to submit justifications for unreasonable rate hikes before they ratchet up their rates.

The administration pushed the limits on the federal government's authority. It doesn't have the legal power to regulate insurance. That authority resides with the states. Merely disclosing proposed premium increases will have little, if any, impact on the cost that Americans will pay.

The states are now on the front lines of fighting against health insurance premium increases. Many are not well equipped. The United States is a patchwork nation in health insurance regulation, and states have varying degrees of consumer protections. Many states don't have the legal authority to reject premium increases.

Less than a year after health care reform was signed into law, Blue Shield of California proposed a 59 percent rate increase for individual policy holders; in New York, WellPoint proposed an increase of 28 percent; in Iowa, Wellmark proposed an 18 percent increase.

The federal government has been helping states that lack the resources or authority to review proposed rate increases that are unreasonable. The health care law includes $250 million in grants for states, or an average of $5 million each, to strengthen their ability to review premium hikes.

Nonetheless, when Secretary Sebelius was asked what Americans should do if they are facing astronomical rate hikes, she replied, "They should contact the governor of their state and state legislature demanding that those laws be changed."

The Obama administration is sending a clear message to Americans. You must buy health insurance, but you are still at the mercy of the insurance companies.

It is understandable if Americans thought that health care reform fixed the problem of exorbitant rate hikes. The public vilification of health insurance companies during the reform debate was great political theater. Then House speaker Nancy Pelosi said that one of the criteria for Democrats in a health care overhaul was making health insurance affordable and companies accountable. Yet the federal government lacks the power to make insurance affordable.

The Obama administration defines an "unreasonable" rate increase as 10 percent or more. Most Americans do not receive a 10 percent raise every year in their paychecks. Americans will have to dig deeper into their pocketbooks every year to pay for health care.

The reform law has a circuit breaker provision—the Independent Payment Advisory Board—that kicks in when Medicare spending increases are too high, but nothing in the law clamps down on private health insurance premiums.

Less than a year after the reform law was enacted, Senator Dianne Feinstein, a Democrat from California, and Representative Jan Schakowsky, a Democrat from Illinois, introduced the Health Insurance Rate Authority Act that would give the federal government authority over health insurance premium increases. It could modify or block health insurance rates deemed excessive, unjustified, or unfairly discriminatory in states whose insurance commissioners don't have the authority or don't exercise it. The chances are nonexistent that the legislation will be enacted because of the power of the health insurance lobby.

At a J.P. Morgan Health Care Conference in San Francisco in 2011, large health insurers were upbeat when they presented their plans to investors about expanding their businesses. Aetna is one company that expects to grow its individual insurance market in anticipation of the boom in 2014 when the mandate starts.

"We have major efforts underway to strategize on how to take advantage of those opportunities," said Joseph M. Zubretsky, Aetna's chief financial officer in a presentation to health investors. "We're clearly understanding the risks . . . but with millions coming on to the health exchanges, one needs to not only balance risk but really understand the opportunity for growth that exists in this market place." The insurers are also angling for contracts with states to manage their Medicaid plans, which will enroll sixteen million more people beginning in 2014.

In a speech at George Mason University before the final vote on health care reform in 2010, Obama asked an assembled crowd, "Do we want to accept a system that works better for the insurance companies than the American people?"

For Americans, the answer is a resounding no. But will private health insurance work better for Americans than for the insurance companies? With no way to control health care costs, private health insurance as we know it today is not sustainable. The benefits will inevitably erode if premiums are to have a modicum of affordability.

Health insurers cannot bear all the blame for out-of-control health care costs. Controlling premium increases is like trying to cap a volcano whose molten lava continues to erupt from deep within the earth's core. Drug companies, device manufacturers, hospitals, and doctors exert powerful pressure to keep it flowing.

• 2 •

The Drug Deal of the Century

The drug industry was expecting the worst. Its lobbying arm, the Pharmaceutical Research and Manufacturers of America (PhRMA), was assembling a war chest and preparing for a fight. It geared up for a multimillion-dollar public-relations campaign to counter a push by the new Obama administration to control prescription drug prices in its health care reform plan.

On the presidential campaign trail in Newport News, Virginia, on October 4, 2008, Obama gave the drug makers fair warning. "First, we'll take on the drug . . . companies and hold them accountable for the prices they charge and the harm they cause. . . . And then we'll tell the pharmaceutical companies, 'Thanks but no thanks for overpriced drugs'. Drugs that cost twice as much here as they do in Europe and Canada and Mexico. We'll let Medicare negotiate for lower prices. We'll stop drug companies from blocking generic drugs that are just as effective and far less expensive. We'll allow the safe re-importation of low-cost drugs from countries like Canada."

At another campaign stop, Obama stirred the crowd. "The pharmaceutical industry wrote into the (Medicare) prescription drug law that Medicare couldn't negotiate with the drug industry," he said, referring to a provision that the drug companies lobbied to include in the 2003 law that established prescription drug coverage in the Medicare program. "That's an example of the same old game playing in Washington. You know I don't want to learn how to play the game better; I want to put an end to the game playing."

Eight months later when Obama was in the White House, he re-
neged on his campaign promises. In a White House–sanctioned deal,
drug companies agreed to give $80 billion in discounts over ten years on
the drugs they sell to people covered by Medicare. This deal was good
only for the drug companies. By offering discounts on their products, the
drug companies can still raise prices and negate the impact of a discount
on their revenue.

Consider a company that offers a 10 percent discount on a drug
that costs $100. A Medicare beneficiary will pay $90. If the drug maker
increases the price to $110, the beneficiary will pay $99. Customers may
think they are getting a discount when, in fact, they are paying more.

The industry had more reason to cheer. The White House agreed
to keep intact the law that prevents Medicare from negotiating drug
prices. Also the White House agreed to continue to prohibit Americans
from buying lower-cost imported drugs from trustworthy sources such as
Canada. The public will still pay the highest prices for prescription drugs
in the world.

The White House made these concessions in return for obtaining the
drug companies' support for health care reform. The drug industry was so
enthusiastic about the deal that it agreed to pay for a $150 million advertis-
ing campaign to garner public support for the health care overhaul.

A portion of the money for the ad campaign went to the Chicago-
based firm AKPD Message and Media, whose founder was David Axelrod,
senior advisor to President Obama when the White House finalized the
deal with the industry, according to Bloomberg News. The AKPD website
features prominently a quote from the *National Journal*, a weekly magazine
that reports on the political climate: "Of those who deserve a place in history for helping Barack Obama win the presidency, atop the list is AKPD
Message and Media."

Axelrod sold his interest in the firm when he joined the Obama administration. His former business associates at the firm reaped substantial
profits from the insider deal for the ad campaign. Axelrod's son worked at
the firm, which reportedly owed the senior Axelrod $2 million in sever-
ance that had to be paid out beginning December 31, 2009.

The drug industry's chief lobbyist was Billy Tauzin, then CEO of the
drug lobby group PhRMA. He gushed in praise of health care reform.

"This plan . . . to better insure Americans for the products we make . . . this should be an optimistic message."

After the deal was made in June 2009, Tauzin forced the White House to publicly acknowledge it. He said about the White House, "We were assured: 'We need somebody to come in first. If you come in first, you will have a rock-solid deal.'" The drug industry was the first and it got a very good deal.

A terse email from Jim Messina, a White House deputy chief of staff at the time, sheepishly acknowledged the deal, the *New York Times* reported. The deal sent a signal that the White House was willing to give lucrative favors to the health care industry in return for support of the president's gamble to reform health care.

The Obama White House had a chance to redeem itself later that year in December 2009 when Senator Byron Dorgan, a Democrat from North Dakota, introduced an amendment to the reform bill calling for the importation of cheaper drugs.

"U.S. consumers are charged the highest prices in the world for FDA-approved prescription drugs, and that's just not fair," Dorgan said. The average prices for patented drugs in other industrialized countries are 35 percent to 55 percent lower than in the United States, according to the nonpartisan Congressional Budget Office.

Margaret Hamburg, the Obama administration's commissioner for the Food and Drug Administration, quashed the idea, saying that importing cheaper prescription drugs could endanger the US medicine supply, a retort that echoes the drug industry's position.

Senator Dorgan excoriated the FDA, saying it was "completely bogus" and "I'm not surprised. I expected this." While in the Senate, Obama had cosponsored Dorgan's drug importation bill but shunned the idea this time.

THE DRUG LORDS

A chief deal maker for the drug companies was the CEO of Pfizer at the time, Jeff Kindler. According to White House visitor logs, he made multiple visits to secure the arrangement. In return for his hard work, Pfizer's board rewarded him with a 13 percent salary increase that boosted his annual compensation to almost $15 million. The company's proxy statement justified the raise:

> During 2009, Mr. Kindler was actively involved, through both Pfizer and external organizations, in developing and advancing U.S. and global public policies that serve the overall interests of our Company and our shareholders. . . . These efforts included constructive participation in the U.S. legislative process to advance Pfizer's goals. . . . Also, through both Pfizer and external organizations, he has sought to ensure the availability of safe medicines by opposing legislation that would allow for importation of prescription drugs.

While the White House was cutting the deal with the drug makers, the industry had reached a milestone. According to the consumer watchdog group Public Citizen, it earned the distinction of being the largest defrauder of the federal government under the federal False Claims Act.

"Step aside, defense industry, there's a new defrauder in town," said Public Citizen when it released its report analyzing federal prosecutions of drug companies. In 2009 the companies paid $4.4 billion in criminal and civil files, a 300 percent increase from the prior year.

The biggest culprit that year was Pfizer. In September 2009 Pfizer pleaded guilty to felony violations involving a subsidiary's drug, Bextra. The drug was used for arthritis, but the company marketed it for uses not approved by the FDA.

A federal judge in Boston imposed a $1.3 billion fine, one of the *largest* criminal fines imposed in the United States for any matter. The company also agreed to pay another $1 billion to settle civil allegations that it fraudulently promoted and marketed Bextra and other drugs and paid doctors kickbacks to induce them to prescribe them.

"Pfizer violated the law over an extensive time period," said Mike Loucks, acting US attorney for Massachusetts. "The size and seriousness of this resolution . . . reflect the seriousness and scope of Pfizer's crimes," he said.

Federal prosecutors had especially harsh words for Pfizer because the company is a serial offender. In 2004 federal investigators prosecuted a subsidiary that Pfizer had acquired, Warner-Lambert, for marketing an epilepsy drug, Neurontin, for unapproved uses.

"When Pfizer was in our office negotiating and resolving the allegations of criminal conduct by its then-newly acquired subsidiary, Warner-Lambert, Pfizer was itself . . . violating those very same laws," with Bextra, prosecutors said. "They've repeatedly marketed drugs for things they knew they couldn't demonstrate efficacy for. That's clearly criminal. . . . Today's enormous fine demonstrates that such blatant and continued disregard of the law will not be tolerated."

Under pressure from the FDA, Pfizer had withdrawn Bextra from the market because it increased the risk of heart attacks, stroke, internal bleeding, and death. It was also associated with a particularly awful life-threatening skin disease called toxic epidermal necrolysis that causes purple, bloody-looking lesions to form on the skin on the head, neck, and chest. When they begin to blister, the skin detaches from the other layers of skin underneath and eventually the entire top layer of the skin dies. Up to 40 percent of the people who have this disease die from it.

If the White House deal with the drug makers was the first cornerstone of health care reform, it was the first step in the wrong direction.

DISMANTLING THE LAW

As the months dragged on during the reform debate, drug company executives began to question Billy Tauzin's deal making with the White House. Health care reform had stalled after Democrats lost the Massachusetts Senate seat once filled by liberal lion Senator Ted Kennedy, who had died from brain cancer. In an upset win that stunned the political elite, Scott Brown, a little-known Republican state legislator, overtook Massachusetts State Attorney General Martha Coakley, who had been poised to carry the Democratic mantle.

Brown won the election held on January 19, 2010, by campaigning against federal health care reform. His election nixed the Democrats' sixty-seat filibuster-proof majority in the Senate and the chances for passage of a bill. Momentum for getting a bill through Congress screeched to a halt.

The early drug deal lost its luster. Speculation swirled that company executives thought the wheeling and dealing Tauzin, who was paid $2 million a year to represent the industry, had given away too much. Tauzin resigned in February 2010. In the end, the drug companies endorsed the reform legislation but had their sights set on killing a key provision after the dust had settled.

The law establishes an Independent Payment Advisory Board (IPAB), the only part of the health care reform overhaul to rein in Medicare spending. It is designed like a circuit breaker. When Medicare's costs exceed a certain threshold tied to the rate of inflation, it triggers the board into action.

A fifteen-member independent board appointed by the president and confirmed by the Senate will recommend ways to keep spending in check. It cannot change Medicare benefits, premiums, or eligibility for the program. Congress must accept the panel's recommendations in their entirety or vote to approve a comparable set of changes with a similar level of savings. If Congress does not act, the recommendations are implemented automatically.

The board is similar in concept to the successful Defense Base Closure and Realignment Commission created by Congress in 1990 as a politically palatable way to close excess military installations and reduce unnecessary spending. Because a military base closure entails the loss of millions of dollars in federal money to the home district of a member of Congress, base closure decisions are politically difficult. The commission depoliticized the process.

The Independent Payment Advisory Board is one of the most pivotal features of the health care reform legislation. The projected growth in Medicare spending is expected to outpace the federal government's financial capacity to pay for it. Without changes in the program, Medicare is financially unsustainable. By making smaller changes now, much deeper cuts in the program's benefits can be avoided in years to come.

The health care industry portrays the Independent Payment Advisory Board as "big government" taking care away from older Americans. They decry giving decision-making power to unelected experts. Yet both Democrats and Republicans have proven to be incapable of making hard choices to ensure Medicare's solvency for the baby boomers and future generations. Congress is surrounded by legions of health care industry lobbyists advocating for their self-interest, not the interest of older Americans and taxpayers.

Drug companies vehemently oppose the board because it could clamp down on drug prices. Eli Lilly has been developing a strategy to repeal the provision in concert with the drug lobby group PhRMA.

Eli Lilly writes on its blog, "We think that the IPAB provision should be repealed. Should we have unelected, unaccountable bureaucrats making health care decisions rather than you and your physician?"

In fact, Eli Lilly's marketing and sales staff, not physicians, have made decisions about the drugs that people are given. Here is one example.

In January 2009, while the drug companies were planning their strategy for health care reform, the US Department of Justice prosecuted Eli Lilly for illegally marketing its drug Zyprexa for unapproved uses. The drug had been approved to treat schizophrenia. To increase sales, Eli Lilly told doctors that it can be used to sedate people with Alzheimer's disease in nursing homes. The drug provided no benefit yet exposed people to great risks from weight gain, diabetes, blindness, and other serious side effects. Despite warnings from the FDA to stop this unapproved use, the company trained its sales forces to violate the law as it continued its brash marketing campaign. The promotion of drugs for unapproved uses "is a serious crime because it undermines the FDA's role in protecting the American public," said the Justice Department.

Eli Lilly heavily marketed the drug because the patent on Prozac, its antidepressant, was expiring and cheaper generics would appear on the market. The company prepared for what it called "Year X," the year when it would lose the patent and revenue would decline. To keep its revenue growing and stock price increasing, the company opened up new target markets for Zyprexa. A brand manager pumped up the company's marketing and sales team with the following message obtained by Department of Justice investigators from internal company documents:

> Dollars pay the bills and boost the stock price, so let's look at $ growth. Again, we are redefining the market. . . . Look at how that Zyprexa sales line jumps. . . . This is Year X for Eli Lilly . . . this trend says we won't just hit our $60 million plan—it says we've got a great shot at exceeding our stretch goal of $100 million in incremental sales. $100 million incremental from this group isn't a nice-to-have; it's a must-have. We need to OWN this target, because the [US] affiliate needs our help. Do I have your commitment on this? I personally challenge each of you [to] drive toward a goal that will help turn Year X into Year X-ceptional.

Later, the product team laid out the stakes for Zyprexa sales, "The Company is betting the farm on Zyprexa. . . . The ability of Eli Lilly to remain independent and emerge as the fastest growing pharma company of the decade depends solely on our ability to achieve world class commercialization of Zyprexa. If we succeed, Zyprexa will be the most successful pharmaceutical product ever . . . we will have made history."

Eli Lilly did make history. In January 2009 the federal government imposed the largest drug company fine ever, $515 million, until this distinction was ceded to Pfizer eight months later. It also paid up to $800 million in a civil settlement.

The company's mission statement says, "We promise to operate our business with absolute integrity and earn the trust of all, set the highest standards for our performance and for the performance of our products, and demonstrate caring and respect for all those who share in our mission and are touched by our work."

The Nobel Prize winner in economics Joseph Stiglitz says that market capitalism works when a company makes money by providing a product or service that is useful to people. Everyone benefits when the market works. The market fails when companies make money by jeopardizing safety and harming the public.

Health care reform architects had a unique moment to make the market work better. They missed the chance to use the enormous leverage of thirty-two million new customers they were giving to the drug companies to hold them accountable to their own standards. That opportunity will never come again.

· 3 ·

Hospitals and Doctors: Their Takeaway

$\mathcal{T}$he hospital industry lined up for its own deal with the White House. As with all the other big players, it received more than it gave.

Hospitals were outspoken critics of the public option and lobbied successfully, along with the insurance companies, for its demise. They opposed it because public programs such as Medicare and Medicaid pay hospitals less than private insurers for the same services.

Hospitals will benefit from thirty-two million new paying customers—sixteen million with private insurance and another sixteen million with Medicaid. They will benefit, too, when gaps in insurance coverage will be plugged with prohibitions against the cancellation of insurance and coverage exclusions. The industry is skittish about whether the penalties are strong enough to enforce the individual mandate.

The newly insured who become patients in a hospital will be better off because they will no longer bear the stigma of being a "charity" case or have a lien placed on their property for unpaid hospital bills. Hospitals with a sincere commitment to caring for people without insurance will have less of a struggle to make ends meet.

Vice President Joe Biden announced the deal with the hospitals saying, "Rising costs are crushing us." Hospitals have acknowledged that savings can be achieved by improving efficiencies and realigning incentives, he said, and the deal represents "real savings in federal health care spending."

Hospital lobbyists agreed to $155 billion in reductions in Medicare payments over ten years. This was a better deal than the $228 billion that the Obama administration had been planning to pare back.

When pressed on the need to reduce health care spending further, the hospital industry was noncommittal. Richard Umbdenstock, the CEO of the American Hospital Association, the chief lobby group for the hospitals, said, "I think all stakeholders have to examine what they can do now. So, very definitely, hospitals already are working hard at improving quality and the related costs. That's been going on now for several years and we want to see that not only continue but pick up in pace."

The most important concession that hospitals won was an exemption from the scrutiny of the Independent Payment Advisory Board. Hospitals are concerned that the law removes Congress from the decision-making process. They say it "threatens the long-time, open and important dialogue between hospitals and their elected officials."

This dialogue and the campaign contributions that go with it are the reason that hospitals have received generous amounts of money from the Medicare program for decades. Members of Congress don't want to disappoint hospitals in their districts, and this time was no different.

Senators Jay Rockefeller, a Democrat from West Virginia, Joseph Lieberman, an Independent from Connecticut, and Sheldon Whitehouse, a Democrat from Rhode Island, tried to eliminate the hospital exemption from oversight by the Independent Payment Advisory Board. They said that no one provider group should "be given special treatment." In vehement protest against the hospital carve-out, Rockefeller spoke on the floor of the Senate:

> I am adamantly opposed to the carve-out for hospitals and other providers as it weaves special interest treatment into the very fabric of a Board created to remove it. . . . It is time to take the special interests out of the process and create an independent, politically-insulated entity whose sole job is to protect Medicare's long-term quality and solvency.

The amendment gained no traction. The White House caved in to pressure from the hospitals in return for their support for the health care reform law. Until 2020, hospitals are exempt from scrutiny of the payment advisory board.

Still, hospitals are trying to postpone the day of financial reckoning. In October 2010, seven months after the reform law was enacted, the American Hospital Association announced its support for repeal of the advisory board. Hospitals want to keep members of Congress in the loop because they hold the keys to the federal treasury.

Charles "Chip" Kahn III, the president of the Federation of American Hospitals, the group that represents more than a thousand for-profit hospitals, had praise for the health care reform deal. He helped defeat President Clinton's plan to reform health care in 1993. This time, the terms of reform were too lucrative for hospitals to turn down. He said, "We support health care reform because we think it will be helpful for hospitals." Indeed, it will.

THE DIVIDED DOCTORS

Unlike the insurance companies, drug makers, and hospitals, the doctors were noticeably split in their position on health care reform. The American Medical Association (AMA) supported the legislation. Its president, J. James Rohack, acknowledged the bill was imperfect but said, "We cannot let the perfect be the enemy of the good."

The chief selling point for the AMA was health insurance coverage for the uninsured. The AMA's support for the overhaul was a departure from its habitually negative stance on major health care legislation considered by Congress. It opposed Medicare in 1965.

The AMA's ambivalence was clear when Rohack said at the press conference announcing the organization's support, "There's an old Texas saying [that] if you're going to have to swallow a bullfrog, the longer you look at it, the bigger it becomes. It's a pretty big bullfrog right now."

The AMA feared that the Independent Payment Advisory Board would cut the payments that doctors receive from Medicare. The AMA did not favor the board but supported reform anyway with the intent to eventually advocate for repealing it. Another chief complaint was that the legislation did not include provisions to deter patients from suing doctors for medical malpractice.

Deep divisions within the medical profession prevented it from speaking with a single voice. The divisions were along ideological lines drawn by more conservative physicians who broke ranks with the AMA. State medical societies and other medical groups representing nearly 100,000 doctors opposed what they believed was government-run health care. Medical societies in Alabama, Delaware, Florida, Georgia, Kansas, New Jersey, Oklahoma, South Carolina, Tennessee, and Texas were among the vocal opponents.

A schism separated primary care physicians, who tended to support the law, and certain specialist physicians, who did not. The rivalry between the two groups is not new and reflects wounds that the medical profession has inflicted upon itself. Primary care doctors have been poorly paid compared to the more powerful and highly paid specialists, who want to maintain the status quo.

The law recognizes the shortage of primary care doctors and provides a 10 percent increase in payment to them for caring for Medicare patients in underserved areas. It also increases payment when they provide care to people covered by Medicaid. Medical students will have their education loans paid if they become primary care doctors and work in underserved communities.

The American College of Surgeons opposed health care reform measures. In a letter to Representative Nancy Pelosi, then Speaker of the House, it highlighted sore points, including the payment advisory board and the failure to reform medical malpractice. It was disappointed that the reform measure did not fix a long-standing problem with how Medicare pays surgeons and other doctors.

Since the law was enacted, state medical societies have expressed their displeasure with the AMA, and some doctors have stopped paying their AMA dues. Splinter groups formed to protest against the AMA's stance. The National Doctors Tea Party and Physicians Against Obamacare characterize doctors as despondent about health care reform. They say it strips doctors of their once elevated and cherished position at the top of the health care system. These divisions among the doctors weakened their stance on Capitol Hill and limited their gains from health care reform.

The health care reform law was not the end of negotiations with doctors. Because of a long-standing provision in federal law, Medicare's reimbursement to doctors would have declined dramatically in 2010, the same year that the reform law was enacted. Architects of the reform legislation deliberately left out a $208 billion "doctor fix" for Medicare reimbursement. It would be so costly that Democrats could not claim that the health care overhaul would reduce the deficit.

Nine months after the reform law was enacted, Congress passed a one-year temporary patch that prevented a large drop in Medicare payments to doctors. A short-term solution was implemented because a long-term fix would cost the federal government so much money and no one knows how to pay for it.

WHEN THE PRICE IS RIGHT

Why did the hospitals, drug industry, and insurance companies receive lucrative deals? The White House was determined to have a reform bill. Health care was the president's signature domestic issue. A deal, any deal, was better than nothing. Industry lobbyists took advantage of the opportunity. They had their price and the White House was willing to pay it.

The backroom deals disappointed progressive Democrats, who thought Obama would not cave in to lobbyists' demands. Journalist Bill Moyers explained the White House surrender to the industry on *Real Time with Bill Maher*: "The Democratic Party has become like the Republican Party, deeply influenced by corporate money. I think Rahm Emanuel, who is a clever politician, understands that the money for Obama's re-election will come from the health care industry, from the drug industry, from Wall Street. And so he's a corporate Democrat who is determined that there won't be something in this legislation that will turn off these interests." Emanuel was the White House chief of staff during the health care reform debate.

In the 2008 presidential race, the health care industry contributed nearly $20 million to Barack Obama's campaign, and it sought a return on its investment. By buying elected officials, too-big-to-fail health care special interests had politicians of all persuasions doing their bidding.

In a more measured way, former senator Tom Daschle explained the give-and-take among lawmakers and special interests to garner support for health care reform: "Lawmakers had to find a way to do that without angering the stakeholders who would have had the most to lose." Daschle acknowledged that helping people get insurance coverage is a popular thing for elected officials to do. But bringing down costs is the least popular for the special interests because they will lose money. Lower costs would be wildly popular among Americans, who would prefer to keep more of their money for themselves. They are the real stakeholders in a democracy and have the most to lose when special interests prevail.

A PERENNIAL FEDERAL STIMULUS

There was plenty of room to cut a deal that was better for America. About 30 percent of the $2.5 trillion spent on health care in 2009, or $760 billion, was spent on things that did not help people become healthier, according to an estimate by the Institute of Medicine, an arm of the National Academy of Sciences. The money comes directly from Americans' paychecks in the form of taxes, premiums, and out-of-pocket payments. The excessive costs occur because of unnecessary tests and surgeries, prices that are too high, inefficiency in how care is provided, failure to prevent disease, excessive administrative costs, and fraud.

How can so much money be spent without contributing to the health of the nation? The answer lies at the heart of why health care is unaffordable.

It has been said that every system is designed to achieve the results it gets. Health care in the Unites States is unaffordable because it is designed to be that way. Wall Street analysts and investors demand that for-profit insurance companies, drug and device manufacturers, hospitals, and every other for-profit health care business achieve constant growth in earnings and share price. Companies' survival depends on satisfying an unforgiving marketplace even if it means that earnings accrue from selling products and services that add no value to Americans' health or cause more harm than good.

The excess spending is equivalent to an annual financial stimulus that props up companies' profitability. In fact, the amount of waste is almost the same amount as the $787 billion American Recovery and Reinvestment Act passed by Congress in February 2009 to jump-start the economy. The country cannot afford an annual fiscal stimulus that pays for waste and inefficiency.

Health care company lobbyists came to Washington during the reform debate to take even more, not to give, and they will be taking for a very long time as trillions more dollars will be transferred from the bank accounts of Americans to the balance sheets of health care businesses for decades to come. When all major players are programmed to be takers, health care will always be unaffordable.

The health care reform law is called the Patient Protection and Affordable Care Act, but the truth is that health care will not be more affordable. It will only seem more affordable to millions of Americans because taxpayer money will soften the impact of costly private health insurance premiums with subsidies and will pay for Medicaid for millions more people.

President Ronald Reagan said in his first inaugural address that "government is not the solution to our problem; government is the problem." In health care reform, the truth is more complicated. Collusion between government and the drug companies, device manufacturers, insurers, and hospitals *is* the problem.

It is an age-old phenomenon. Throughout history, private-sector interests have been among the principal architects of public policy for their own benefit. Adam Smith, the Scotsman who wrote the 1776 classic book on economy more than two hundred years ago, *The Wealth of Nations*, warned against the collusion of companies that manipulate government policy for their benefit at the expense of the public. In the present-day collusion, members of Congress and the president conspire with the industry to obtain excessive amounts of public money.

In contrast, good government creates conditions in which business and the economy operate efficiently. An efficient economy allocates public and private resources to achieve the maximum benefit to society. Health care reform perpetuates deep inefficiencies and massive misallocation of money. And in a competitive global economy, the United States doesn't have money to waste.

HEALTH CARE CEO COMPENSATION: THE HIGHEST OF THEM ALL

Executives of health care companies and nonprofit providers of medical care are paid to maximize their organizations' revenues. In other words, they are paid to make sure that health care spending continues to increase. They are succeeding, and they are rewarded handsomely for it.

When the health care overhaul was passed, the *Wall Street Journal*'s chief executive officer compensation survey found that health care company chief executives had the highest median compensation of any industry. In fact, their compensation was higher than the reviled banking and financial company CEOs who pillaged America's families during the mortgage and housing debacle.

In 2010, the year that the reform was signed into law, the roster of the top ten highest paid CEOs in the United States included CEOs of three health care firms: Thermo Fisher Scientific, which produces diagnostic testing products ($33 million); Boston Scientific, a medical device maker ($32 million); and McKesson, which provides a range of services to hospitals and other health care providers ($24.5 million).

Among health insurers, the CEO of Unitedhealth Group had $106 million in total compensation in fiscal year 2009, including stock option exercises totaling $98.6 million.

The compensation for chief executives of for-profit hospitals can be enormous. In 2010 the CEO of Community Health Systems, which owns more than one hundred hospitals, had the highest compensation, $20.8 million, of any hospital or hospital system executive in the country, according to Modern Healthcare's annual compensation survey of hospital executives.

Nonprofit, tax-exempt hospitals can be among the most aggressive billion-dollar enterprises in the country disguised as charitable organizations. They are not immune to paying their CEOs enormous compensation. The CEO of University Health Systems in eastern North Carolina received $9 million in compensation in 2009, according to an analysis of tax records by the *Beaufort Observer* newspaper in North Carolina.

THE DEAL AMERICANS DIDN'T GET

The White House and Congressional Democrats could have used the leverage of thirty-two million new customers to negotiate more affordable care for the American public. Instead, industry players were treated as if they were doing a favor for Americans when, in fact, the deal did *them* a favor by giving them 10 percent of the US population as future customers. Negotiators let stand most of the $760 billion in waste that could have been recycled to pay for the uninsured.

A brief glance at history offers lessons about the misplaced power of industry. In 1961 President Dwight Eisenhower gave a farewell address to the nation. He warned of the defense industry that would wreak havoc on the society if left untamed. He referred to it as the military-industrial complex.

His words apply to the medical-industrial complex, which didn't exist at the time. It is the combined force of the medical, hospital, insurance, drug and device industries, and others who rely on government largess. Eisenhower said,

> The total influence—economic, political, even spiritual—is felt in every city, every Statehouse, every office of the Federal government. . . . We must not fail to comprehend its grave implications. Our toil, resources, and livelihood are all involved. So is the very structure of our society. . . . In the councils of government, we must guard against the acquisition of unwarranted influence. . . . The potential for the disastrous rise of misplaced power exists and will persist.

Eisenhower's words describe the battle over health care. The reform bill became the law of the land only with the consent of the medical-industrial complex. The spoils of the political war were divided among the insurance companies, the drug companies, the hospital industry, doctors, and other players. They will consume an even larger share of the country's entire income.

PAY IT FORWARD OR PASS IT FORWARD?

Proponents of the individual mandate say that Americans should look beyond their own self-interest and obtain health insurance so they don't shift the cost of their care to others.

Yet proponents of reform did not mandate that the health care industry do the same and sacrifice a portion of their earnings and compensation so they are not a burden on society.

Today, the federal government borrows from China and other lenders more than forty cents of every dollar it spends to pay its bills. When government intervenes to advance a worthy social goal, it has an obligation to ensure public resources are used wisely. Health care reform does not stop the cost shift to future generations. Instead of paying it forward, health care reform passes it forward.

Eisenhower warned,

> We . . . must avoid the impulse to live only for today, plundering for our own ease and convenience the precious resources of tomorrow. We cannot mortgage the material assets of our grandchildren without risking the loss also of their political and spiritual heritage. We want democracy to survive for all generations to come, not to become the insolvent phantom of tomorrow.

Elected officials from both political parties are enablers of the medical-industrial complex. Republicans in Congress were the driving force behind the Medicare prescription drug benefit legislation enacted under President George W. Bush in 2003. Americans will pay dearly for decades to come for that highly lucrative deal with the drug companies.

In a speech to Congress in the heat of the health care reform debate, President Obama asked a question about the cost of the war in Iraq and the country's priorities. "Is America a society that squanders $900 billion on a dishonest war but refuses to spend the same amount to give its citizens affordable health care?" A related question is whether Americans can afford to squander a nearly equivalent amount of health care waste *every year*. The answer is an unequivocal no.

A TWO-SIDED GAME OVER REPEAL

As the battle hymn of health care reform continues to play, Republicans seem to be playing a two-sided game over its repeal.

Under pressure from Tea Party backers, the Republican-led House of Representatives voted in January 2011 to repeal the law by a margin of 245–189. Three Democrats joined the Republicans in voting for repeal. Republicans knew they could not succeed in the Senate because Democrats controlled it, led by Majority Leader Harry Reid. One month later, forty-seven Senators voted for repeal, thirteen votes short of the sixty votes needed.

Behind the scenes, a different story is playing out. Traditional Republican supporters—big insurance companies, drug companies, and hospitals—are lobbying to keep the individual mandate intact. It is too lucrative for them to advocate for repeal.

Republicans have not offered their own solutions to help people who cannot afford needed medical care. They have tended to stay on the offensive and attack the law rather than suggest ways to solve a vexing public policy issue.

Representative Dan Boren, a Democrat from Oklahoma, was one of thirty-four Democrats who voted against the reform law and among the three who voted for repeal. In a statement to his constituents, he criticized the law and acknowledged, "We have many uninsured Oklahomans who need assistance. Many voters also agree that reforms are needed to address the issue of rising health insurance premiums, the staggering number of medical bankruptcies, and the burden that health care costs have on small-business growth and job creation." But he offered no solutions to help the people in his state obtain affordable health care. He introduced a bill in Congress that would allow every small-business owner or average American the opportunity to apply for a waiver from the health care law, but it offers no help for people who are uninsured and need costly care.

Other Democrats acknowledge that the law can be improved. Senator Tom Harkin, a Democrat from Iowa, said, "It's not like the Ten Commandments, chiseled in stone. It's more like a starter home—suitable for improvement."

DEATH PANELS

In a toxic political atmosphere, the public's interest vanishes in the crossfire. Washington is at war with itself. The public is confused because the warring factions spin their own version of the truth. The confusion causes panic and fear.

Consider the story of an older gentleman who called the Alzheimer's Association asking for help for his wife who had this devastating and frightening disease. He asked the person who answered the phone, "When is the government death panel coming to take my wife?" The representative gently explained that he didn't need to worry because there was no such thing as a death panel.

The "death panel" accusation by Republicans stoked unnecessary fear. Here is the truth about the so-called death panels.

When people are diagnosed with a serious and life-limiting illness, they want to talk to their doctor. They have a lot of questions and want answers. Difficult decisions may have to be made about treatment options, and it can be a very confusing time. A common complaint in health care today is that doctors don't have enough time to spend with their patients because they are on the productivity treadmill. Conversations are hurried, and patients and families are dissatisfied.

The health care reform bill included a provision that would have compensated doctors for the time they spend talking with patients and their families about their treatment options and their wishes. Medicare doesn't pay doctors for this now. The reform law would have compensated doctors when their patients want to have a conversation about important decisions they have to make.

Sarah Palin started the ruckus by coining the term *death panel*, and Betsy McCaughey, the former lieutenant governor of New York, spread the rumor that the government would be telling everyone on Medicare how they should end their life. This false accusation traveled as fast as the speed of light. The provision was removed from the legislation.

Almost thirty years ago, Congress voted to include hospice care as part of the Medicare program. High quality hospice care helps people when they are nearing the end of their lives make decisions that are consistent with their wishes.

Since then, millions of Americans—Democrats, Republicans, and everyone else—have chosen hospice care. Grateful family members volunteer at their local hospice, and families and friends donate gifts to hospices in their loved one's memory.

If Congress had voted in 2010 rather than in the 1980s on whether hospice care should be included as a benefit in the Medicare program, it would probably have been shouted down in a self-serving chorus of misinformation. This would have been an enormous loss of a valuable service to the public.

WAS HEALTH CARE REFORM REALLY REFORM?

Has health care reform restrained the heartless? Or has health care reform unleashed the medical-industrial complex on thirty-two million unsuspecting Americans?

Throughout history, great reform movements have transformed the nation, shaped its future, and inspired hundreds of millions of people around the world. Among the most profound were the abolition of slavery, women's suffrage, civil rights, and the women's movement. They occurred because of sacrifice and suffering by ordinary people who did extraordinary things. Compromise was a word that did not exist in their dictionary. As Mahatma Gandhi said, "Great achievement is born of great sacrifice and is never the result of selfishness."

With this as the measure, was health care reform really reform? Or was it politics as usual?

Health care reform is all about money, lots of it, and who got it. The people who didn't have a seat at the table—those who go to work every day and are too busy to sort fact from fiction—have no voice. They will pay dearly for what Washington politicians of all persuasions failed to do, which is to make health care affordable. The reform law pumps more money into an industry whose purpose is to maximize revenue, not improve health. This is fundamentally incompatible with the country's dire need for affordable care for all Americans.

· *4* ·

Who Will Pay for
Trillion-Dollar Health Care Reform?

$\mathcal{T}$he price tag for the sweeping health care overhaul is estimated to be $940 billion over ten years. The money to pay for it will come from two main sources. The first is taxes on individuals and families and fees on health care companies, which will generate about $450 billion in revenue over ten years.

The second source of revenue—about $500 billion—will come from paying hospitals and other Medicare providers slightly less every year than the amount they would have received. A closer look reveals a predictable pattern in who will really pay for health care reform.

NEW TAXES ON PEOPLE WITH HIGHER INCOMES

If you earn more than $200,000 a year as an individual or $250,000 as a couple, you will pay a higher Medicare payroll tax on your income. The current Medicare payroll tax is 2.9 percent. Workers and employers each pay 1.45 percent. Beginning in 2013, higher income earners will pay 2.35 percent. The proceeds will not be used to bolster the Medicare trust fund, which is projected to be exhausted in 2024 and will lack the revenue to pay all the cost of medical care for baby boomers and future generations. The proceeds will be used to pay for the uninsured. The tax increase may be offset partially by a 2 percentage point payroll tax cut in the 2010 legislation that extended unemployment benefits and the Bush-era tax cuts.

Higher-income individuals will pay a new 3.8 percent tax on un-earned income from interest, dividends, capital gains, annuities, and income from rental property. If you sell a second home or a principal residence that yields a capital gain of more than $250,000 for an individual or $500,000 for a couple, you will pay the new 3.8 percent tax.

Consider a single woman who is the president of her own company and earns $225,000 a year. If she sells her vacation condo on the North Carolina Outer Banks for a substantial profit, she will pay the new health care tax in addition to the capital gains tax.

Together, these taxes are the largest source of new revenue to pay for health insurance for the uninsured and will generate $210 billion over ten years.

HOW HEALTH CARE REFORM REDISTRIBUTES INCOME

Health care reform redistributes income. According to the Tax Foundation, taxpayers in the top 1 percent income bracket will pay an average of $52,000 a year in additional taxes. Those with incomes in the top 20 percent of the income distribution will pay $3,800.

People with lower-middle incomes will benefit the most, about $2,000 per person. They won't receive the money directly. It will be used to pay for expanded coverage under Medicaid and subsidies to help individuals buy private insurance.

THE CADILLAC TAX AND OTHER FEES

If you have a comprehensive health insurance plan, be prepared for a so-called Cadillac tax, which is like a tax on gas-guzzling vehicles.

Insurance companies that sell expensive health insurance plans to employers whose premiums cost more than $10,200 annually for individual coverage and $27,500 annually for family coverage will pay a 40 percent tax on the excess premium over these amounts.

Consider an employer that offers comprehensive insurance that costs $12,000 a year for an employee. The 40 percent tax will be applied to $1,800, the amount over $10,200. The total tax will be $720.

The tax will begin in 2018 and is expected to generate $32 billion in revenue over ten years. Instead of paying this tax from their own revenue, insurers will pass it on to employers in the form of higher premiums. In turn, employers will pass the cost on to their employees.

Drug companies, medical device manufacturers, and others will pay fees assessed as an excise tax in return for millions of new customers. The fees are based on the volume of a company's sales to Medicare beneficiaries and government programs. They are expected to generate revenue totaling $107 billion over ten years. The businesses will pass the costs on to the public through higher prices for their products. The Congressional Budget Office, which reviews budgets and legislative initiatives with budget implications, estimates that drug company fees will likely increase the price of drugs purchased through federal programs by about 1 percent.

PENALTIES

Employers will pay a $2,000 penalty for each full-time employee (excluding the first thirty employees) if they have more than fifty workers, don't provide health insurance coverage, and have at least one employee who receives a subsidy for health insurance. The penalty is estimated to yield $52 billion in revenue over ten years.

Americans who decide not to buy health insurance will pay a penalty. Beginning in 2014, the penalty is $95 or 1 percent of a person's income, whichever is higher. The penalty increases to the higher of $695 or 2.5 percent in income. It doesn't apply to people whose incomes are so low that they don't file income taxes.

How will the Internal Revenue Service know whether tax filers are uninsured and have to pay the penalty? Insurance companies will send information to the IRS confirming that a person has health insurance, just as banks inform the IRS about interest income a taxpayer receives from a savings account.

The health care reform law prohibits the government from criminally prosecuting people who refuse to pay the penalty. The IRS cannot file a notice of lien on any property for failure to pay. The federal government expects to receive $4 billion in revenue from penalties from individual taxpayers from 2017 to 2019.

THE SUNTAN TAX

A new tax of 10 percent is being collected from customers who use indoor tanning services. Studies show that exposure to ultraviolet light used in tanning salons increases the risk of skin cancer. The tax is expected to bring in $300 million a year.

ARE HEALTH CARE PROVIDERS REALLY PAYING?

The second major source of funding for health care reform is $500 billion in spending cuts over ten years. Here is how they work.

Every year, Medicare pays providers an increase, or "raise." Medicare will continue to provide an annual increase, but it will be slightly less than projected. Hospitals are slated to receive $155 billion less over ten years. Even with slower growth in payments, hospitals will receive nearly $1.7 trillion from Medicare through 2019.

When Medicare reduces payments, hospitals will have the incentive to increase the number of tests and surgeries they perform to make up the difference in revenue. The "real savings" that Vice President Biden mentioned could be a mirage. Also hospitals are likely to shift their costs and charge higher fees for privately insured patients.

The law was intended to clamp down on how much Medicare pays to Medicare Advantage plans, an alternative to the traditional Medicare program offered by private health insurance companies. Millions of people on Medicare select this option. The health care reform law cut payments to the plans by $136 billion over ten years.

The plans have already received a partial reprieve. A week after the November 2010 midterm election, Medicare announced that additional Medicare Advantage plans will receive bonuses—and more money—for providing high-quality care. Previously, health plans had to score four out of five "stars" to receive bonuses. Now, they can be a "three-star" plan and still receive a bonus. The Obama administration justified the change by saying that the bonuses increase the incentive for health plans to improve the quality of care they provide. By lowering the bar, though, Medicare sends the opposite message: lower quality care is just as acceptable.

An independent commission that advises Congress on the Medicare program, the Medicare Payment Advisory Commission, confirmed that the revised bonuses would reward poorly performing plans. The extra bonuses reduce planned Medicare savings by $5 billion, but some analysts believe the reduction could be much higher.

While budget hawks worry about fewer dollars being available to pay for health care reform, Wall Street analysts heralded the good news. An equity analyst with Citigroup Investment Research mused that the star rating bonus is "a big positive for 2012 rates, as it will offset much of the expected cuts."

HOW MUCH WILL YOU PAY
FOR THE INDIVIDUAL MANDATE?

If you don't have insurance from your employer and are not eligible for Medicare or Medicaid, you will be required to buy health insurance in 2014 from a one-stop-shop health insurance exchange in your state that will function like an online travel website. If your state has decided not to implement health care reform, the federal government will set up an exchange for your state.

To make the cost more affordable, you may be eligible for a subsidy. To qualify, your household income must be between $11,000 and $44,000 for individuals and $22,000 and $88,000 for families. The amount of the subsidy gradually declines as your income increases.

A person with $50,000 in annual income and $1 million in savings receives the same subsidy as one with the same income and no savings.

If the mandate applies to you, and if you are eligible for a subsidy, you might feel relieved that you can buy insurance that is more affordable. Others may feel differently, especially if they are not eligible for a subsidy.

So far, little information has been publicized about the cost of the individual mandate. The answer is that it all depends. While it is impossible to predict how much health insurance will cost in 2014, here are a few estimates of how much you might have to pay.

A forty-five-year-old parent of a four-person family whose total income is $45,000 a year will pay about $2,700 a year for insurance and receive a subsidy worth $11,500. The maximum out-of-pocket costs for copayments and deductibles (not including the premium) will be about $4,100.

A sixty-year-old person earning $48,000 a year or more will pay an estimated $10,000 a year for individual insurance coverage and is not eligible for any subsidy. Premiums for older Americans will be higher than for younger Americans with the same income because they tend to use more health care. The limit on out-of-pocket costs will be $6,250. Total spending could amount to one-third of income.

The high cost that some Americans will pay is determined by how the subsidies were allocated in the health care reform bill. Also, the high costs represent the failure of policy makers of all political stripes over many decades to ensure affordable health care.

As for the penalty that kicks in if you decide not to buy insurance, consider a forty-two-year-old single woman with $40,000 a year in income who decides not to buy insurance. She will pay a $1,000 penalty every year, or 2.5 percent of her income.

Not everyone has to pay the penalty. Undocumented immigrants are not permitted by the law to buy insurance through the health insurance exchanges, so they won't pay a penalty. Veterans who receive care from the US Department of Veterans Affairs are exempt, as are individuals and families who claim exceptional hardship. Those who don't use medical care because of their personal religious beliefs are exempt from the requirement to buy health insurance.

REALITY CHECK

A consistent pattern is emerging about who will pay for health care reform. The health care industry's lobbyists are pressuring Congress to roll back provisions that require them to pay for a portion of health care reform. For example, medical device companies have lobbied Congress to roll back the excise taxes they are required to pay under the reform law. Five industry-supported bills were introduced in 2011 by members of Congress to overturn the tax, which is slated to generate $20 billion over ten years. Meanwhile, Americans who lack political lubricant to lobby Congress have little opportunity to reduce their burden.

Does the health care overhaul add to the federal deficit? This hotly debated question has consumed gigabytes of coverage in the media. A far more important question looms. Does the overhaul improve the outlook for the federal government's ability to pay for health care?

Health care spending in the year 2030 will be half a percent of the country's gross domestic product (GDP) below what it would have been without health care reform, said two architects of the plan: Peter Orszag, who was the White House budget director during the reform debate, and Ezekiel Emanuel, Orszag's former health care advisor and the brother of Obama's former chief of staff Rahm Emanuel. By then, health care will devour 25 percent of the country's income. A half a percent is lost in the shuffle of the deck chairs on the *Titanic*.

Part 2

HOW HEALTH CARE REFORM
DID NOT REFORM HEALTH CARE

*W*hen health care reform was born, it had a long to-do list. Reforming health insurance was at the top. Reforming health care was lower down on the list.

We begin with an analysis of how the overhaul did not fix three parts of the health care system that are badly in need of repair: the lack of primary care doctors and nurses, the enormous number of medical mistakes and other causes of preventable harm, and the financial engineering that has increased production of more health care but not more health. These fixes are not "nice-to-have" features. They are essential to any system that will assume responsibility for the lives of more Americans.

Health care reform built a big house without a first floor. As millions of people obtain health insurance, precious few will have a primary care physician, nurse practitioner, or physician assistant to take care of them. Primary care is the foundation of any endeavor to improve and sustain health. Chapter 5 describes how an American Medical Association committee has deliberately weakened primary care in recent decades and endangered its very existence. This has hurt the health and well-being of the public and is one of the most significant reasons that health care costs are out of control. We describe tactical changes that the health care reform law made but highlight how it didn't fundamentally shift course. The country is still headed in the wrong direction that will keep costs spiraling out of control and prevent millions of people from having access to basic medical care.

Chapter 6 reveals how patient safety was put on the back burner in the reform legislation. The overhaul is like a plan to build a new solar-powered car that neglects the legions of people dying from design flaws in the millions of vehicles already on the road. Because the safety failures are not understood by most policy makers, they will be built into the care provided to thirty-two million more people. An inconvenient truth is that 225,000 people die each year from preventable health care harm. We provide the basis for this estimate and predict that this number, sadly, will increase. The Obama administration's patient safety initiative that was launched a year after the reform law was enacted is a welcome step forward. The solution, though, rests with hospitals and other health care providers, many of whom still deny that a public health crisis exists.

While hospitals mismanage billions of Medicare dollars every year, their lobbyists set off pyrotechnics when Congress tries to rein in Medicare spending. The National Academy of Engineering and the Institute of Medicine, which are part of the National Academy of Sciences, put their finger on the problem. Most hospitals have never adopted modern-day management practices that all other business enterprises began using decades ago to improve safety and manage resources wisely. Chapter 7 offers a solution for how hospitals can provide better and safer care while being good stewards of the public's money. We predict, though, that hospitals will default to their usual financial engineering and increase the volume of services they provide so they can continue to fatten their bottom lines.

· 5 ·

How the AMA Killed the Family Doctor

$\mathcal{A}$ good friend of ours, Dr. Larry Jassie, trained at Bellevue Hospital in New York City and has exquisite diagnostic skills honed by years of experience and continuous study. He tells the story of a patient who had a lump on his neck and was worried it might be cancer. Dr. Jassie performed a physical exam and concluded that the lump was nothing to worry about. He reassured his anxious patient.

Dr. Jassie helped him avoid unnecessary visits to specialists who would have performed a bevy of expensive and scary tests that would have yielded no benefit, provoked fear, cost too much, and possibly caused more harm than good. "I saved him thousands of dollars and lots of worry," he said.

Although many people would like to have a doctor like Dr. Jassie, he is among a vanishing breed of primary care doctors. The loss to society is profound and dismaying but without fanfare. No one is sounding the alarm except the primary care doctors themselves.

Meanwhile, many Americans have no trouble finding a cardiologist to insert an unnecessary stent or a neurosurgeon to perform an inappropriate and risky back surgery, which is the most overused surgery in the country, according to *Consumer Reports*. In fact, in some communities there are so many proceduralists, as they are called, that they drum up lucrative business and perform operations on people who don't need them. We wrote about this unfortunate aspect of medical care in our book *The Treatment Trap*.

It is no accident that primary care doctors are scarce. The situation is the direct result of a deliberate strategy carried out from within the medical profession itself.

An AMA advisory committee called the Relative-Value Scale Update Committee (RUC) has been meeting in secret since 1991. It calculates the value of services that doctors render in a variety of medical fields. The committee gives a higher value to services provided by specialists, such as radiologists, and a lower value to the work performed by family doctors and internists like Dr. Jassie. Medicare uses the values recommended by the AMA to calculate payments to doctors. It might pay $190 to a gastro-enterologist for the time spent performing a colonoscopy but only $90 to a primary care doctor for the same time spent diagnosing and treating a patient with diabetes.

Specialists dominate the AMA committee. Since the RUC was established, Medicare's payments have favored specialists at the expense of primary care doctors.

The government's watchdog, the Government Accountability Office, has criticized the AMA's cozy arrangement with Medicare. It says the AMA overvalues expensive high-tech medical procedures and diagnostic tests and undervalues keeping people out of the hospital and away from unnecessary tests and procedures. Congressman Jim McDermott, a Democrat from Seattle, Washington, said in hearings in the House Ways and Means Subcommittee on Health, "Why should the medical association be setting their own fees?" We are letting "the fox decide what the keys to the henhouse will be used for."

In our example, Dr. Jassie would have been paid very little for his careful and accurate diagnosis of a patient. His work is based on his years of experience, skill, and commitment to continuous learning about new developments in medicine. As a result, many primary care doctors have difficulty making their practices financially viable.

Medicare and the government are often blamed for the imbalance. An opinion editorial published in the *Wall Street Journal* was titled "How Medicare Killed the Family Doctor." The truth is that one group of doctors has cannibalized another group.

The AMA touts its influence over the government and says that the RUC allows the medical profession to continue to shape its own payment environment, and it is merely "exercising its First Amendment right to petition the federal government."

The impact of the AMA's price-fixing is far-reaching. It determines how more than $60 billion annually in Medicare spending for doctors is allocated. It contributes to the imbalance in the types of doctors who practice medicine in the United States and the entire structure of the health care system.

The AMA's price-fixing affects medical school students' career choices. They tend to choose lucrative subspecialties such as radiology, orthopedic surgery, anesthesiology, or dermatology. In fact, they have a nickname for these specialties—"ROAD." Few students choose careers as family doctors or internists.

Money is not the only factor in a career choice. Many students are told by their professors that they are too talented to be "just" a primary care doctor and they should be a surgeon or other specialist. This attitude creates a false impression about the importance of primary care to maintaining and sustaining health.

Primary care physicians are overworked and have little say about their work life. One doctor described her experience in a blog in the journal *Health Affairs*: "It was factory work; we were interchangeable cogs in a vast machine. The people who saw patients, especially 'primary care providers' like me, were at the base of the pyramid and the bottom of the pecking order. . . . Professional administrators, and physicians who see few if any patients, will schedule every moment of every primary provider's day, critique every decision, continually scrutinize and evaluate every aspect of one's practice. . . . We were on teams, but given no time to communicate with one another. We were forced to complete clunky electronic records we had no time to read."

A primary care doctor told us about a new radiologist in his poor, rural community who had just completed training and was offered a starting salary of $500,000 for working only two of every three weeks. Meanwhile his primary care practice is barely making ends meet.

The American Academy of Family Physicians predicts a shortage of 39,000 family physicians by 2020. Internists are in very short supply too. In fact, they are both endangered species.

In 2010 and 2011 a slight increase occurred in the number of medical students choosing to train to become family doctors and internists. This trend will need to continue for a generation if the United States is to over-come the imbalance that exists.

The imbalance between primary care doctors and specialists will likely continue as twenty new medical schools are expected to be built in the next several years. Medical students who graduate from the new schools will have every incentive to work in medical fields that are more lucrative than primary care.

Their career choices will affect the care that millions of Americans will receive for decades to come. While future doctors should use their talents, medical practice is still a public service. Medical schools need to produce the doctors that can keep people healthy.

A family doctor in Kentucky, Dr. Phillip Bale, helps prevent his patients from having heart disease, stroke, and diabetes. For some patients, he helps reverse disease. He tells the story of one of his patients, a policeman, who was overweight and had diabetes and high cholesterol. Dr. Bale and a nurse practitioner worked with the policeman over many months to create a plan that would help him reverse his poor health. They helped him understand the reasons he should make changes in his life and showed him how to track his progress. After five months, the policeman saw the impact of his hard work and the good results. He lost almost sixty pounds, his diabetes was under control, and his cholesterol level was dramatically reduced.

"Heart disease can be reversed," Dr. Bale says. He knows that individual lifestyle changes, like stopping smoking, walking every day, and eating a cautious diet, along with medications, can reduce heart disease.

Dr. Bale says, "Patients do really well. It's cheap to do this," compared to the usual care people receive that includes surgery and stents. "You just have to slow down and have a conversation," Dr. Bale says.

But because primary care doctors receive so little payment, they can barely afford to spend more than a few minutes with each patient. Anyone who has been to a doctor's office knows how brief the visits are. That's why most people are not fortunate enough to receive personalized care to keep them healthy or restore them to health. As Dr. Bale says, patients are like "deer in the headlights with the avalanche of procedures they have to go through."

For all the money spent on health care in the United States, life expectancy is no better than that of Cuba, which emphasizes basic primary care and spends pennies for every dollar the United States spends.

HOW SPECIAL INTERESTS DECIDE THE CARE *YOU* GET

During the health care reform debate, Republicans said that government bureaucrats would make decisions about your care, not your doctor. A closer look reveals a more troubling reality.

We met a primary care doctor in Cleveland who told the story of how he helped two of his patients avoid an unnecessary hospitalization. Other doctors wanted to admit his patients, but he knew his patients' medical histories and realized their symptoms were minor and no cause for concern. "Patients are being overtested and overtreated," he said. "It only creates more anxiety for them."

One day a hospital official came to see him and announced that the hospital was terminating his contract. The doctor was stunned. His main concern was his patients, many of whom he had known for a long time. A partner in his practice who cared for 1,500 patients, mostly older adults, was also terminated.

"I was terminated because of lack of productivity," the primary care doctor said. "We weren't seeing enough patients." He said that it can take ten minutes just to help an elderly patient move from a wheelchair to an exam table.

The hospital where he worked was intent on increasing revenue. He recalls how the hospital's chief financial officer had told a medical staff meeting that if all the doctors could admit one more Medicare patient a month, the hospital would meet its revenue targets. "This suggests we should go out and commit fraud," the doctor said. "It's unconscionable," he continued.

Did the hospital want to use the doctor's office space for a specialist physician who could generate more revenue per square foot? We don't know if that happened, but it would not be surprising. Specialists are more valuable to a hospital because they perform surgeries and procedures that generate hospital revenue.

The care that many Americans receive depends on the treatment that hospitals, drug companies, and device manufacturers want you to get. Hospitals want to fill their beds. Drug companies want to sell as many drugs as possible. Device manufacturers want to sell as many cardiac stents and screws for back surgeries as they can. They lose money when doctors keep you healthy.

The health care reform law did not correct the imbalance between primary care doctors and specialists. Instead, it requires the Secretary of the Department of Health and Human Services to begin a process to validate the AMA committee's recommendations. Proponents of reform avoided making the hard decision. In return, the AMA supported health care reform.

The AMA ranks fourteenth in the list of all-time donors to political campaigns and is ahead of Goldman Sachs and the American Bankers Association. Campaign finance records show that national organizations of radiologists, orthopedists, and anesthesiologists were among the "heavy hitters" for contributions to Barack Obama's 2008 presidential campaign.

The health care reform law gives a nod to primary care by funding bonus payments to primary care doctors and training for five hundred primary care doctors, six hundred physician assistants, and six hundred nurse practitioners. While well intended, these provisions don't fix the fundamental imbalance.

Taxpayers are paying for a Band-Aid rather than a real solution. The RUC needs to be pulled out from under the AMA. An independent entity needs to take the lead in allocating Medicare physician payments and give primary care doctors a larger share.

This policy change will be as popular as kicking a beehive. Special interests will play the "rationing" card and claim that the government is intruding on the doctor-patient relationship. These changes are needed if Americans are to have access to a health care system rather than a sick care system.

THE BIGGEST THREAT TO THE
HEALTH OF OLDER AMERICANS

During the turbulent debate on health care reform, President Obama convened a national summit with Congressional leaders at Blair House, the president's official guest house located across the street from the White House on Pennsylvania Avenue. During the summit, Senator Kent Conrad, a Democrat from North Dakota, talked about his father-in-law's health care. Here is what he said:

My own father-in-law [was] in his final illness. [I] went to his kitchen table. Didn't know it was the final illness. Got out all his prescription drugs. Sure enough, he was taking sixteen. I get on the phone to the doctor—I go down the list . . . of what my father-in-law was taking, sixteen prescription drugs. And I get on the line to the doctor, and he says, "Well, Kent"—and I get down to about the third one—"He shouldn't be taking that. He shouldn't have been taking that the last five years." I get a little further down the list, two drugs, and he says, "Well, Kent, he shouldn't be taking those two drugs, they work against each other." I said, "Doc, how does this happen." He said . . . "We've got chaos." And my conclusion, after all of these hundreds of hours of hearings and meetings . . . was that indeed we do. We have a system that is characterized, especially for those people, by chaos.

Why didn't the health care overhaul fix this dangerous and costly chaos? The health care reform law provides a small amount of funds to train more doctors and nurses to become primary care doctors and nurses that specialize in the care of older adults. The amount of money is miniscule compared to the enormity of the need. There are too few doctors, nurses, and other professionals who can properly care for the forty-six million people covered by Medicare.

Yet the law closes Medicare's prescription drug "donut hole" in 2020. Currently, Medicare beneficiaries lose coverage for drugs after spending $2,700 in a year, and coverage begins again when they have spent about $6,100. The gap can be an enormous burden.

Why did policy makers fix the donut hole but not address the shortage of trained people to help older Americans navigate the chaos?

Several years ago during a conversation with a drug company executive about the shortage of pharmacists, we were surprised to learn the company's perspective on the shortage. "We think it's a good thing," he said, smiling. His company makes brand-name drugs, hospital supplies, medical devices, and health care equipment. He explained that pharmacists tend to substitute generic drugs rather than use brand-name drugs, which is bad for his company's bottom line.

Do the drug companies stand by and watch the shortage of pharmacists? Is the dearth of people trained in geriatrics and primary care no accident?

Drug companies, biotech firms, and their lobby groups dominate Capitol Hill. During the first six months of 2009, they spent more than $609,000 a day to influence legislation, according to the Center for Responsive Politics, a nonpartisan watchdog group. There are more than twice as many registered lobbyists for the drug and biotech firms (1,200) than there are members of Congress (535). As one high-level Senate staffer said, "The drug companies own this place."

This is why the donut hole was fixed. More money will flow to the drug companies. Meanwhile, the chaos will worsen for older Americans. The chaos is not just about drugs. It's about tests, surgeries, treatments, and everything else the medical-industrial complex can do to make money.

Take the case of Arthur, an eighty-four-year-old former newspaper publisher. His family doctor, whom he had known for nearly twenty years, coordinated all his care. When Arthur went to a specialist, his family doctor reviewed the specialist's findings and recommendations and talked to him about them. When his doctor retired in 2005, Arthur said that everything fell apart. His care is fragmented now, and he feels as if no one has time to talk to him or look out for him. Like many people, he can easily fall through the cracks.

He says that health care is like going to multiple mechanics to get his car repaired. Each one knows only about a certain part of his car, not the entire vehicle. If the brakes need to be replaced, a mechanic who specializes in brakes fixes them. If the car needs new tires, another mechanic who specializes in tires selects new ones and puts them on. No one person takes care of the whole car. No one person assures that interdependent systems function well together. Nor does anyone keep track of whether preventive maintenance is performed so the car doesn't break down on the highway.

Arthur is not an expert and has to guess what type of doctor he should go to when he has a medical problem. This arrangement is costly and time consuming for him but highly lucrative for the medical-industrial complex. When his experience is multiplied by that of millions of older adults, the negative consequence for their health is immeasurable.

The health care reform overhaul includes provisions that encourage doctors, nurse practitioners, and other professionals to work together in teams and better coordinate care. Up to one million people on Medicare could benefit from expanded primary care practices, called medical homes, which are expected to be established. Primary care providers coordinate care and take responsibility for the ongoing treatment of their patients. They commit to communicating with them by email and telephone and are accessible at night. Regular checkups are provided to prevent problems from getting out of hand.

If you are fortunate enough to find doctors who work in practices such as this, you will be among a relatively small number of people who will benefit from the important incentives in health care reform. Most people will not.

The greatest threat to the health of older Americans is not Medicare spending cuts or the donut hole. The greatest threat is too few doctors and nurses who know how to care for them. The donut hole is fixed, but the shortage of trained health care professionals is not. Older Americans are bereft of anyone to guide them through the phalanx of specialists. They have no choice but to go where the medical-industrial complex takes them.

Meanwhile, Medicare pays teaching hospitals handsomely to train doctors. In fiscal year 2008, Medicare paid $8.4 billion toward doctor training, but the funding is not being used to train the kinds of doctors that older Americans need.

The chaos in health care for Arthur and millions of other people is no accident. It is nurtured by the special interests that want you and everyone else to be a patient always and forever. Their ideal patient is on sixteen drugs, has multiple surgeries and hospitalizations, and has doctor appointments every week, with no one coordinating it all. Every system is designed to achieve the results it gets.

· *6* ·

Why Hospitals Don't Stop Harming Patients

*T*hink about this. By 2020 the populations of North Dakota, Rhode Island, and Vermont vanish. The cause will not be an earthquake or other natural disaster. It will be a man-made disaster.

In the decade ending in 2020, we predict that more than 2.25 million Americans will have succumbed to medical mistakes, hospital-acquired infections, overuse of radiation-emitting CT scans, and other causes of preventable health care harm. This is more than the populations of the three states.

This prediction does not account for the thirty-two million more people who are expected to be newly insured beginning in 2014. They will use more health care than they are now and be exposed to potential harm.

What is behind the numbers? Why do hospitals continue to harm patients?

A TALE OF TWO HOSPITALS

In April 2010 two California hospitals in Riverside County, Rancho Springs Medical Center and Inland Valley Regional Medical Center, received letters from Medicare saying that it was going to terminate them from the program. The hospitals had multiple and ongoing violations of federal requirements for safe patient care and failed to fix them. The hospitals' governing board was apprised of the problems and Medicare's intent to terminate, but it was unable to eliminate clear threats to the public's health and safety, according to Medicare officials.

The hospitals had been cited by government regulators for a string of safety failures. Beginning in 2007, patients with life-threatening injuries waited in the emergency department for up to eight hours to see a doctor because not enough doctors were available to treat them.

In the intensive care unit, patients were placed in an illegal satellite unit that was not properly staffed. Regulators issued a cease-and-desist order because peoples' lives were placed in immediate jeopardy.

Doctors performed caesarean sections on three women using electrical cauterizing instruments in a delivery room with dangerously low humidity, which could have sparked a fire. Mold was found in delivery rooms. Food for patients was not stored safely.

Both hospitals are owned by Universal Health Services (UHS), a for-profit entity based in King of Prussia, Pennsylvania, that owns 25 hospitals and 102 mental health facilities.

In December 2009 Medicare officials sent a letter to the board of directors and the president of UHS to express concern with the hospitals' ability to pass the upcoming full validation survey. The survey was billed as a "make-or-break" inspection. The hospitals failed the inspections.

On April 15, 2010, Medicare sent a letter of termination to each of the two hospitals. It cited multiple failures, including lack of proper infection control, the failure of pharmacists to safely handle medications, and the lack of competent hospital staff, among other serious safety concerns.

Medicare rarely terminates a hospital from the program. The situation must constitute a significant threat to the public's health.

Five days later, the California Department of Public Health, which had been monitoring the hospitals, notified them that it was planning to revoke their licenses to operate.

Hospitals can appeal a Medicare termination, and the two California hospitals appealed. They continue to operate and are included in the Medicare program under the close scrutiny of regulators.

On its website, UHS describes itself as maintaining "one of the strongest balance sheets in the industry. . . . This strong capital position has enabled the company to develop and acquire many new facilities over the past few years. The UHS strategy is to build or purchase healthcare properties in rapidly-growing markets and create a strong franchise based on exceptional service and effective cost control. The company owes its success to a responsive management style and to a service philosophy that is based on integrity, competence and compassion."

While two of the company's twenty-five hospitals were under imminent threat of being barred from the Medicare program, on March 11, 2010, the compensation committee of the UHS board of directors authorized incentive bonuses to the chief executive officer and other executive officers for their exemplary performance in 2009.

According to company filings with the Securities and Exchange Commission, the CEO received a $3.375 million bonus for meeting financial performance targets for earnings per share and return on capital. A younger executive, the CEO's son, who was co-head of the hospital division, received a $537,000 bonus and a 15 percent salary increase in recognition of his promotion to president in 2009.

This case illustrates the disconnect that exists in many hospitals between executive compensation and the safety of patients. Compensation is based on financial performance, not the quality of care patients receive. Regulatory action concerning risks to the public's health is relegated to a few sentences buried in annual reports and in government filings with the Securities and Exchange Commission.

The hospitals were able to provide substandard care for so long because regulatory agencies have limited power to intervene. Restaurants can be shut down because of poor food handling but hospitals are rarely shut down for egregious acts that place the public in danger.

A BIGGER PICTURE OF HEALTH CARE HARM

In November 2010 the Office of Inspector General of the US Department of Health and Human Services reported national estimates on the number of people on Medicare who are harmed in hospitals. It estimates that in a single year, 79,200 people covered by Medicare experience preventable harm that contributes to their deaths.

The American Hospital Association issued a response to the report that was unapologetic and offered no reassurance to the public. In its statement, the hospital association said, "While hospitals have made great strides in improving care, this report highlights that there is more we can do. Hospitals are already engaged in important projects designed to improve patient care in many of the areas mentioned in the report. We are committed to taking additional needed steps to improve patient care. That is why we support the report's recommendations for further research."

The government report was issued around the same time that automaker Toyota was thrust into the national spotlight because of sticky accelerator pedals and poorly positioned floor mats in its vehicles that contributed to car crashes and nineteen deaths since 1999.

The contrast is striking between Toyota's response to the public to its safety failures and the hospital association's response to far greater numbers of fatalities.

Toyota issued a public apology for the company's failure to ensure public safety. "First, I want to sincerely apologize to Toyota owners," said Jim Lentz, president and chief operating officer of Toyota's US sales. "I know that our recalls have caused many of you concern and for that I am truly sorry."

The company made no excuses. It invested its own resources to identify and fix safety hazards, and kept the public apprised of its plans to repair their vehicles. It reduced the compensation of its top management by 10 percent to acknowledge their responsibility for the recall of vehicles. The company president, Akio Toyoda, and other company executives forfeited bonuses.

The federal government held Toyota accountable. Secretary of the US Department of Transportation Ray LaHood said, "Safety is our number one priority. . . . We are holding Toyota's feet to the fire. We will stay on this until every car is safe. We feel an obligation to the drivers of Toyotas." The government conducted a full investigation into the cause of the crashes and concluded that electronic systems in the vehicles were not responsible for the mishaps.

In contrast, the US Department of Health and Human Services offered no assurance that it was doing everything possible to protect the public. Nor did it commit to hold hospitals accountable for improving safety. Pundits and politicians didn't provoke a frenzy about the real "death panels" that occur in hospitals every day.

THE FIRST REPORTS OF HEALTH CARE HARM

The American public had its first exposure to the extent of health care harm with the 1999 landmark report *To Err Is Human*, prepared by the Institute of Medicine of the National Academy of Sciences. It concluded that up to 98,000 preventable deaths occur every year from medical mistakes. Its estimates were based on studies conducted in the 1980s and included deaths that happen primarily in hospitals. They did not include harm that occurs in nursing homes, dialysis centers, ambulatory surgery centers, and other health care settings.

The federal government does not have a tracking system to monitor deaths from preventable harm in health care similar to how it tracks deaths from diseases such as cancer and AIDS. Researchers who conduct studies of health care harm use different methods to count incidents of harm. This explains the varying estimates of harm.

Medical Mistakes

The impact of medical mistakes can be understood best when compared to other causes of death. Arlington National Cemetery and its 612 acres of rolling hills in Virginia overlooking the Potomac River is the final resting place for about 330,000 soldiers, patriots, and their families, some of whom fought in the American Revolution. The Pentagon overlooks the rows of white marble stones lined up in perfect formation. The life-and-death consequences of its decisions are always within sight. A new Arlington Cemetery would need to be established every three years to provide a resting place for all the people who die from errors in hospitals.

Medical mistakes are an equal opportunity event and affect people from all walks of life. Former secretary of defense Donald Rumsfeld said in an interview with Diane Sawyer on *ABC News* that his wife nearly died from a medical error.

Actor Dennis Quaid made headlines when a medical mistake almost killed his ten-day-old twins at Cedars-Sinai Medical Center in Los Angeles. The newborns were to be given a dose of a blood thinner but were given two doses of an adult version of the drug. "While my wife and I were in the room, a nurse unintentionally gave our children 1,000 times the safe dosage," said Quaid. The heparin turned the blood in their tiny bodies into the consistency of water. Fortunately, the twins recovered.

Hospital-Acquired Infections

Hospital-acquired infections are another cause of preventable health care harm. Nearly 100,000 people die each year from infections they acquire while in the hospital, according to the Centers for Disease Control and Prevention. Another Arlington Cemetery would need to be constructed every three years for them. Ambulatory surgery centers, nursing homes, and dialysis units for people with kidney disease are other places that can be breeding grounds for infections.

Every data point is a person. Diana is one of them. At age twenty-four and fifteen weeks pregnant, she had emergency surgery to remove her gallbladder, one of 750,000 people a year who have this surgery. Diana suffered from a medical mistake and an antibiotic-resistant hospital-acquired infection that turned her pregnancy into a nightmare. She was hospitalized during the final four months of her pregnancy and lost fifty pounds during that time.

Diana gave birth to a healthy daughter named Julia. At two pounds thirteen ounces, she survived the nine surgeries her mother endured to stem the harm that ravaged her body.

A photograph of Diana in a rocking chair holding Julia, swaddled in a blanket, is reminiscent of Michelangelo's *Madonna and Child*. It was the only time Diana could muster the strength to hold her newborn daughter. Two days later, she succumbed to the assault that was too much for her body to bear.

Overtreatment

Other causes of preventable harm occur. Researchers at the National Cancer Institute estimate that radiation exposure from CT scans causes 14,500 deaths a year. Unnecessary surgery causes an estimated 12,000 fatalities. Overprescribing of prescription drugs contributes to untold numbers of deaths. Malfunctions from poorly designed medical devices such as implantable defibrillators are another cause of preventable harm.

When the toll is tallied, a conservative estimate is that 225,000 people die every year from preventable harm in the health care system. This is equivalent to about 10 percent of the total deaths in the United States every year from all causes.

When health care reform takes effect as planned, more people will have health insurance and use more health care. More Americans will be exposed to the risk of preventable harm. Doctors, nurses, and other health care professionals who are already working at a breakneck speed will be required to work even faster. When a complex system is forced to operate at higher speed, more mistakes will occur.

THE CULTURE WARS

Health care in the United States is a tale of two very different worlds. The private sector and government spend billions of dollars on research to advance knowledge about how to prevent and treat disease. This aspect of American medicine is unparalleled in the world.

Yet hospitals and other health care facilities have failed to apply the most basic quality-control practices to deliver the benefits of research and new treatments to patients safely.

The National Academy of Engineering and the Institute of Medicine, which are part of the National Academy of Sciences, recommend that the health care industry use systems-engineering tools that have revolutionized the quality and performance of the transportation, telecommunications, and manufacturing sectors. The health care industry lags decades behind these industries.

If solutions exist to improve patient safety, why don't hospitals adopt them? The culture in many hospitals is toxic. They are composed of fiefdoms. Departments are ruled by doctors who stake out their turf. Hierarchies exist within and among doctors, nurses, administrators, and other professionals. The lack of cooperation among them is a primary cause of safety failures in health care today.

To illustrate this point, a few years ago a doctor told the story of his first few weeks as CEO of a hospital where multiple wrong-site surgeries had occurred in the months before his arrival. He announced a policy that every surgery will be preceded by a "time-out" when the team would verify the patient's identity and the procedure to be performed, and mark the site of surgery.

One day after the new policy began, he was informed that a surgeon was about to begin an operation without the required time-out. The CEO scrubbed and went into the operating room to inform the surgeon that if he went ahead with the operation, it would be the last one he would perform in that hospital.

The surgeon complied. The hospital was located in a rural area and the nearest hospital was a long distance away. The surgeon could not threaten to take his patients—and the revenue—to a competing hospital.

This example is not an isolated occurrence. In Colorado, 25 wrong-patient surgeries and 107 wrong-site procedures, such as an operation on the wrong leg, occurred from January 2002 to June 2008. Thirty-four people were significantly harmed or impaired. These incidents were voluntarily reported to COPIC, a medical malpractice insurance company.

These safety failures occurred because doctors ignored a standard protocol, or checklist, similar to one that pilots use before they start airplane engines and take off down an airport runway. A checklist requires doctors, nurses, and others to make sure they are performing the right procedure on the right patient and the right part of the body. A brief "time-out" is called to allow anyone to raise questions or concerns.

Across the country, these types of errors continue to occur about forty times a week. If passenger airplanes took off on the wrong runway forty times a week, the Federal Aviation Administration would ground all flights until the causes of the safety failures were identified and corrected. Health care has not adopted this forceful but effective approach to safety.

"THEY HARM YOU AND THEY BILL YOU FOR IT"

A family member whose loved one suffered from health care harm once said, "They harm you and they bill you for it."

It has been standard practice in health care that when patients are harmed, hospitals and doctors bill them for the treatment and follow-up care to repair the harm. When they do this, providers convey the belief that they are not accountable for the harm they cause. It reflects the habit of privatized financial gain by hospitals but socialized losses whereby the public, employers, and the government pay for the cost of harm.

In a giant leap forward, the federal government stopped paying hospitals and doctors for wrong-site surgeries, surgery on the wrong patient, bed sores acquired while in the hospital, and other preventable mistakes and poor care. Private insurance companies adopted similar practices.

So far, the financial impact on hospitals has been minimal compared to the billions of dollars they receive from private and public insurers. Nonetheless, the federal stance sends a clear message that hospitals and doctors should no longer assume that someone else should pay for their mistakes.

The health care reform law expands this sensible approach. Medicare will stop paying for more causes of preventable harm. Also, Medicare payments will be reduced by 1 percent for hospitals that rank in the worst 25 percent for rates of preventable harm.

With real money at stake, the hospital industry is pushing back. Rich Umbdenstock, the AHA's CEO, says the penalties are counterproductive. "Rather than punishing hospitals for their efforts to improve, we should encourage them to continue to work together to develop new and better tools to deliver the safest possible care." In fact, proven approaches to reduce preventable harm already exist and need to be applied consistently for the benefit of patients.

A GOAL TO REDUCE HOSPITAL-ACQUIRED INFECTIONS

In a bold and welcome step, in 2009 Secretary Sebelius set a goal for a 30 percent reduction in hospital-acquired infections. Hospitals used this opportunity to lobby Congress for more money. They convinced lawmakers to give $50 million in taxpayer funds to help them learn how to reduce the number of people harmed by infections in their facilities. Even with the public funding, many hospitals chose not to participate, citing other priorities.

As the work progressed, the government took charge. It convened a public meeting to provide an update on hospital infections. Few in the hospital industry attended. Government officials led the effort. The solution rests, however, with hospitals. Only a sustained, never-ending commitment of hospital personnel to apply proven practices will reduce infections. Here is an example.

A hospital in California trained its housekeeping staff in important cleaning techniques in intensive-care rooms that had been previously occupied by a patient who had been infected with a potentially deadly antibiotic-resistant bacteria. To prepare the room for the next patient and avoid transmission of the bacteria, simple steps were used. Hospital staff immersed cleaning cloths in disinfectant rather than pouring disinfectant on the floor or on the cloths. They used black lights to shine over the area where they cleaned to see how effective they were in removing bacteria. The result? Life-threatening infections were cut nearly in half.

While some hospitals have made great strides in reducing infections, have they met the goal of a 30 percent reduction in hospital-acquired infections? The federal government stated in its 2010 annual report to Congress on health care quality that very little progress has been made. In fact, certain types of infections increased. Hospitals have used their special status as a place where life-saving care is provided to avoid being held accountable for their failure to provide care safely. Under the health care reform law, hospitals that have high rates of infections will be penalized financially. Whether this strategy will compel better care cannot be assured. Reducing infections requires hospitals to be high-functioning organizations in which staff cooperate with each other to achieve a common aim.

BUILDING A PATIENT SAFETY INFRASTRUCTURE

The extent of health care harm is a public safety crisis and demands a robust response by government and the health care industry. A brief examination of highway and aviation safety illustrates the commitment and cooperation needed to address this crisis. In both sectors, an infrastructure was established that engages the government, the private sector, and consumers. Health care safety requires a similar sustained commitment.

How Highway Safety Improved

For many years, auto manufacturers blamed drivers for vehicle accidents. Consumer advocate Ralph Nader wrote *Unsafe at Any Speed*, the 1965 book that showed that drivers were not the cause of many accidents. The subtitle of his book is less catchy but critically important: *The Designed-In Dangers of the American Automobile*.

By exposing the design flaws in vehicles, Nader proved that responsibility for safety needed to shift from consumers to the manufacturers. He was relentless in the face of harsh rebuke from an auto industry that fought his efforts to promote public safety.

The escalating number of traffic fatalities compelled Congress to enact the 1966 National Traffic and Motor Vehicle Safety Act. The federal law was a turning point. For the first time, manufacturers were held accountable for the safety of their vehicles. A new federal agency, now called the National Highway Traffic Safety Administration, was established and gave the federal government the authority to set and regulate standards for motor vehicles. Vehicles were required to include safety features such as seat belts, shatter-resistant windshields, and head rests to prevent whiplash.

Lee Iacocca, the chief executive officer of Chrysler who had voiced loud opposition to government regulation, eventually had a change of heart. He realized that safety features could be a competitive advantage in the marketplace. Now the auto industry boasts safety features in its consumer advertising.

Great strides have been made in highway safety. In 2010 the number of traffic deaths—33,000—reached its lowest point since 1949, even as billions more miles were driven.

What does highway safety have to do with health care? It provides a useful contrast. Health care professionals say that their work is more complex and that it is harder for them to improve safety. To some extent this is true. It can also be an excuse for poor performance.

Every day, millions of people step into slabs of molded steel and travel at speeds of up to sixty miles an hour carrying twenty gallons of flammable fuel that can trigger an inferno. Each vehicle travels within several yards of other steel hunks doing the exact same thing. Miraculously, fatal harm is relatively rare and becoming more rare.

A commitment from government, vehicle manufacturers, insurance companies, consumer advocates, and others has made this feat possible. The contentious battles have yielded an enviable safety record that everyone can be proud of. Mission impossible is possible.

How Aviation Safety Improved

Passenger airlines have made remarkable progress to improve safety in the past fifteen years. In 1997 the White House Commission on Aviation

Safety and Security set a goal to reduce the fatal accident rate in commercial aviation by 80 percent in ten years. Many in the industry believed that the goal was unattainable, but that did not stop progress.

A joint industry and government team was established and led the effort. It was composed of airline companies, airplane manufacturers, pilots' associations, Federal Aviation Administration safety officials, and technical experts. The team was called the Commercial Aviation Safety Team (CAST).

All the airlines and federal agencies cooperated with each other and contributed their own staff and financial resources. No federal money was appropriated to reach this goal.

The team analyzed information from five hundred accidents and thousands of safety incidents worldwide. They distilled lessons and identified ways to improve safety and save lives. A leading cause of accidents occurred when pilots inadvertently flew planes into mountains, trees, or water, a situation called "controlled flight into terrain" accidents.

One of the first improvements the team developed was a ground proximity warning system that gives pilots a computerized map that shows oncoming obstacles such as mountains and trees. It sounds an alarm to prevent pilots from inadvertently flying into mountains or water. All the airlines voluntarily installed this technology on every airplane.

Because of this and other improvements, fatalities in commercial aviation declined by 83 percent in twelve years. The safest aviation system in the world had been created. This improvement occurred even when the complexity of air passenger travel increased dramatically in the aftermath of the tragic events on September 11, 2001.

Despite the significant cost of implementing a full array of safety features, airlines gained a $620 million per year return on their investment. The aviation field demonstrated that safety is good business and saves lives and money. It also showed that what seems impossible is possible.

ENGINEERING UNSAFE CARE OUT OF HOSPITALS

Just as the airlines successfully engineered unsafe conditions out of the system, hospitals can do the same. Here is an example of how it can be done.

A patient in a Midwest hospital with asthma and pneumonia was being transported to have a chest X-ray. The patient was placed on oxygen. While in the elevator with the transporter, the patient's skin began to turn blue. The patient was not getting enough oxygen circulating to his vital organs. The transporter realized that the oxygen tank was empty. The patient was rushed to the intensive care unit where he eventually recovered.

Nurses, respiratory therapists, and doctors at the hospital tried to fix the problem so it would not happen again. Here's what they did.

First, they wanted to know how many hospital staff could accurately calculate whether an oxygen tank has enough oxygen for an hour trip to the X-ray department when a patient is on a designated level of oxygen. They conducted a short, anonymous survey and learned that very few people could answer the questions correctly, with the exception of respiratory therapists and anesthesiologists.

One solution they considered was to teach hospital staff how to calculate the oxygen remaining in a tank. They dropped this idea because arithmetic mistakes can be made. The team needed a reliable method. The Apple iTunes store sells an iPhone and iPad application that calculates remaining oxygen time in a tank, but not all hospital staff have an iPhone or iPad.

The respiratory therapists developed a chart with the hours and minutes that oxygen would remain depending on the flow of oxygen that the patient needed and the amount of oxygen in the tank. They placed this chart on every oxygen tank in the hospital.

A nationwide solution would require every manufacturer of oxygen tanks to include a chart on all the tanks they sell so that thousands of hospitals don't have to reinvent ways to ensure safe patient care.

WILL HEALTH CARE EVER BE SAFE?

In the mid-2000s patient safety captured the attention and enthusiasm of many dedicated doctors, nurses, pharmacists, and administrators who wanted to learn how to redesign error-prone systems in which they work. People who have been patients are alive today because of their commitment to fixing broken systems and making them fail-safe.

We sense that some of this enthusiasm has waned. The weak economy is a major distraction and interrupts the laser-like focus needed to create and sustain fundamental transformation. This is a missed opportunity because safer care costs less money.

The health care reform law has been a distraction too. Hundreds of thousands of people who work in hospitals and other facilities are assessing the impact of the law on their organizations and positioning themselves to survive in a rapidly changing world.

In private conversations with health care leaders, we sense a growing unease that while safety has improved in certain units in individual hospitals and doctors' offices, the health care system is not becoming safer overall. In fact, seasoned observers say they believe it is becoming more unsafe. When we talk to nurses who work at the bedside in hospitals and have made safety improvements in their units, many of them witness growing chaos.

Are people simply becoming more aware of health care harm? Or are Americans using more health care and being exposed to the potential for more harm? Both are probably true, but the explanation is more profound.

We have come to believe that the unrestrained, market-driven approach to health care is a chief cause of the chaos that is reaching a tipping point beyond which it is impossible to remedy. Compounding this progression is the lack of cooperation in the health care sector that is essential to achieve the high levels of safety attained in other industries. Exceptional organizations with insightful and informed leaders can buck this trend. They will be oases in the desert.

· 7 ·

Hospitals: Do This, Not That

$\mathcal{A}$s the frenzy of health care reform continues to unfold, hospitals and other health care providers are looking for advice about how to survive and thrive in the new world that lies ahead.

High-priced consultants are advising hospital executives on how they can increase profitability. The usual advice is to reduce costs and increase revenues. As with any business, this approach seems reasonable. Consultants tend to suggest that hospitals reduce costs by cutting nursing and housekeeping staff because labor costs are a hospital's largest expense.

After hospitals exhaust that approach, they are advised to recruit more physicians who can bring patients—and the revenue they generate—to the hospitals. Says one expert, "New physicians will bring in more cases and grow your profits." She recommends "polling your medical staff for names of local physicians to target and inviting them into the facility." During the visit, hospitals should work to "wow" the target physician.

If every hospital followed this advice, the health care system would be in big trouble. In fact, most hospitals follow this advice and that's why health care *is* in trouble.

The public is in trouble too. Who wants to be a patient at a hospital that encourages doctors to perform surgeries with the sole purpose of increasing revenue?

Recently, one of us was invited to give a presentation at a hospital in New Jersey. At the time, this hospital was enticing a group of physicians in its community to admit their patients to its facility. An ethical physician

77

at the hospital refused to give the sales pitch because the doctors had a reputation for overtreating patients. The hospital continued to pursue this approach to increase market share and revenue.

We predict that the sweeping overhaul of health care will cause a surge in this business model. Americans with private insurance will have unlimited lifetime insurance benefits. Hospitals, ambulatory surgery centers, and other providers will take advantage of these benefits and perform unnecessary and inappropriate surgeries, tests, and procedures. Nothing in the health care reform law curtails this business model.

THE FREE SURGERY GIVE-AWAY

Lap-band surgery for obesity illustrates the madness. During the surgery, an inflatable silicone ring is wrapped around the stomach to control the urge to eat. It is widely marketed as a solution to weight loss. The company that makes the inflatable device, Allergan, proposed to the FDA to increase the number of people eligible for the surgery. Its sales of lap bands were declining, so the company was looking for new customers.

The surgery is marketed as an alternative to more invasive gastric bypass surgery. The lap band was originally approved by the FDA for morbidly obese people. A 5'6" person who weighs 216 pounds and has diabetes or hypertension would be eligible to have the procedure. In December 2010 advisors to the FDA recommended broader use of lap-band surgery to include people who weigh less. A person who is 5'6" tall and weighs 187 pounds and has diabetes or hypertension, for example, would be eligible for the procedure.

Video testimonials from patients on the company's website say the surgery benefited them. A closer look reveals troubling risks. The company reports on its website that 25 percent of people who had the surgery had a second operation to remove the band because they had so much trouble with it.

If 25 percent of Toyota owners were so dissatisfied that they called up their dealers and asked them to come and take their cars out of their driveways, the US Department of Transportation would launch an investigation into the reason for consumer dissatisfaction.

Another 18 percent of people needed a second surgery to fix problems with the band. Four people had the band erode into their stomachs. Some doctors have stopped using the device.

ABC Nightly News reported the FDA advisory panel's recommendation to expand the use of the surgery. Chief health and medical editor, Dr. Richard Besser, weighed in with his recommendation, saying that the surgery "is growing in popularity" and "should be approved."

The segment mentions the risks, but it also included a video clip of a doctor who suggested the FDA should approve the device for broader use. The network did not interview a physician with an opposing view. The segment also aired a testimonial from a satisfied patient who had the procedure. No one who had the band removed was interviewed.

The manufacturer of the lap band, Allergan, conducted a marketing campaign to promote lap-band surgery. It included a contest to give away free lap-band surgeries. A doctor in Arizona, who is billed as "Arizona's Premier Lap-Band Specialist," advertised the contest on his blog. Three lucky "winners" will receive free surgery and follow-up care. Serious surgery is being marketed as a game to be won.

Websites advertise the surgery as if it were a luxury vacation. "Hurry and Book Now! Ask About Our Specials! Only $3999." The hype creates perverse incentives. Bloggers report that some people are *gaining* weight so they can weigh enough to qualify for the surgery.

The company shies away from making any commitment about whether the surgery succeeds in helping people lose weight and keep it off.

The FDA approved the manufacturer's request to lower the threshold of eligibility for the surgery. Now the company has millions of new potential customers.

Hospitals and doctors reap enormous financial benefits from this lucrative business. Repeat surgeries and multiple office visits to manage complications are highly profitable. The device maker will earn profits to help satisfy Wall Street's insatiable expectations for higher stock prices and earnings per share. Lap-band surgery is just one example of the perfect storm that conspires to place the health of Americans at risk.

There is nothing wrong with performing a procedure that may help some people. The decision to perform an operation should take into account the significant potential to cause more harm than good. Unfortunately, companies have every incentive to ignore this basic principle. And no one is protecting the public's interest.

The reform law does not fix this profound and deeply disturbing problem. Health care was meant to be a public service. Now it is a means for private gain at public expense.

THE DEATH OF TRUTH

The medical-industrial complex squelches the truth when it gets in the way of financial gain. Take the case of an Aurora, Wisconsin, physician, Dr. Kiran Sagar. She did an internal quality assurance project at St. Luke's Medical Center in Aurora where she worked. She found that nearly 30 percent of the 235 echocardiograms performed at the hospital had been interpreted incorrectly. An echocardiogram uses ultrasound to show images of the heart.

Because of the faulty interpretations, eighteen people had to have even more tests in which a probe was inserted down their throats; nineteen had a coronary angiography, a test that uses dye and a special X-ray of the heart to determine whether arteries are blocked. People having these unnecessary and inappropriate procedures bore the risks of harm and paid for the privilege.

According to an account in the *Milwaukee Journal Sentinel*, Dr. Sagar presented her findings at a meeting of the American Society of Echocardiography because she thought the problem needed to be discussed with other doctors around the country to help improve medical care. Two months later, she was told by hospital officials that she was fired and had to leave the hospital immediately. The hospital said in a statement that her termination was not related to the study.

Dr. Sagar has trained dozens of doctors in echocardiography over the years and is one of the first female cardiologists to practice in Wisconsin. Widely regarded as a good doctor, she came to Aurora in 2003 after leaving a tenured position at the Medical College of Wisconsin.

She believes she was fired because her study shed an unfavorable light on the hospital. "The cardiologists weren't happy," she said. "I think behind the scenes they were saying, 'How can you expose our dirty laundry?'"

Dr. John Birkmeyer of the Center for Healthcare Outcomes and Policy at the University of Michigan estimates that $150 billion a year is spent on surgery that doesn't make people better and could actually make them worse.

The manipulation of medicine for financial benefit fits well with the building construction binge among hospitals in recent years. The financial hangover will last for decades. Empty beds are a money loser for hospitals. They need to find patients who can fill them. Medical device manufacturers are pleased to oblige and develop new products that can be used in surgeries that help to fill those empty beds.

Full-page advertisements in the *New York Times* and other major newspapers tout hospitals' brand-name images and draw patients from other parts of the country. The marketing material does not say whether a hospital achieves better outcomes than other hospitals. Instead, it advertises the newest and most expensive robots and the nicest atrium.

Desperate for more money, some hospitals pay kickbacks to doctors to induce them to admit patients and perform surgery and tests. Two Texas hospitals owned by Universal Health Services, the same firm whose two hospitals in California received Medicare termination letters, engaged in similar acts. Two months after those termination letters, UHS paid $27.5 million to settle claims that from 1999 to 2006 it committed fraud and paid bribes to doctors in McAllen, Texas. The settlement with the Justice Department involved allegations that the hospitals had entered into financial relationships with several doctors to induce them to refer patients to UHS hospitals. The government alleged that these payments were disguised through a series of sham contracts including medical directorships and lease agreements.

The *New Yorker* profiled McAllen, Texas, in a June 2009 article that suggested that hospitals in the community were performing too many surgeries at Medicare's expense and implied that a portion of them were unnecessary.

Years ago, hospitals provided a community service. Now many of them are a means to enrich their top brass. Nonprofit hospitals are not immune. With high salaries and private airplanes for company executives, some nonprofit hospitals are not what the public has in mind when they think of a tax-exempt charitable organization. A beehive that needs to be kicked is the tax-exempt status of the hospitals that believe charity begins at home.

WHAT HOSPITALS *SHOULD* DO
TO SAVE A TRILLION DOLLARS

Instead of financial gimmickry, hospitals should be doing more operations engineering. Here is an example of what we mean.

Imagine if the airlines scheduled all their flights only when pilots want to fly. Assume that few pilots want to fly before six o'clock in the morning or after seven o'clock at night. Assume, too, that pilots want to take Fridays off to play golf. The consequences are predictable.

Flight schedules are compressed. Airline and airport staff—air traffic controllers, flight engineers, flight attendants, baggage handlers, and maintenance staff—work around pilots' schedules. Airports are more crowded as passengers cool their heels waiting in longer security lines that snake outside the airport. Bad weather and flight cancellations wreak havoc when passengers try to rebook. More frequent takeoffs and landings in a compressed time period increase the risk of a near miss on the runways, or worse. Underused airport capacity in downtime drains efficiency.

In most hospitals, elective surgeries such as knee replacement are scheduled according to doctors' convenience. Nurses' and other hospital staffs' schedules revolve around the doctors. Mondays might be a peak period and crammed with elective surgeries.

During the rush, nurses work unexpected overtime, which means they can't pick up their child from day care or be home for dinner with their families. Patients spend more time anxiously waiting for their operations. Others lie on gurneys after surgery waiting to be safely transferred to units in the hospital to recover. Surgeries may have to be rescheduled because the surgeons are backed up. The risk of mistakes increases when everyone works faster. Meanwhile, Fridays are calm and quiet because the doctors are in their offices seeing patients, attending a conference, or taking the day off.

Professor Eugene Litvak, adjunct professor in operations management at the Harvard School of Public Health, hails from Russia, where he helped the trains run on time. Litvak is an expert in queuing theory and variability methodology, common tools in management science.

He quickly observed an anomaly in US hospitals. Why do hospitals seem to be overcrowded when only about 66 percent of the hospitals' beds are filled?

Litvak mused that hospitals think they are overcrowded and build a new wing at an average cost of $1 million per bed. In reality, they haven't properly managed the flow of their patients through the hospital.

Operations management, variability methodology, and queuing theory are among the tools of management science that are beginning to be applied in hospitals. Predictably, the use of this science is improving care, increasing efficiency, and reducing waste.

Take the example of Cincinnati Children's Hospital. Its progressive leaders were looking for solutions to improve how it organized its operations. Hospital officials were candid about the problems. They wrote,

> As the hospital has grown and expanded, the number of referrals increased, along with the complexity of the care required. Emergency surgeries were considered unpredictable and were done at the end of the day or forced into slots between scheduled cases. The result was a long list of add-on patients at the conclusion of the regular day and long waiting times for children with urgent needs.
>
> Complex cases were often done in the evening or at night, when resources were limited. The competition for available beds in the pediatric intensive care unit resulted in patients being held in the emergency department . . . causing those locations to back up and causing elective surgeries to be delayed or cancelled. Patients sometimes were placed in beds that were not optimal for their condition. . . . Clinicians and families were left frustrated.

Initially, hospital officials tried to reduce overcrowding in the emergency room by hiring more staff to work during peak periods. Professor Litvak helped them realize this was not a solution. They had to look at the whole hospital, not just the emergency department. He showed them how backups in one part of the hospital can cause backups in others.

Litvak traced the long waiting times in the emergency department and backups in other parts of the hospital to how elective surgeries were scheduled. He helped the hospital improve how it organized its work.

Hospital administrators took control over operating-room time and assigned times when doctors perform elective, nonemergency surgeries. This was a major feat because doctors prefer to set their own schedules. The frenetic rush hours were eliminated.

The hospital set aside operating rooms for emergencies so that scheduled elective operations would not be disrupted if unexpected emergencies occur. To avoid backups, a bed in the intensive care unit was reserved at the same time a surgery was scheduled for patients requiring intensive care following the operation.

Litvak predicted that the hospital could perform more surgeries by using the same capacity more efficiently. He was right. The hospital treated more children using the same staff and physical capacity and boosted revenue by $137 million. Hospital occupancy increased from 76 percent to 90 percent.

The hospital had been planning to build an expansion with one hundred new beds, but administrators and doctors realized that it was not needed. They had learned how to use their existing capacity efficiently.

Doctors are enthusiastic about the new system. Fewer surgeries are cancelled and the chaos that can occur during peak periods is engineered out of the system. Nurses can spend more time with patients and can go home as planned. Overtime hours decreased by nearly 60 percent, which saved $559,000 a year.

If all hospitals in the United States used their capacity efficiently, Professor Litvak estimates the savings to be $35 to $112 billion annually.

He predicts that enough capacity exists in the system to take care of all the newly insured. This would save $12 billion to $35 billion a year by avoiding construction of more hospital beds.

The Institute of Medicine has recognized the importance of variability methodology and queuing theory and stresses that "hospitals can identify and eliminate many of the patient flow impediments caused by operational inefficiencies."

Although the American Hospital Association's Quality Center has also recognized variability methodology as a key principle for making care safe, timely, effective, efficient, equitable, and patient centered, only a handful of the nearly five thousand hospitals in the United States are using management science to improve their operations. They are reluctant to disrupt the schedules of their doctors. Another reason is that hospital executives and chief medical officers don't know about this science-based approach to effective hospital management.

The overcrowding "crisis" caused by poor hospital management contributed to a building boom that will cost hundreds of billions of dollars for decades to come. All of the costs are hidden in higher health insurance premiums.

Hospitals consume more than 5 percent of the country's gross domestic product. Their collective inefficiency represents a monumental loss of productive efficiency in the American economy.

Health care reform pours billions of dollars more into these poorly organized and managed institutions. Few policy makers understand why hospitals and other health care providers require more money every year. By plowing even more funding into health care, the reform law cements inefficiency in the system.

If you drive by Cincinnati Children's Hospital today, it looks like any other modern hospital. You wouldn't know that it has engineered some of the inefficiencies out of its day-to-day work. The hospital acknowledges that it has a lot more work to do to transform health care.

As an added bonus, patients receive better care in smoothly running facilities. Professor Litvak discovered that the chaos in poorly run hospitals can cause patients to be placed in units that have an open bed but which may not be optimal for patient care. A child recovering from orthopedic surgery, for example, might be placed in an oncology unit. Because the doctors and nurses in that unit are not accustomed to caring for children recovering from surgery and the drugs they are prescribed, they are prone to miss clinical signs and symptoms that require immediate attention.

This is what happened to Lewis Blackman at the Medical University of South Carolina Children's Hospital. After elective surgery to correct a condition called sunken chest syndrome, fifteen-year-old Lewis was admitted to an oncology unit. To control the significant pain following the surgery, he was administered a powerful drug, Toradol. The doctors and nurses were not familiar with this drug, as they would be with chemotherapy drugs. Lewis died from a perforated ulcer, a known complication of the drug.

A more mundane example illustrates that hospitals are in the very early stages of rooting out the most rudimentary inefficiencies. A hospital in the Midwest noticed that its staff prepared a giant stack of documents every time one of its patients went to a nursing home. A team was assigned the task to review the papers and find out whether all of them were necessary. The team had one week to complete its assignment.

Team members called the nursing homes and learned that they didn't use or need much of the information. In fact, they threw most of the paper away. By the end of the week, the team whittled down the big stack to less than an inch. Staff that had been assigned to produce the useless documents were reassigned to perform value-added work.

Improvement in operational efficiency is routine in businesses that must compete to survive in the marketplace. Health care is not like any other business. If McDonald's Corporation or Apple Inc. were managed like hospitals, they would be out of business. Poor customer service, long waiting times, and defective products would drive customers away. Staff turnover would be in the stratosphere because of workplace chaos. Balance sheets would be awash in red ink.

Real efficiency and transformation in health care can happen only if hospital executives and doctors are as fixated on smart operational engineering as they are on financial gimmickry. The transformation would be miraculous. We advise young doctors and nurses to obtain degrees in engineering instead of an MBA.

As health care organizations come under financial pressure, those that don't have the knowledge and skill to improve efficiency the right way won't know what to do. Incentives in the health care reform law try to promote more efficiency, but if hospitals and other providers don't know how to do it, the incentives will have unintended consequences.

Imagine you are walking down a street in Boston and are offered a million dollars to hit a baseball out of Fenway Park. If you are like the average American, you probably couldn't do it. That's because you don't know how. Even if you know theoretically how to hold the bat to hit a home run, you won't have the strength or skill that comes from training.

Hospitals and other health care providers will default to what they know, which is to cut nursing and other staff and encourage doctors to admit more patients. A bad situation will become worse. Once again, hospital lobbyists will swarm the halls of Congress and explain why perpetual increases in funding should be showered upon them.

The reform law makes a good-faith effort to bring more efficiency into the health care system. Here are a few examples of what is planned.

Prevent Hospital Readmissions

Almost one in five people on Medicare who are admitted to a hospital returns within thirty days. Most of them don't see a doctor after they leave the hospital the first time. Doctors say that better care after a hospital stay can avoid readmissions. The law imposes financial penalties on hospitals whose patients with certain conditions have to be admitted to the hospital again because of preventable complications. The intent is to encourage hospitals to provide good care the first time.

Bundle Up

In the months ahead, Medicare will test different ways of paying hospitals and doctors to encourage them to provide better care and possibly control spending. Currently, if a person has heart surgery, Medicare pays the hospital and each doctor separately. If the patient returns to the hospital because of a complication, the hospital and doctor are paid again. They have no incentive to work together to prevent complications.

Medicare is testing an idea to pay hospitals and doctors a lump sum payment for treating people throughout an episode of care. The approach is like paying for a car rather than buying parts of the car, putting it together, and hoping it runs.

These so-called bundled payments are meant to give hospitals and doctors motivation to coordinate care, keep people healthy, and prevent unnecessary hospitalizations. If successful, the pilot projects can be expanded around the country.

We predict that the savings will be modest and won't materialize for a long time. The Congressional Budget Office estimates $1.3 billion in savings but acknowledges that the savings are uncertain because the ideas haven't been tested.

Know What Works

The reform law established the Patient-Centered Outcomes Research Institute, which is intended to give doctors, nurses, and patients information about how well tests and treatments work. Opponents of health care reform have stirred up a tizzy of opposition, saying that government will come between you and your doctor. It is unfortunate that they have stoked unfounded fear among the public.

Here's the truth about what is intended. If you are lying on a gurney and waiting to be wheeled into an operating room for surgery, the research aims to ensure that you receive the best care that science can offer.

Information Technology

Federal government investments in health information technology aim to boost the use of electronic health records. A time-and-motion study in hospitals found that nurses spent one-third of their time documenting patient information and often manually transferring information from different electronic systems that are not interoperable. Well-functioning electronic health records will give doctors and nurses more accurate and real-time information about their patients.

Cut the Paperwork

The reform law takes aim at unnecessary paperwork. It creates uniform electronic standards for all private insurers, Medicare, and Medicaid. This sensible change will save the federal government $20 billion over ten years. Private insurers, physicians, hospitals, and other providers will save tens of billions of dollars too.

Each of these measures has the potential to improve health and lower spending, but they don't tackle the heart of the problem. The health care system in the United States supports a business model driven by volume. Health care reform will offer needed protection from the cost of health care for millions of Americans in the next few years. We predict that the benefits will erode because the cost of care will continue to increase as volume increases. Eventually, comprehensive health insurance will be unaffordable even with government subsidies.

The medical-industrial complex has an addiction, and no antidote exists to cure it except a slow and painful withdrawal.

Part 3

HOW HEALTH CARE CAUGHT
THE WALL STREET FEVER

$\mathcal{T}$he first chapter in this section, chapter 8, draws parallels between the inner workings of the banking and financial sector and the health care industry.

With the near collapse of the banks in 2008, the public learned new language that had been "inside baseball" in the world of Wall Street: price bubbles, toxic assets, conflict of interest, and too big to fail.

For the first time, Americans saw what was really going on behind the shimmering steel and glass towers on Wall Street and what highly paid people were really doing with their money. Regulatory agencies designed to keep the banks in check were no match for the behemoths that showered Washington politicians with cash.

We describe symptoms of the Wall Street fever and how the contagion has spread to the health care industry. Behind the veneer of the mighty-looking towers of drug companies, device manufacturers, and hospitals is their own version of price bubbles, toxic assets, conflict of interest, and too big to fail. We examine what they are really doing with your money. Yes, they do a lot of good. But they do more than that as they follow in the footsteps of the banking industry.

Chapter 9 explains how the Wall Street fever has permeated virtually every crevice in health care. A cascade of devices and equipment flows into hospitals that add to chaos but increase companies' bottom line. At Johns Hopkins Hospital in Baltimore, the top-rated hospital in *U.S. News and World Report* rankings, an average of 942 alarms sounded from multiple devices every day on a fifteen-bed patient care unit, about one alarm every ninety seconds. Devices and equipment routinely malfunction and can harm patients. If these devices were iPhones, manufacturers would be held accountable for safety and reliability. Not so in health care.

· 8 ·

Too Big to Fail Just Got Bigger

The near collapse of the financial industry in 2008 revealed profound weaknesses in government regulation that was supposed to rein in excessive and unlawful activities. The financial meltdown that nearly brought the country to its knees offers lessons for health care. If an unfettered marketplace can mess with your wealth, it can also mess with your health.

Let's begin in the good old days when banks helped people who wanted to buy a home. The terms of mortgages were straightforward. Borrowers understood they had to pay a certain amount of money every month for thirty years. Bankers verified borrowers' income and credit, and they had a vested interest in ensuring that borrowers had the financial wherewithal to pay back the loan. If the borrower defaulted, the banker bore the risk.

Bankers earned a reasonable rate of return on the money they loaned, and millions of Americans enjoyed the satisfaction of owning their own home. Money was allocated efficiently, and it helped people live a better life.

During the housing boom, many would-be homeowners were attracted to loans with low teaser rates. Although large balloon payments would kick in a few years later, borrowers were told that their houses would increase in value before the higher interest rates and payments came due. They could refinance their mortgages and obtain a lower interest rate. Even better, they could use the equity in their houses as if they were ATMs that could be tapped to pay for a new car or family vacation.

Many borrowers didn't have enough income to qualify for their loans. Banks and mortgage brokers lent hundreds of thousands of dollars to individuals and families without asking for proof of their income. No one enforced commonsense rules of lending, so the companies broke the rules. As long as everyone was making money, and as long as homeowners saw the value of their homes rise, bankers continued the lending spree. Of course, they were lending other peoples' money.

Worthless mortgages from Main Street were bundled into complicated bonds and sold to investors on Wall Street and around the world. The risks of these toxic assets were passed on to unsuspecting investors who didn't know what they were buying. The firms that sold the repackaged mortgages didn't have any incentive to tell the buyers what was in them.

When the bubble burst in 2008, housing values crumpled. People lost their jobs and couldn't pay their mortgages. Higher interest rates kicked in on adjustable-rate mortgages. Refinancing was impossible for many families because their houses were worth less than the balances on their mortgages. Millions of people defaulted, and the banks foreclosed on the properties.

When Wall Street bankers and investment firms realized that the house of cards was collapsing, they were at risk of losing billions of dollars, including their own personal wealth. They went to their friends in Washington and asked for a bailout. The Washington insiders were the same people who allowed them to break the rules.

The economy screeched to a halt. No one trusted anyone, so loans dried up and a credit crunch ensued. Businesses reduced investment. Consumer spending slowed to a crawl. The economy contracted. Even worse, the country lost its confidence and belief that the future will be better for the next generation.

During the financial meltdown, people saw a different side of their banks than the friendly teller in their neighborhood branch. For the first time, Americans got a look behind the scenes at what the big bankers did at work every day: create price bubbles, sell toxic assets, and collude with politicians in Washington to weaken any possibility of meaningful regulation and oversight.

The same Wall Street mentality influences the health care industry, which has its own price bubbles, sells toxic assets, and colludes with politicians to keep the money flowing and pesky bureaucrats at bay. This is not the health care system that people see when they go to the hospital or doctor's office. It lurks behind the scenes in the shadows.

PRICE BUBBLES

Just as housing prices jumped during the height of the frenzy, health care has its own price bubble. What lies at the heart of these bubbles?

Consumption is king in America. Economic growth is highly dependent on Americans buying lots of stuff. During Thanksgiving weekends, Black Friday is an unofficial national holiday when millions of Americans race to the shopping malls. The economy rises and falls on retail sales as the barometer of Americans' willingness to part with their money.

Even after the tragedy of September 11, 2001, President George W. Bush urged Americans to go shopping to jump-start an economy that had grown quiet as people hunkered down in their homes.

How can consumption continue to drive America's economic growth when middle class Americans have not seen their real incomes rise in decades?

Years ago, big business and Wall Street had to find a solution to this vexing problem. Their stock prices and earnings per share depended on people spending more money. But how could American families spend money they didn't have?

American ingenuity found a solution. The answer was to loan them money. If Americans could borrow money, they could continue to shop. Banks would earn huge profits from interest on unpaid bills and credit card fees. Retail businesses that sell clothing, electronics, and other consumer goods and services would reap big profits.

This is how America changed from being a nation of thrifty savers to a nation of shop-until-you-drop spenders and credit card debtors.

American ingenuity didn't stop there. If more Americans could buy houses, the economic engine would really roar. America's mantra, "Charge it!" triggered a frenzy in the housing market. Low teaser rates in adjustable-rate mortgages fueled the frenzy.

Homes became houses. Their value was measured in dollars and cents, not as a place to live and raise a family. Speculation drove prices up. The bubble was bound to burst. And it did. That's why housing prices have dropped from the stratosphere to the dismay of their owners, who thought they could only go up.

Health care is consumption too. Most Americans have health insurance that protects them from the true price of health care. If you are like most Americans, you use more medical care, and more higher-priced care, than if you had to pay with your own money.

The biggest spenders are the hospitals, doctors, drug companies, and device manufacturers who use your insurance card as their credit card.

A perceptive nurse described the trend this way, "Health insurance used to be about giving patients access to providers. Now it's about giving providers access to patients."

Before health care reform, price bubbles became visible as companies announced new $100,000 therapies to treat cancer. They set their prices so high because they *can*. More blockbuster pricing will occur now that lifetime health insurance benefits can no longer be capped.

Adding to the surge is the belief of many Americans that more care will always make them better. It's not their fault that they believe this. As we wrote in *The Treatment Trap*, the medical-industrial complex has marinated the minds of Americans in an endless stream of marketing and media hype that creates consumer demand for their products.

As the price bubble has grown, it is impossible for the middle class and even the upper middle class to pay for their health care from their own pockets, especially if they have a serious illness.

Instead of deflating the price bubble and making health care affordable, health care reform papered over the problem with more health insurance, subsidies from the federal government, and no caps on benefits. This approach will fuel the price bubble even more.

Just as American families watched their mortgage debt grow larger than the value of their houses, the world watches as the federal government's debt is on par with the value of all the goods and services the country produces annually.

CONFLICT OF INTEREST

The financial meltdown was lubricated by conflicts of interest where the private financial interests of bankers were at odds with their obligations to their customers. Without a moral compass, their private financial interests came first. Health care is riddled with conflicts of interest too.

In the banking industry, a borrower depends on a banker to know about mortgage options and suggest loans that suit his or her circumstance.

In the housing debacle, bankers made enormous amounts of money by hiding the risks that unsuspecting borrowers were taking.

In health care, patients expect doctors to make decisions that are in their best interests. Here is one example where the financial interests of the medical-industrial complex took precedence over patients' health and safety.

Americans who had hip or knee surgery from 2002 to 2006 had a surgical device implanted that was the subject of a massive bribery scandal involving device manufacturers and doctors. Five companies that sold about 95 percent of all artificial hip and knee surgical implants in the country had paid orthopedic surgeons bribes to encourage them to use their products, according to a US Department of Justice investigation that ended in 2007.

In the bribery scandal, hundreds of orthopedic surgeons were paid tens to hundreds of thousands of dollars per year for consulting contracts and received expensive trips and other perks.

According to Christopher Christie, then US attorney in New Jersey and now the state's governor, "Prior to our investigation, many orthopedic surgeons in this country made decisions predicated on how much money they could make—choosing which device to implant by going to the highest bidder. . . . We expect doctors to make decisions based on what is in the best interests of their patients—not the best interests of their bank accounts."

The companies that paid the bribes were Zimmer, DePuy Orthopaedics (a subsidiary of Johnson & Johnson), Biomet, and Smith & Nephew. They were the subject of federal criminal complaints and paid fines totaling $311 million. A fifth company, Stryker, avoided a criminal complaint because it was the first to cooperate with prosecutors. Despite the breadth and depth of the crimes, neither company executives nor doctors were prosecuted. The public expects doctors to be different from bankers. They expect hospitals to be different from banks. Many are different and guided by a moral compass.

Ethical physicians who practice medicine for the right reason are deeply distressed about the tidal wave of money that has seeped into every nook and cranny in health care. A physician wrote a letter to us expressing his concerns. He graduated from three Ivy League universities and is board certified in two medical specialties.

"The system is awash in money," he wrote. "The whole emphasis of medical care appears to be on the making of large amounts of money. This is accomplished by the machinations of drug companies, surgical equipment companies, surgi-centers, hospitals, and the medical profession . . . [which] has increased the cost and harm to patients. I can't say enough about this."

Conflicts of interest reach the highest levels. President Obama took $20 million from the health care industry to help pay for his 2008 presidential campaign.

Obama's director of the White House Office of Health Reform during the reform debate, Nancy Ann DeParle, had been a member of the boards of multiple health care companies before accepting that position. According to American University's investigative reporting unit, she received $6 million from firms that stood to benefit from health care reform. DeParle was also a decade-long board member of Cerner, a software manufacturer specializing in electronic medical records, until the day after her White House appointment. Meanwhile, the Obama administration is spending billions of taxpayer dollars to encourage hospitals and doctors to use electronic medical records.

Conflicts of interest explain why the health care industry was rewarded handsomely on the political battlefield of health care reform and why they are handled gingerly by prosecutors.

TOXIC ASSETS

After the mortgage mess unfolded, banks had billions of dollars of toxic assets on their books. Toxic asset values had been inflated by a noxious brew of fraud and speculation but plummeted when the gimmickry was uncovered. Owners of these assets had buyer's remorse because no one would buy them at a price acceptable to the holder.

A "toxic" asset was a term used by Angelo Mozilo, the founder of Countrywide Financial, once the nation's largest mortgage lender. In a 2006 email uncovered by the Securities and Exchange Commission in its investigation of the lender, Mozilo acknowledged, "In all my years in the business I have never seen a more toxic product." He was referring to the 100 percent loans that required no down payments from borrowers with awful credit histories. "Frankly, I consider that product line to be the poison of ours," he continued.

Health care has its own unique form of toxic assets. Here's how they work. A new blockbuster drug comes on the market. Investment bloggers and public relations firms hype a new drug that promises the fountain of youth. Excitement grows about how much money the drug will generate for the company.

An expensive marketing campaign is a success. Six million people have been lured into taking the new drug. Wall Street likes what it sees and the company's stock price jumps. The drug is the most profitable product for one of the biggest drug companies in the world.

Meanwhile, the federal government funds an independent study and discovers that the drug increases the risk of cancer. With all the trappings of a toxic asset, hordes of people stop taking the drug and sales plummet 50 percent.

Doctors notice a remarkable trend. Cancer rates drop nearly 15 percent, the first time in recorded history that rates drop so dramatically. A few years later, another study shows that the drug not only causes cancer but doubles the risk of dying from it. It also increases mortality from another kind of cancer by 70 percent. Curious minds will observe that the same company that sells the drug also makes chemotherapy to treat cancer.

The toxic asset was Prempro, the hormone replacement therapy for women sold by Pfizer. Millions of women trusted the information they received from their doctors and the drug companies. By the time they knew about the dangerous side effects, many women had developed breast cancer. The company continued to rake in billions of dollars.

Women sued Pfizer. The company has been winning many cases because it has convinced juries that women were warned that the drug increased the risk of breast cancer. In one case, a jury in federal court in Alexandria, Virginia, decided unanimously that a sixty-five-year-old woman who had taken Prempro and developed breast cancer was unable to prove that the drug company hid or downplayed risks.

Pfizer's defense is that it communicated the risks and benefits. It points to FDA-approved warnings for physicians and patients about the risk of breast cancer and says that information was available to help doctors determine whether and how to prescribe the drug.

The company uses similar language when warning people who are thinking about buying its stock. An excerpt from the Pfizer prospectus reads as follows: "Achievement of future results is subject to risks, uncertainties and potentially inaccurate assumptions. Should known or unknown risks or uncertainties materialize, or should underlying assumptions prove inaccurate, actual results could differ materially from past results and those anticipated, estimated or projected. You should bear this in mind."

Health care is meant to be different from buying a share of a company's stock. When people take drugs prescribed by doctors, they believe that benevolence lies behind a brightly colored pill. Science, not hype, brought the drug to market, they believe. They rely on trained professionals to warn them of lurking dangers. If a drug is so dangerous, a company would not sell it. Nor would the government allow it to be sold, or so it would seem.

Today patients must read drug labels as if they were reading a stock prospectus. The conflicts of interest in health care are widespread, and unfortunately, the public cannot always trust those who should be protecting them.

The Wall Street mentality has changed health care in America forever. The discovery of new treatments, drugs, or diagnostic tools that are a significant advance in the diagnosis, treatment, or cure for a disease can take years to bring to market. Yet venture capitalists and investors, intent on quick returns, want financial results now not later.

When companies cannot satisfy Wall Street's demands for a legitimate new blockbuster every year, they market their existing drugs and devices so more people use them. The risks are passed on to the patient with the mentality of "buyer beware." A health care company's worth is measured by its stock price, not by whether it helps or hurts its customers. The stock price becomes the almighty indicator that is watched with an intensity matched only by farmers watching for rain during a drought. Ethical investors could make socially responsible decisions if they had an index that measures the social good that a company does and the harm it inflicts.

PRIVATIZED GAIN, SOCIALIZED LOSS

Before the financial meltdown, banks and investment firms pursued high-risk strategies that yielded enormously high returns. Multimillion-dollar salaries and bonuses paid to company executives financed Madison Avenue homes and Nantucket beach villas. When the house of cards came tumbling down, the American taxpayer was forced to bail out the banks. It is a classic case of privatized gains and socialized losses.

Health care has its own privatized gains and socialized losses. When Pfizer sold toxic assets like Prempro, it gained profits from the sale of the drug but passed the cost of treatment for breast and lung cancer to women and their health insurers. In turn, insurers spread the cost among all their insured and everyone pays higher premiums. Similarly, when hospitals fail to apply standard practices to prevent hospital-acquired infections, they make money from the extra services to treat the infection, as do drug companies that manufacture antibiotics, but pass the cost on to the patients and their health insurers. As the federal government and private insurers expand the no-payment policy when patient harm occurs, they are appropriately privatizing the losses.

ROBO-SIGNING

As the housing market was undergoing a wrenching correction, the robo-signing scandal surfaced. Employees at Bank of America, JPMorgan Chase, and other banks routinely signed thousands of foreclosure documents without knowing or verifying the information contained in them. The courts used these documents to decide whether to foreclose on properties when borrowers defaulted on their mortgages. Families were forced out of their homes when they should not have been.

The health care sector has its own form of robo-signing. Drug and device makers pay marketing company ghostwriters to write so-called research articles for medical journals that extol the benefits of their products. Doctors are solicited to have their names used as authors. They may not have conducted the research nor verified the validity of the data or the conclusions drawn. The articles are published in medical journals, and other doctors and patients rely on the information to make medical decisions. Company sales representatives distribute the information to doctors to convince them to use their products.

In medicine, science was meant to be the compass guiding the allocation of human and financial resources in service to humanity. The perversion of science for financial gain has unleashed a torrent of misinformation to deliberately mislead and confuse honest doctors, patients, and policy makers. Chaos ensues. Few doctors have time to sort fact from fiction, so they surrender to whatever information sticks.

The former editor of the *New England Journal of Medicine*, Dr. Marcia Angell, wrote, "It is simply no longer possible to believe much of the clinical research that is published, or to rely on the judgment of trusted physicians or authoritative medical guidelines. I take no pleasure in this conclusion, which I reached slowly and reluctantly over my two decades as an editor of the *New England Journal of Medicine*."

THE RATING GAME

Imagine a failing student who gets an A in every class. That is how the credit ratings agencies graded the quality of mortgage-backed securities that were chock full of subprime mortgages. The AAA ratings from Standard & Poor's and Moody's were a mistake. Pension funds, banks, and other investors relied on these ratings to make investment decisions.

Says economist Joseph Stiglitz, "I view the rating agencies as one of the key culprits. . . . They were the party that performed the alchemy that converted the securities from F-rated to A-rated. The banks could not have done what they did without the complicity of the rating agencies."

The rating agencies are rife with conflicts of interest. They are paid by the investment banks that organize and sell debt to investors, and they reap larger profits when they inflate the ratings.

Health care has its own rating agencies. The Joint Commission, the Chicago-based group that accredits health care facilities, gives hospitals that meet its highest standards a "Gold Seal of Approval." The Joint Commission is funded by the hospitals it accredits.

The ratings don't tell the full story. Accredited hospitals are to report serious events such as the preventable death or serious injury of a patient. An investigation by the federal Government Accountability Office found that hospitals report a tiny fraction of these events to The Joint Commission, which acknowledges low self-reporting. Its own information shows that fewer than five thousand events had been reported in fifteen years. One-third of them had been reported by other sources.

Like the credit rating agencies, The Joint Commission's information paints a rosier picture than warranted. Unlike the credit rating agencies, most prospective patients don't bet their health on The Joint Commission ratings. In fact, most people don't know about the ratings. Nonetheless, the ratings can give a false sense of security about the safety and quality of care.

TOO BIG TO FAIL

A company that is too big to fail is considered too important to the economy to be allowed to declare bankruptcy or be liquidated. The banking and health care industries are riddled with entities that are considered too big to fail.

In the immediate wake of the financial crisis, the federal government poured billions of taxpayer dollars into the big banks—Bank of America, Citicorp, JPMorgan Chase, Wells Fargo—and hundreds of other smaller banks to bolster their capital and support new lending to jump-start a sputtering economy. The government would never let them collapse because the economy would collapse. The banks were too big to fail and they knew it. In a classic case of moral hazard, they assumed the government would bail them out even if they continued their streak of risky behavior.

The federal government encouraged stronger banks to take over weaker ones to stabilize them. In a wave of consolidation, big banks became even bigger. Two years later, the assets of the six largest banks totaled 63 percent of GDP. Fifteen years earlier, the assets of the six largest banks totaled only 17 percent of GDP.

In health care, the government doesn't allow too-big-to-fail companies to fail. When Eli Lilly was found guilty of misusing its drug Zyprexa on nursing-home patients with Alzheimer's disease, it was convicted on a misdemeanor rather than a felony. If the offense had been a felony, the company would be excluded from receiving any money from the Medicare and Medicaid programs. The court was unwilling to take this action because of what it called collateral consequences that would befall stockholders and Medicare and Medicaid enrollees who benefit from insulin and other beneficial medications the company makes. Eli Lilly was too big to fail.

Soon after health care reform became the law of the land, a torrid pace of mergers and acquisitions ensued. As one example, Johns Hopkins health system, a $6 billion behemoth based in Baltimore, acquired Sibley Memorial Hospital, a small community facility in Washington, DC, for the princely sum of $1. Sibley gave its resources to Hopkins in return for Hopkins' brand name and infrastructure.

Consolidation means fewer choices for the public. Big hospital systems wield more negotiating power over insurance companies and demand higher payments. Patients who are harmed by bad care have a more intimidating battle when seeking redress. In the *Wealth of Nations,* Adam Smith understood this when he wrote, "People of the same trade seldom meet together, even for merriment and diversion, but the conversation ends in a conspiracy against the public."

TOO BIG TO BE HELD ACCOUNTABLE

After the reckless activity was uncovered in the banking industry, company executives were not held accountable for massive irregularities: issuing fraudulent loans, failing to disclose risks on company books, knowingly giving themselves bonuses based on illusory profits, and misleading regulators, among many other failings. When companies such as Pfizer and Eli Lilly have been found guilty of paying bribes or selling drugs in violation of the law, their executives are not held accountable.

The big clout wielded by hospitals with undue influence came to light in a first-of-its-kind study in Massachusetts. The state attorney general reviewed the contracts between private insurance companies and hospitals—a study every state should do—and found startling variation in prices the insurance companies paid to different hospitals.

Blue Cross Blue Shield paid a hospital on Nantucket nearly 200 percent more than it paid a similar hospital. Another insurer, Harvard Pilgrim Health Care, paid about 300 percent more to one hospital compared to another. In some instances, hospitals that provided *better* quality care received less money than hospitals with *lower* quality. A hospital's brand-name recognition and market clout explained the differences in price.

During public hearings in Massachusetts to discuss the price variation, giant Blue Cross Blue Shield of Massachusetts said it didn't have the power to negotiate lower prices with hospitals wielding clout in the marketplace. The hospitals threatened to withdraw from the insurer's provider network if they didn't receive the amount of money they wanted. The Blues relented because they didn't want to lose customers. Higher payments to hospitals were passed on to employers, employees, and others who bought health insurance.

In California, hospitals with clout demanded and received higher payments too. Sutter Health is California's priciest large hospital system, according to an analysis by Kaiser Health News. It was paid 37 percent more than the state average. Catholic Healthcare West, another nonprofit chain and one of Sutter's main competitors, was paid 4 percent below the state average. The California Hospital Association wants to keep secret the rates that its members receive from insurers. Employers who are footing the bill want the information public, as it should be.

The Obama administration vilified greedy insurance companies but was silent about the practices of hospitals and other providers. In years to come, a Darwinian battle of survival of the fittest will occur where big hospitals will win and weaker hospitals will barely survive or fade away.

ACCOUNTABLE CARE ORGANIZATIONS: NEW BULLIES ON THE BLOCK?

Let's face it. Health care is a mess. Hospitals, doctor's offices, imaging centers, home health care, and other health care providers operate in their own silos. Their staffs don't talk to each other to coordinate a patient's care. When people become patients, they are frustrated because they often receive different and conflicting information. They must become the coordinator-in-chief of their own care.

The health care reform law encourages providers to work together. It authorizes accountable care organizations (ACOs) that will be alliances among health care providers. They will be paid to take care of a whole patient, rather than paid for individual services. The intent is to fill in the cracks in the system through which patients can fall.

This is a complicated problem to fix. A few months after the law was signed, a hospital executive created an animated cartoon video that went viral on YouTube. In the video, a befuddled executive who didn't know where to begin to start an accountable care organization asks a health care consultant what to do. Health care insiders found the video amusing because many felt the same way.

To whom will accountable care organizations be accountable? Most will be structured to profit their managers and doctors, not the public. Others will be created by good people who will design a system with the patient in mind. They will be few in number and smart patients will look for them.

Like a game of musical chairs, no hospital wants to be left standing. Some hospital executives are using accountable care organizations to create mega-institutions. Small, independent hospitals in urban and suburban areas will likely vanish.

Oligopolies are accountable to no one and are free to roam like bullies at school. Health care reformers wanted to solve a problem, but they may have created a bigger one.

THE HARVARD SCHOOL OF REGULATION

An unfettered free market could not deliver a banking system that creates and protects wealth. In fact, it destroyed wealth and nearly brought down the country.

An unbridled health care market can't deliver health either. In fact, it destroys health when errors, infections, and overtreatment occur. Meanwhile, it is on track to bring down the country financially.

Big business needs adult supervision, a countervailing force to keep it honest. Government supervision of the financial players was virtually nonexistent. If the Securities and Exchange Commission (SEC) could not stop Bernard Madoff, even when it was provided detailed information about his scheme that robbed people of billions of dollars, surely it could not stop wayward investment firms and banks from wreaking havoc across the country and around the world.

Two days before the global investment bank and securities and trading brokerage firm Bear Stearns collapsed in 2008, the SEC chairman announced infamously that the company was in good shape. Government regulators could not grasp the company's finances, funding strategy, or relationship to the overall financial system.

In the 1980s regulation became a bad word. Free-market ideology prevailed, and unfettered markets were viewed as more efficient and self-correcting. Eventually, markets self-correct, but the collateral damage can be widespread. Free-market proponents assert that regulation stifles innovation. In fact, oligopolies stifle innovation by barring competing ideas, products, and services.

Health care lacks a meaningful regulatory system to ensure patients' safety. This absence is remarkable considering the magnitude of preventable health care harm. The reservoir of talent for regulation of a complex market is scarce. Business schools train corporate executives but who trains leaders to regulate markets so they enable private gains that benefit society, not harm it?

The Harvard Business School dean, Nitin Nohria, said in a speech to the business school, "As business itself has lost society's trust, so has business education. People are no longer sure we are educating leaders who have the requisite competence and character to fulfill the responsibilities that come with their positions of power and privilege." Nohria acknowledges that some Harvard Business School graduates seem to be responsible for the financial meltdown. To repair its sullied reputation, the school has added required ethics classes and team-based teaching.

A more robust solution is needed. There is no Harvard School of Regulation, but there should be if the country is to cultivate public leaders with the savvy to regulate the excesses of health care and other businesses and preserve the benefits of capitalism.

THE PATHOLOGICAL MUTATION

John Bogle, the legendary founder of Vanguard mutual funds, describes the pathological mutation that has occurred in capitalism in his book, *The Battle for the Soul of Capitalism*. Bogle observes that in the latter part of the twentieth century, businesses changed from focusing on their "intrinsic corporate value to the momentary precision of stock price," a change that he says lies at the heart of what has gone wrong in American capitalism.

Companies began to reward their executives not for creating real economic value but for creating the perception of pumped-up short-term stock prices, he says. CEOs and their teams figured out how to do that.

"The first is the old-fashioned way by increasing volume, cutting costs, raising productivity, using technology and developing new products and services. . . . Then [when that] isn't enough, meet your goals by . . . pushing accounting principles to their very edge. And when that isn't enough, *cheat*."

We believe that the pathological mutation that Bogle describes has migrated to health care. The intrinsic value of healing, rooted in science and ethics, has been forsaken. In its place, the momentary glee of a rising stock price or a giant royalty payment has forever changed what was once a mission. It became a business. Now it is a racket. This is the corruption of a human enterprise that should be the noblest of them all, and it lies at the heart of where American-style health care went wrong.

When people become patients, they expect benevolence. They may find it among the doctors and nurses who care for them. But they cannot expect it from the people who operate behind the scenes, the financial engineers that calculate sales and earnings per share and update Wall Street analysts every quarter. Nor can they expect benevolence from the marketing gurus who have mastered the exploitation of human fear of illness, or marketing experts who exploit the human frailties of doctors. The sacred space between the patient and the healers becomes polluted.

CEOs are accountable to investors and Wall Street analysts who flock to the likes of Goldman Sachs Global Health Care Conferences. A powerful brew it is—the bankers and the health care executives. Their allegiance is to their companies and themselves. The global economy won't come crashing down because of the transgressions of the too-big-to-fail health care companies. But the worlds of millions of invisible people harmed by price bubbles, toxic assets, and conflicts of interest do come crashing down.

Must companies deceive and destroy to survive? Must device manufacturers pay bribes to doctors to survive? Must for-profit and nonprofit hospitals overtreat to survive? If survival is defined as meeting Wall Street–type expectations for constant growth, the answer is yes. With this as the inevitable answer, it is clear that the business model for health care companies is incompatible with the purpose of health care, which is to improve health.

Bogle says that America has become a bottom-line society, but it measures "the *wrong* bottom line: form over substance, prestige over virtue, money over achievement, charisma over character, the ephemeral over the enduring." Bogle believes that capitalism requires a value system so it can flourish. Without it, capitalism will collapse.

The pathological mutation has entered the bloodstream of the health care industry and permeates every organ. The nation's elite have no immunity to this mutation. Eli Lilly's board members are a "Who's Who of America" and include academics from elite institutions such as Dr. Martin Feldstein, a noted Harvard economist. Board members received fees and stock awards worth $292,545 in the year that Eli Lilly paid its record fine for marketing drugs for unapproved use on people with Alzheimer's disease. The material abundance of a few creates a chasm of indifference to the plight of many.

So far no antidote exists to curb this mutation. It has become a cancer. Barack Obama succumbed to this systemic disease when he took campaign contributions from the industry. So did John McCain. The moral high ground was lost.

No amount of better Medicare management is sufficient to make the fundamental changes needed for a sustainable system. The business model needs to be reoriented to produce health not health care. This is where intrinsic value lies.

Health care reform did not weed out the seeds of the system's own collapse. Too big to fail just got bigger.

· 9 ·

If Only They Were iPhones

*I*magine if airplane cockpits had a cascade of new gadgets every year, each with its own promise of innovation to make flying safer. Imagine further that pilots have not tested them to see how they work before starting the engines and taking off down the runway. A chorus of beeping sounds and blinking lights cause confusion for pilots during takeoffs and landings. Near misses on airport runways increase because pilots are distracted by the bells and whistles.

Airline pilots and the aviation industry would never allow this scenario to occur. Aviation has a culture of safety built into its DNA. Personnel are steeped in the science of safety. Health care is entirely different.

At Johns Hopkins Hospital in Baltimore where an average of 942 alarms sounded every day on a fifteen-bed unit, nurses did not hear, or ignored, many of the alarms. "Alarm fatigue" occurs when humans tune out the sheer number of alarms that are impossible to respond to in a timely way. Technology that is meant to help patients fails to do so.

At another hospital, a cardiac monitor sounded at least nineteen alarms over two hours, signaling that a patient was in distress. The nurses turned off the alarm without checking the patient, who later died. If an airplane cockpit had this many alarms that sounded, pilots could not fly planes safely. In fact, pilots would *refuse* to fly and the airlines would take note.

If nurses had a choice, they would refuse to work in hospitals where it is impossible to care for patients safely, but hospitals hardly ever take note.

A former hospital chief nursing officer, researcher, and educator, Bonnie Jennings, helped us understand the cacophony from the surge of devices that are used routinely in hospitals.

At any one time, respiratory monitors sound an alarm if the patient is breathing too slowly. Intravenous pumps deliver medicine, fluids, and nutrition into the veins of patients. The pumps "beep" if the dose has been fully administered or if there is a blockage in the line. Compression stockings that are wrapped around patients' legs to reduce blood clots sound an alarm if they are not working properly. Bed monitors alarm nurses if patients at risk of falling try to get out of bed.

Silent technology is another distraction. Screens resembling a flat-screen TV are used in some hospitals to communicate information. On the display for each room, symbols are used to highlight the patients who are at high risk of falling. More than sixty different symbols might be used. When a patient leaves the unit for a procedure, different symbols are displayed to indicate where they went, whether it is to the radiology department for an X-ray or the dialysis unit for kidney dialysis. The screen has a symbol for when the blood bank signals that blood is ready for a patient. This avoids the need for a phone call. The nurse must be attentive to the silent summons to retrieve the needed unit of blood. Symbols can change every few seconds.

Cell phones are used throughout the health care workplace. Calls are usually taken while the nurse is walking from one patient room to another, getting supplies, or retrieving and administering medications. The conversations are brief and might be about when a procedure is scheduled or the results of a blood test. A unit clerk might call to relay patient requests or information about patient admissions and discharges. Families call to get updates on patients. Technicians who monitor patients' heart rates call to indicate a problem with the technology or an abnormal heart rate. Nurses call one another for help.

THE HUMAN FACTOR

Most hospitals have poorly designed work environments, and the cascade of devices and equipment is emblematic of the chaos that proliferates. Hospital executives often view nurses' concerns about safety as mere complaints. In facilities where nurses are unionized, battles rage about adequate staffing. Even seasoned nurses say they are overwhelmed.

The nurses are usually right because their work has not been designed with safety in mind. Very few hospital executives and health care professionals are trained in the science of human factors, which recognizes the complexity of human interaction in systems and organizations in which people work. Human factors engineering is a body of knowledge and skill that devises solutions to help ensure that people can use multiple devices and equipment safely and reliably.

The health care industry has been reluctant to engage experts in human factors engineering and related fields to identify and implement solutions, although this situation is beginning to change. If hospital staff had this expertise, every purchasing decision for technology and equipment would be studied and assessed for its safe use in the health care cockpit. End users of the products would be actively involved in decisions and thoroughly trained in their use. Companies that sell products would be required to ensure safe interoperability with other firms' products before the product could be sold. This rational approach to creating a safe working environment occurs too rarely.

Equipment and device manufacturers take advantage of the knowledge vacuum and pitch an avalanche of new products as quick fixes to hospital executives. There is no quick fix. Every so-called fix creates its own safety challenges and adds to the chaos. The solution is intelligent design of work to ensure safe care for every patient, every time.

ELECTRONIC HEALTH RECORDS
IN THE HEALTH CARE COCKPIT

The Obama administration has plowed billions of dollars into electronic health records so doctors and nurses will have better information in real time about their patients. Hospitals are complex organizations, and creating a workable information technology system is challenging. Unintended consequences occur. Doctors who have studied the installation and use of electronic health records say, "Once installed, they do not routinely meet safety standards of other safety-critical industries. The aggressive timeline . . . means that a large number of practitioners and health care organizations will soon be attempting a monumental feat without the time or ability to customize these systems to their local workflows."

In the health care cockpit, computer failures are frequent occurrences, not rare events. Systems often "time out" quickly and require password reentry. Screens freeze and the systems must be rebooted and previous work that was lost needs to be redone. Each malfunction requires troubleshooting the source of the problem, which takes time away from patient care. The computer becomes the patient.

Mobile computers offer special challenges. Because they rely on wireless systems, they may lose connectivity in some locations in the hospital. Because computers are used almost continuously, there is limited time to recharge their batteries.

Nurses have a name for the mobile computers on wheels: "COWs." The wheels can stick—like the wheels on a grocery cart that will not turn. Nurses have to drag the computers and their carts, which weigh more than sixty pounds. The computers are in constant use, and protocols to maintain them are not well established. In the airline industry, the lack of preventive maintenance programs would be cause for grounding airplanes. Not so in health care.

None of these operational pitfalls suggests that electronic medical records should not be used. The health care industry has been an unabashed laggard in adoption of electronic information systems. They are not an immediate panacea, though, and the unintended safety consequences are real in the mad dash to use them.

Bar code scanners used in grocery stores and express mail delivery have finally been introduced in hospitals. They are designed to help prevent medication errors and ensure that patients receive the right medication meant for them, not another patient with the same name.

The scanners are handheld devices that scan bar codes on a patient's identification wristband and bar codes on drug packaging. It is a potentially very beneficial technology to ensure that people receive the drugs that are meant for them, but real world use demonstrates questionable reliability.

Imagine being in the grocery store at a self-serve checkout line and trying to scan your groceries but running into problems when trying to scan an item and no store clerk is available to help.

A study in the *Journal of the American Medical Informatics Association* identified these and other problems with the design and implementation of bar code technology. Researchers examined half a million instances where nurses and other staff scanned bar codes on patient identification bands and drug packaging. Nurses overrode the system for 10 percent of the drugs administered, a very high percentage, because they are under extraordinary pressure to administer many doses of drugs to patients in a timely way. The technology can be programmed to report when a medication is delivered late and the nurse can be reprimanded. The main reasons for the overrides were smudged or torn bar codes on drug packaging, unreadable or missing patient identification bands, drugs that were not bar-coded, loss of wireless connectivity, failing batteries, and patient emergencies.

Each piece of equipment and technology is intended to make care safer. Individually and together, however, they can be disruptive and potentially life threatening. Even with the best intentions, the health care cockpit becomes a confusing, chaotic, and dangerous place. This is why errors are so common.

Another unintended consequence is that the purpose of health care—the care of patients—is sidelined as technology pulls doctors' and nurses' attention away from the patient. It can be a source of unhappiness and moral distress among dedicated nurses, doctors, and other health care professionals who are in the healing professions for all the reasons that the public wants and expects. Some of them have managed to create safe oases where the best of medicine, nursing, and caring is manifest, a lingering reminder of what health care is really all about. They are the real health care reformers, motivated by the intent to heal always and harm never.

FIRE IN THE OPERATING ROOM

Six hundred fires occur in operating rooms every year in the United States. Here is how one of them happened.

When a fire erupted in the operating room of a Midwest hospital, the smoke was so dense that the doctor could not see the patient. The fire alarm was pulled and the flames were snuffed out with fire extinguishers. The hospital did a thorough root-cause analysis to find out the cause of the fire.

Before the surgery was to begin, a nurse used an alcohol-based product to sterilize the patient's skin. This practice is encouraged because surgical site infections occur in 2 to 5 percent of patients who have operations and can be deadly.

Operating room fires have been reported when alcohol-based products are used. They occur because operating rooms have equipment that can cause sparks when used during surgery. Alcohol-based products can be the fuel that ignites the fire. Flammability can be avoided by allowing the skin to completely dry when the product is used.

In this case, hospital staff used an alcohol-based product manufactured by a company whose brochure says it kills major pathogens in one minute and is flammable until completely dry. The solution is 70 percent alcohol. The company that makes the product sells it in applicators that come in two sizes. A small applicator contains six milliliters of solution and is used for operations involving less exposure of the body such as surgery on the head or neck. A large applicator contains twenty-six milliliters, more than four times the amount in the small applicator, and is meant for major abdominal surgeries and Caesarean sections. The company's brochure states that the large applicator should not be used to prep a patient for head-and-neck surgeries.

As the hospital investigated the source of the fire, it learned from an article in the Cleveland newspaper, the *Plain Dealer*, that the Cleveland Clinic had had six fires in its operating rooms. Flammable skin-preparations had been used during surgery. Three people suffered superficial burns. The Midwest hospital staff concluded that its operating room fire was a symptom of a system-wide problem occurring in multiple hospitals.

The hospital discovered that three of the large applicators of the alcohol-based product were used to sterilize the surgical site, about ten times more than should have been used. The alcohol had soaked into the mattress that the patient had been lying on.

The hospital also discovered that the company sales representative had sold the hospital only the large-size applicators. The representative was fully aware that the hospital performs more than two thousand head-and-neck surgeries a year. The fire occurred during a head-and-neck surgery.

The chief of patient safety at the hospital recognized that errors were made by hospital staff. He also questioned whether the sales representative was under pressure to meet his sales targets and sold the hospital only the large applicators to generate more profit for his company.

SHOW STOPPERS

When Apple Inc. released the iPhone 4, excitement swirled. *Consumer Reports* confirmed what customers already knew. In areas with weak reception, the voice and data connection was lost when users touched the external antenna band.

Consumer Reports called the flaw a "show stopper" even though the iPhone 4 had lots of snazzy features. Before the consumer watchdog group would recommend the device, Apple had to provide a free fix.

The antenna glitch that caused an inconvenience triggered an outpouring of dissatisfaction from customers. Apple promptly offered dissatisfied customers a full refund or a free case, which was a fix for the reception issues. This is an example of the free market working. The company was held accountable by its customers.

In hospitals, "show stoppers" are common in medical devices and equipment. There is no *Consumer Reports* to bring them to the public's attention, but there should be. They are hidden from public view.

Unlike Apple iPhone users, nurses who use equipment or devices that malfunction have little clout with manufacturers. They must use the equipment that companies sell to hospitals. Too often manufacturers are not held responsible for ensuring that doctors, nurses, and other health care professionals can use their products safely and effectively in the real world.

An infusion pump is a widely used pump to provide chemotherapy drugs or pain medication as well as fluids intravenously. Nurses or doctors program the pump to deliver a controlled amount. Pumps are manufactured by different companies and have different designs. Programming the pumps can be confusing and subject to human error. Patients can be harmed.

Infusion pumps have had persistent safety problems. From 2005 to 2009, the FDA received more than 56,000 reports of adverse events associated with the use of infusion pumps. Serious injuries and more than five hundred deaths occurred. Eighty-seven infusion pump recalls were conducted during this period because of safety concerns.

Just as auto manufacturers used to blame drivers for highway accidents, pump manufacturers blame users for mistakes. An FDA analysis of complaints found that product design and engineering were the primary causes of errors. Software defects and mechanical and electrical failures were common.

The FDA has been working with infusion pump manufacturer Baxter since 1999 to correct numerous flaws in one of its infusion pumps called Colleague. It was subject to recalls for battery swelling, inadvertent power off, service data errors, and other issues.

In June 2006 the FDA obtained a consent decree allowing it to require Baxter to stop manufacturing and distributing all models of the Colleague pump until the company corrected manufacturing defects. The company made changes, but they didn't correct the defects. Four years later, the company submitted a proposed correction schedule to the FDA with plans to begin another round of corrections to its pumps beginning in two years. This response was unacceptable. In 2010 the FDA ordered Baxter to recall and destroy all Colleague infusion pumps, reimburse customers for the value of the recalled device, and help find a replacement for these customers.

Shortly after the recall, the FDA announced that it was planning a new and welcome initiative requiring additional premarket requirements that manufacturers will be expected to meet before they can sell their products.

Infusion pumps are another example of how the health care industry privatizes profit and socializes losses. Companies have been able to get away with poorly designed devices and equipment at immense human and financial cost. Hospitals don't hold product manufacturers accountable for product defects. In a stark contrast, it is inconceivable that Apple would tell its iPhone customers that it had plans to fix the glitch on the antenna in a few years. This abysmal level of customer service is pervasive in the health care industry.

Other devices are sold with widespread product defects too. In fiscal year 2006, for example, the FDA received reports of 116,086 potential device-related injuries, 2,830 potential device-related deaths, and more than 200,000 adverse events occurring because of medical devices. The FDA uses these reports to help determine whether a device should be recalled.

Most people probably think that medical devices are thoroughly tested before being marketed, sold, and placed in the human body. That's not true, according to researchers who studied all FDA high-risk recalls of medical devices from 2005 through 2009.

High-risk recalls are those that the FDA determined could cause serious health problems or death. More than three-fourths of these recalled devices had been approved without any scientific review of their safety and effectiveness.

Cardiovascular devices were the most common category of high-risk recalls. Automatic external defibrillators are one such device. They are used to resuscitate patients with a certain type of heart rhythm problem and can be found in shopping malls, sports arenas, cruise ships, airports, and airplanes. More than 20 percent of the almost one million defibrillators had to be recalled by the FDA, and hundreds of people have died due to malfunctions.

The FDA is supposed to ensure that devices are safe and effective. The researchers discovered that the FDA's Center for Devices and Radiological Health must review thousands of devices each year, but Congress has not appropriated sufficient funds to enable the FDA to conduct thorough reviews.

Lobbyists for device manufacturers want fast-track approval. Government red tape stifles life-saving innovation, they say. With government out of the way, they can reach sales targets, yet another symptom of the pathological mutation that has gripped health care. If the products were iPhones, consumers would say, "Not so fast."

Toyotas, iPhones, and other commonly used consumer products are held to a higher performance and safety standard than many medical devices. Apple must ensure that the human-computer interface works as intended. Toyota must design and build cars that are safe when all kinds of drivers use them. Consumers and patients should expect no less from devices that enter the sacred space of the human body.

Part 4

UNTIL DEBT DO US PART

*H*istory has shown that nations are often overcome by forces whose significance they were unable to grasp at the time. The health care reform debate occurred against the backdrop of a fast-changing global economy that will have profound implications for the future of health care in the United States.

In chapter 10 we examine the future trends for employer-provided health insurance. This workplace tradition has helped millions of working Americans and their families. It began at a time when US businesses were dominant in the world economy. Their dominance is fading. The rise of China will have an increasingly greater impact on American companies. Many American firms that have provided generous health insurance benefits for decades will continue to be buffeted by events thousands of miles away. We predict that global competition will have a profound impact on the future of employer-provided health insurance.

Chapter 11 tells the story of promises made and promises broken. State governments are on the front lines of health care reform implementation, and many are coping with record levels of fiscal deficits. The fiscal ill health of many states is forcing cuts in essential services ranging from street lights to health care. Meanwhile, new promises have been made in the health care reform overhaul. Massachusetts was the model for many of the provisions in the national health care law, and it too faces challenges to rein in spending and ensure the sustainability of near universal coverage. At the national level, Medicare is vulnerable to unwise slashing that will jeopardize the health and well-being of older Americans. We highlight ways to prune Medicare so it remains financially viable and serves its intended purpose.

In chapter 12 we challenge industry critics of the Medicare Independent Payment Advisory Board who are lobbying Congress to dismantle it. The same critics oppose the proposals from the president's Debt Reduction Commission to make dramatic cuts in health care, far greater than the comparatively modest reductions in the reform law. Progress to reduce the ominous burden of the federal debt can be made only if health care spending is reduced. If this does not happen, we pose the only remaining alternative, a bailout from the International Monetary Fund (IMF), and describe what it will mean for the country. Industry critics can pick their poison.

· *10* ·

Good-bye Busboys

$\mathscr{T}$ake this test. When you get up tomorrow morning, look at the products you use and where they were made. Your clothes, sheets, toothbrush, coffee mug, toaster, and iPad were probably manufactured in China. Thirty years ago, at least some of these products were made in the United States.

Browsing the aisles of Target and Walmart and the catalogs of L.L.Bean and Nordstrom, it is abundantly clear that America has shifted away from its manufacturing base that created economic prosperity. When retailers cheer strong sales on Black Friday, they are actually celebrating the profits of Chinese businesses because the United States has become an outlet mall for their factories.

Americans understand the threat of global competition to the country's economic security and way of life. A *Washington Post*–ABC News poll found that 61 percent of Americans surveyed perceive China as a threat to jobs and the country's economic security. Only 29 percent see China as an opportunity for new markets and investments.

ECONOMIC SECURITY IS HEALTH CARE SECURITY

The country's economic security—and the jobs and benefits that come with it—is one of the most significant determinants of Americans' health care security.

The Great Recession demonstrated this stark reality. In 2008, 68 percent of Americans obtained insurance from their employer. A year later, only 59 percent did. The recession caused millions of people to lose their jobs and health insurance. Some businesses stopped offering health insurance because it was a better alternative to laying off employees. More than twenty years earlier, 76 percent of wage and salary workers had health insurance through their employers, a figure that remained nearly constant until 2001.

Workers who are fortunate to have employer-provided insurance are paying more for it. In 2010 employers tended to shift all premium increases to their employees, a harbinger of the future. Wages and salaries have not kept pace with health care inflation, so workers' take-home pay is shrinking. Because there is no end in sight to escalating costs, employees will continue to bear the brunt.

Employers that have calculated the impact of the reform law may have found that paying the penalty instead of paying for health insurance for their employees would be financially beneficial to them. For example, AT&T calculated that it spends $2.4 billion a year for health insurance but would spend only $600 million if it paid the penalty.

Governor Philip Bredesen, a Democrat from Tennessee, figured that his cash-strapped state would save $146 million if it stopped providing health insurance for forty thousand state employees and instead provided them money to purchase insurance from a state exchange. Another two hundred and forty thousand employees in local governments and school systems in the state would find it financially attractive to do the same.

Will employers continue to provide insurance? Most large companies say they will. Only 6 percent of firms with five hundred or more employees say they are likely to drop health insurance benefits, according to a survey by Mercer, a human resource consulting firm. Small employers have a different reaction. Twenty percent of them say they are likely to stop providing insurance.

After the reform law became effective, more small businesses began to offer health insurance because of a federal tax credit. In 2010, 59 percent of employers with three to nine workers offered insurance compared to 46 percent in 2009. Beginning in 2014 small companies with fewer than twenty-five employees will continue to be eligible for a tax credit but only for two years. Without subsidies, small employers may pare back insurance coverage.

In the coming years one trend is certain. Employees will pay an increasing share of the cost of their health insurance coverage. More employers will offer a defined contribution rather than a defined benefit, much like the pensions most employees in the private sector receive. In the early 1990s, 40 percent of workers had a predetermined or defined pension when they retired. By 2007 only 17 percent did as employers cut back on their pension liabilities.

A traditional employer benefit that is going the way of the typewriter is retiree health insurance. In 1997 two-thirds of employers provided coverage to their former employees under age sixty-five and not yet eligible for Medicare; in 2010 only 28 percent did so. This trend is continuing. The health care reform law provides a one-time subsidy of $5 billion to employers as an incentive to continue providing benefits to early retirees until 2014 when they can buy individual insurance on the exchanges. The one-time subsidy sought to protect this group from the cost of an individual health insurance policy, which, at their age, can be prohibitively expensive.

The future of employer-provided health insurance will depend on the affordability of health care. With no end in sight for skyrocketing health care costs, the future of comprehensive employer-provided health insurance is bleak.

Adding to the burden will be extra costs shifted to employers and employees. Medicare and Medicaid pay doctors and hospitals less than private insurers do. In fact, the amount they pay might be less than the cost of providing the service, even among providers who render good care efficiently. To compensate, hospitals and doctors will continue to shift more of the cost to employers and other private health insurance purchasers.

GOING GLOBAL

Employers' decisions to provide insurance will depend on how well American businesses fare in global competition and whether they maintain and grow well-paid jobs at home. The golden age of employer-provided health insurance and other benefits occurred from the 1950s to the mid-1980s, the same period in which the American economy was unparalleled in the world. Competition from other countries was virtually nonexistent. Today global competition is forcing American companies and their workers to operate in unprecedented ways.

The Fortune 500 list of the world's largest companies lists sixty-two firms from emerging economies, a number that has doubled since 2003. In the coming decade, American firms will face a greater torrent of competition from China and other countries that have honed carefully crafted industrial strategies aimed at growing their manufacturing base and competing successfully against the American worker.

America's comparative advantage is in technology and its knowledge-driven economy, but this advantage is slipping. China is manufacturing increasingly sophisticated products and by 2020 is expected to surpass the United States as the world's largest economy. Its huge workforce will be well educated, English-speaking, and motivated to succeed.

The United States had developed the fastest supercomputers, but in 2010 China took the world lead with a machine that far surpasses the speed of those developed in the United States. In 2011 Japan superseded China with its even faster supercomputer. With the capability to simulate weapons defense systems, break codes, and test new drugs, a country's supercomputers are a mark of competitiveness and rising prowess.

Aerospace blogs buzzed when China reverse-engineered a Russian fighter jet, the Sukhoi-27, that had been the pride of the Russian Air Force. After the fall of the Soviet Union in the 1980s, the Russians were in need of cash and eagerly sold billions of dollars of arms to China, including the jet. China cloned the jet rather than spend money to buy it. In fact, China is undercutting its former supplier and sells its home-grown fighter jets at a lower price to customers that had previously bought the jets from Russia.

China's strategy is to force United States and other countries' companies to disclose sensitive technological information in return for lucrative contracts and access to the country's vast domestic market. Once it has amassed the world's cutting-edge knowledge, it will build a great wall around its economy. Where possible, it will buy from its own domestic companies, not American or European firms. The American worker will be shut out of the soon-to-be world's largest economy.

This strategy is evident already. According to a business confidence survey conducted by the European Union Chamber of Commerce, 36 percent of European businesses perceive that China has become less friendly toward foreign companies that want to do business inside the country. More worrying, 39 percent of respondents expect China's internal regulatory environment for foreign companies to become more restrictive in the coming years.

The International Finance Corporation's annual ranking of countries for their business-friendly environment confirms this trend. China ranked eighty-ninth in 2010, three notches lower than its place in 2009. It ranks behind Asian economies such as Thailand (twelfth) and Malaysia (twenty-third). Surprisingly, it has a lower ranking than the economies of Mongolia (sixtieth) and Pakistan (eighty-fifth).

The US-China Economic and Security Review Commission, a congressionally mandated entity that examines the two countries' relationship, warns that the Chinese government is pursuing policies of indigenous innovation whereby China sets standards for products that foreign companies must meet if they want to do business. This strategy makes it hard for American and other overseas firms to operate and compete in China. These policies have harmed US businesses, and although the United States has sought remedies from the World Trade Organization, the lengthy process has impeded US companies' access to the Chinese market.

American firms have taken advantage of investment incentives, subsidies, and lower labor costs to shift production to China. The price of entry is steep, and they are taking a monumental gamble. Firms are folding parts of their worldwide operations into partnerships with Chinese companies to do business around the globe. For example, General Electric is finalizing plans for a fifty-fifty joint venture with a Chinese military jet maker to produce nonmilitary avionics, which are the electronic brains of aircraft. GE will have access to a Chinese government project aimed at competing with Boeing and Airbus to produce passenger jets. When that happens, China will undercut Boeing and threaten American jobs.

American companies are cannibalizing their crown jewels—their know-how—which has been created by American workers over decades. In return, the companies receive short-term financial gain. When the jewels have been given away, the companies will have little remaining intrinsic value.

China is encircling American businesses and their workers and keeping them out. Jeffrey Immelt, the CEO of General Electric, told Italian business leaders about the challenges of doing business in China: "It's getting harder for foreign companies to do business there. . . . I really worry about China. . . . I am not sure that in the end they want any of us to win, or any of us to be successful."

In a speech at the American Chamber of Commerce in Shanghai, Immelt admitted, "The hardest thing to do in China is to get a win–win relationship. The negotiating, the ability to find a space where both people make money, that is something that we always have to continue to, not just think about, but insist on."

If General Electric, one of the largest manufacturing companies in the world, is having trouble garnering business opportunities, this portends trouble for the American worker. Immelt expressed growing dismay among international business executives about China's systematic strategy to grab technology from western businesses and use it to compete against them in China's own domestic market and other countries.

What does all this have to do with health care? The American worker is being cut out of business in a high-stakes economic battle being waged around the globe.

Here is one example. A giant Indian conglomerate, Reliance Industries, signed a $10 billion contract with Shanghai Electric to purchase power-generation equipment. The Indian firm could have purchased the equipment from General Electric at a price that was 30 to 40 percent higher. To seal the deal, the China Development Bank and other Chinese banks provided generous financing that gave the buyer a 60 percent discount. With these terms, it is impossible for the American worker to have a share of business opportunities.

WHILE CHINA INVESTS, AMERICA CONSUMES

While the health care reform law commits the federal government to spend billions of dollars more on health care, China is using its money for investment, not consumption.

According to the National Science Foundation's Science and Engineering Indicators Report, recent growth in research and development expenditures has been most dramatic in China, averaging just above 19 percent annually in inflation-adjusted dollars over the past decade. By comparison, the US pace of growth averaged 3.3 percent.

China targets strategic industries to accelerate their development: telecommunications, information technology, aviation, automobile manufacturing, construction, energy, and steel. Other favored industries include biotechnology, computer chip design, and software, which all receive low-interest loans and loan forgiveness from government-owned banks.

While China invests in infrastructure, US roads, bridges, dams, power lines, water treatment plants, and telecommunications systems are crumbling. The American Society of Civil Engineers estimates that the United States needs to invest $2.2 trillion in the next twenty years to restore the nation's infrastructure. Eleven billion dollars of this amount is to ensure the supply of safe drinking water. "In 10 years, China will have better infrastructure than the U.S.," said Jim Owens, the former CEO of Caterpillar.

Because the United States spends more than 18 percent of its national income on health care, government and business have less money to invest in industries where Americans can be competitive in the global marketplace. Health care will swallow an even larger share of national income by 2020. This means that less money will be available for investment in productive economic activity to enable the country to keep up with the rest of the world, let alone remain in the top tier.

In an increasingly unfriendly global business climate that deliberately seeks to cut out the American worker, it will be difficult to maintain high-quality American jobs. Employment has already suffered. China's export-led growth policies have produced excess capacity in steel and automobiles and contributed to a loss in US jobs.

While America's trade deficit with China is enormous, its changing composition is even more compelling. The United States had a record $72.7 billion trade deficit in advanced technology products, a sign of the future threat against high-wage and high-benefit American jobs.

AS GLOBAL COMPETITION GOES, SO GOES HEALTH CARE

"The best action we can do to create jobs and strengthen our economic security is pass health care reform," said then Speaker of the House Nancy Pelosi when the reform law was being debated.

We disagree. When $760 billion a year in health care spending is wasted on products and services that do not add value to health, the expenditures represent an immense loss of missed opportunity for productive investment and an enormous drain on the American economy. A portion of that money should be invested in public goods: strengthening the country's competitive edge in science and innovation, upgrading and expanding its infrastructure, and enabling the country to become energy independent.

The massive unemployment and underemployment that spiked during the recession and its aftermath have been impervious to billions in federal stimulus funding. Like a dose of caffeine, federal stimulus funds can usually kick-start an economy when it is in a cyclical lull. But this time, highly caffeinated economic policies did not work in the aftermath of the Great Recession because the medicine didn't fit the disease.

Jobs—and health insurance benefits—follow the money. The Business Roundtable reported that the share of profits of US-based multinational companies from operations in other countries jumped from 27 percent in 1994 to 48.6 percent in 2006.

When GE's Immelt was appointed by President Obama to lead the president's Council on Jobs and Competitiveness, he seemed to be apologetic when he acknowledged that 60 percent of GE's profit comes from its operations in other countries.

The United States faces a tough future that will affect jobs and employer-provided health insurance. They will be an ongoing target for cost cutting. Here are some examples. A *Los Angeles Times* analysis found that American companies hired workers during the economic downturn, but they hired them overseas. More than 700,000 workers had new jobs at their foreign subsidiaries and affiliates from 2006 to 2008. During the same period, 500,000 domestic jobs were cut.

Higher-end engineering jobs for products manufactured in China are being performed near the centers of production. By moving jobs overseas, US multinationals cannibalize their domestic business. When jobs are moved away, Americans' purchasing power is reduced. They have less money to buy American companies' products and services, and the vicious cycle repeats itself.

A reader of the *Los Angeles Times* weighed in on the shift in jobs, saying, "When I had to call Amazon the other day for help with my Kindle, I asked the guy where he was based. Imagine my surprise when he told me 'Costa Rica.' So I guess we can add Costa Rica to the list of places our jobs are going. Nice going, Amazon."

Closer to home, the Chili's restaurant chain is buying new ovens to replace more labor-intensive grills. Each restaurant is being designed to operate with three chefs instead of six. Busboys are being engineered out of their jobs. CVS Pharmacy and other retailers are installing self-service checkouts in their stores.

The country's economic standing in the world is its destiny. The best way to sustain health insurance coverage for Americans is a robust economy that creates manufacturing jobs that pay good wages and benefits, along with a strategy to lower health care costs.

Warren Buffett, the oracle of Omaha, said that health care costs are like a tapeworm eating into the competitiveness of American firms. Without this two-pronged strategy, the health care that most Americans have come to expect will be a shadow of its former self.

In a worst-case scenario, which is not out of the realm of possibility, employers will stop providing health insurance to their employees. Their workers will obtain health insurance from exchanges where some will be eligible for federal subsidies. Under the health care law, the federal government will absorb the costs that employers had paid. The shifting financial burden from employers to the federal government will be impossible for the public treasury to bear.

Whether health care reform is considered by conservatives to be socialism, or by liberals to be corporate welfare, one fact is indisputable: when someone else is paying the bill, eventually the money runs out.

· 11 ·

Promises Made, Promises Broken

$\mathcal{T}$he Obama administration promised millions of Americans that they won't need to worry any more about the cost of their health care. As these new promises were being made, promises made years ago to millions of other Americans are being broken.

In Arizona the state government sold its capitol and supreme court buildings to raise money. Now it rents the space from the new owners. To close more budget holes, state officials eliminated 280,000 people from its Medicaid program, about one-fifth of its participants. This cut comes on the heels of a highly controversial state decision to stop paying for bone marrow transplants for people with certain medical conditions.

California and New York, two of the most populous states led by Democratic governors, are slashing spending for people on Medicaid. Governor Jerry Brown of California proposed steep cuts to save $1.4 billion in the Medicaid program, including a 10 percent reduction in payments to doctors and hospitals. He called for copayments for doctor and emergency room visits, hospitals stays, and prescriptions, and proposed to limit visits to a doctor and spending caps on wheelchairs and hearing aids.

New York Governor Andrew Cuomo said his state was "functionally bankrupt." He axed $2.85 billion in state-only funds for Medicaid in 2011 after a panel of health care stakeholders made recommendations.

The Obama administration recognizes that Medicaid poses fiscal challenges to state coffers. Secretary Sebelius wrote to the country's governors advising them how they can curb Medicaid spending by cutting benefits: "In 2008, roughly 40 percent of Medicaid benefits spending—$100 billion—was spent on optional benefits for all enrollees," she wrote. "Many services such as prescription drugs, dental services, and speech therapy, are optional. States can generally change optional benefits or limit their amount, duration or scope."

The letter shows how the federal government is giving health insurance with one hand but taking away benefits with another. These steps are being taken *before* sixteen million more people become eligible for Medicaid beginning in 2014, which raises doubts about the program's financial viability. The federal government will pay 100 percent of the cost of covering newly eligible Medicaid beneficiaries but will reduce its share to 90 percent in 2020. States will pay the rest. And they will have an additional financial burden. Because the individual mandate requires everyone to have health insurance, many people will see if they are eligible for Medicaid's free insurance. In fact, many people who are already eligible are not enrolled. The federal government will pay only fifty cents on average for every dollar spent for them because they are eligible under the rules that existed before the reform law was enacted. States will pay the remainder.

California is expected to have more newly insured people than any other state, approximately 3.4 million. State officials estimate that it will cost $2 to $3 billion annually. Kim Belshe, the chief of the Department of Health and Human Services under Governor Arnold Schwarzenegger, said, "Medicaid provides care that is invaluable but it is reeling under its own weight. States are now being asked to implement the largest social program since Medicare and Medicaid began. Medicaid is falling apart as states cut benefits as enrollment increased because of the recession. It makes little sense to build on a house that's falling apart."

THE MASSACHUSETTS FIX—FOR NOW

The federal health care reform law contains provisions that are modeled on the reform that Massachusetts enacted in 2006. Republican Scott Brown voted for the state overhaul when he was a member of the Massachusetts legislature, and Republican Mitt Romney signed it into law.

Massachusetts is unique because it is a state where health care plays an important role in the economy and politics. The state government has the capacity to implement new ways of doing business. The state medical society was supportive of the state's reform, as are 70 percent of doctors.

In Massachusetts the health care reform debate in the years leading up to the law was cordial compared with the national debate. Employers, health care providers, and consumers achieved consensus about how to ensure that everyone had health insurance. The state's individual mandate requires most individuals to have health insurance and the state provides a subsidy for people with incomes up to about $66,000 a year for a family of four.

About 98 percent of people have health insurance. Employers are maintaining their insurance coverage for their employees. In fact, 150,000 more people have employer-sponsored coverage and 40,000 people obtained private coverage.

When the Massachusetts model was brought to Washington, a similar chance for consensus building did not exist. Any public policy change, big or small, encounters headwinds when it is imposed rather than when it emerges from the engagement of stakeholders. States have different politics, cultures, and financial capacities. What works in one state may not work well in another state. This reality should not be used, though, to shortchange Americans and expose them to the high cost of health care because of where they live.

Massachusetts postponed tough decisions to rein in spending, and there is no plan for how to do so. It is much easier for public-policy makers to create new benefits than to curb them. Health care spending in the state is projected to nearly double by 2020, and the growth will be faster than that of the state's gross domestic product. If costs are not controlled, it will be impossible to sustain the gains in access to care and they will erode over time.

The Greater Boston Interfaith Coalition, whose mission is to tackle social ills and economic inequality, supported the state's health care reform and has called for cost-control measures to preserve the gains that have been made. Hospitals and other health care providers have shown little interest.

A SHORT-TERM BLIP OR LONG-TERM TREND?

Many states will be in the fiscal doldrums for years to come. The Great Recession caused millions of Americans to lose their jobs. State revenues from income taxes plummeted. People stopped shopping and sales tax revenues dropped. States were so strapped that they didn't have money to pay unemployment benefits, and thirty-two states had to borrow $41 billion from the federal government to pay the unemployed. Meanwhile, people who were unemployed became eligible for publicly funded services.

Hawaii was so short of cash that it closed schools on Fridays for seventeen weeks. In California, the head of the Department of Finance read the US Constitution to determine if the state could return to territory status and be absolved of its financial obligations.

The cuts rolled down hill as states pared back their funding to local governments. Communities made tough choices. In Vista, California, city council members voted to reduce the number of ambulances from four to three to save more than $600,000 a year. The city of Colorado Springs sold police helicopters on the Internet. Trash cans were removed from public parks to save money, and signs were posted encouraging patrons to take their trash with them. Brainerd, Minnesota, turned off four hundred street lights to save $90,000 a year. Another town in the state, Zumbrota, sent a $4.75 bill to each household to keep the lights on.

Schools faced shrinking budgets and parents were asked to pick up the slack. In the depths of the recession, schools sent parents back-to-school shopping lists that included the usual pens and pencils but also paper towels, toilet paper, liquid soap, and paper for the printer in school principals' offices.

State treasuries have improved during the shaky economic recovery. But the recession exposed long-term financial vulnerabilities that are the culmination of years of mismanagement by Republicans and Democrats who went on spending sprees with the public's money and that of future generations. Beneath the fiscal icebergs is a ticking time bomb of retiree benefits promised to public-sector employees. For years, many states have paid only a fraction of the payments needed to cover future liabilities. Twenty states have paid nothing toward these liabilities, according to the Pew Center on the States. Altogether, the states have a $1 trillion shortfall in funding to meet their obligations.

What is the impact of these commitments? California spends more money on state employee pensions than on its flagship state university system. In Kentucky almost all of the state's additional spending (97 percent) on primary and secondary education since 1992 has been for employee health and pension benefits. In other words, for the past twenty years, hardly any additional money allocated for education has been for the benefit of children.

Republicans Jeb Bush, former governor of Florida, and Newt Gingrich, perpetual presidential aspirant, floated the idea to allow states to file for bankruptcy to get out from under crushing debt. The proposal was a cynical ploy to weaken the power of public-sector unions, traditional Democratic supporters, at the expense of the country's financial well-being. Harmful ripples would reverberate throughout the financial system if states were allowed to file for bankruptcy. States could rewrite pension contracts with the unions. But companies that do business with states may never be paid, and construction projects would be postponed. States would find it harder to borrow cheap money because lenders will see them as risky borrowers and charge higher interest rates.

As for policy proposals designed for political gain rather than to solve a serious fiscal problem, allegiance to the country must come before allegiance to party. The country's ideals should not be sacrificed at the altar of ideology. A political ideology may make for fine speeches and generate campaign contributions, but if it doesn't solve the problems people have in their daily life, it has no place in public discourse or public policy.

DO THIS, NOT THAT

For decades, elected officials have avoided honest, mature conversations with the public. Tradeoffs are a fact of life. People make them every day. Americans aren't as foolish as the politicians treat them.

Because these conversations have been avoided for so long, people have become accustomed to having it all with the least amount of financial pain, which makes it more difficult to break the habit of living on piles of borrowed money.

Breaking bad habits is hard. In Illinois the Democrat-led legislature voted along party lines in 2011 to increase income taxes by a whopping 66 percent. At the new rate, an Illinois resident who paid $1,000 in state income taxes will pay $1,666.

Tax increases are not enough to solve the fiscal mess. A crucial conversation is needed about what it means to spend so much of the nation's income—more than 18 percent—on health care. States spend more of their own money on Medicaid than higher education. As health care costs and use increase, money is automatically diverted from other important priorities.

THE RIGHT WAY AND THE
WRONG WAY TO OVERHAUL MEDICARE

Representative Paul Ryan, a Republican from Wisconsin and chair of the House Budget Committee, proposed a dramatic overhaul of Medicare. His plan converts Medicare from a defined benefit program to a defined contribution. People covered by Medicare would use the contribution to pay the premium for a health plan. If the plan costs more, they would pay the extra cost.

Republicans believe that if Medicare beneficiaries use their own money to buy health care, they will use fewer health care services. While this is true, the amount of money that would be saved is small when compared to the real reason that Medicare is financially unsustainable: the medical-industrial complex wants to relentlessly increase revenue. Neither the Republican plan nor the Democrats' health care reform fixes this fundamental flaw in Medicare.

Instead, the Ryan plan shifts the burden of a financially unsustainable program to people who are least able to negotiate with too-big-to-fail health care companies. A healthy and empowered seventy-year-old person is no match for a hospital, drug company, or insurer whose aim is to garner as much revenue as possible. By 2030 nine million Americans will be over age eighty-five, and half of them are expected to have Alzheimer's disease and will have no negotiating ability.

It is too late to place the onus of failed leadership on older Americans. They cannot be the bulwark that holds the line on Medicare spending.

Ryan says, "Americans have been lured into viewing government—more than themselves, their families, their communities, and their faith—as their main source of support." He calls this the expanding culture of dependency.

In fact, the health care reform debate showed the expanding culture of dependency on government by drug companies, device manufacturers, equipment makers, and every other health care business. Neither Ryan nor other elected officials on both sides of the aisle wants to talk about *that*.

Nancy Pelosi said that the Republican plan would be the end of Medicare as we know it. This is true. It is also true that Medicare is already on track to cease to exist as it is today. But it is not too late to change course.

Here is what Congress *should* do. Sixty members of Congress from both political parties sought to break the collusion between the federal government and the drug industry in March 2010 when they introduced the Medicare Prescription Drug Price Negotiation Act, which would have given Medicare the same authority as the Department of Veterans Affairs to negotiate drug prices with the drug companies.

Congressman Pete Welch, a Democrat from Vermont, said that $15 billion in taxpayer money could be saved each year if Medicare paid the same prices that the Department of Veterans Affairs (VA) negotiates on behalf of America's veterans. During a press conference announcing the bill, Congressman Welch compared the amount that Medicare and the VA pay for the exact same drugs.

For Nexium, a drug prescribed to reduce the amount of acid in the stomach, Medicare pays a non-negotiated price of $1,433 and the VA pays $848. For Zocor, a drug used to reduce cholesterol levels, Medicare pays $1,486 and the VA negotiates a price of $127.

"There is no justification to rip off the American taxpayer, make them pay retail when we are purchasing wholesale," Welch said.

The health care reform law did not give Medicare the authority to negotiate drug prices. Nor did it give hospitals the incentive to negotiate better prices for the expensive devices, equipment, and supplies they purchase. In fact, health care businesses are lobbying to stop Medicare from competitive bidding for certain kinds of durable medical equipment and supplies that Medicare pays for.

A Medicare overhaul that preserves and protects Medicare must apply these commonsense ways of doing business throughout the program. As long as the money that has corrupted health care continues to flow to members of Congress and the president, the political will to muster enough votes to change the status quo is absent.

The US Supreme Court enshrined the status quo when it comes to money and politicians in its decision in *Citizens United v. Federal Election*

Commission. The 5–4 majority ruled that the government cannot ban political spending by corporations in candidate elections. By overturning the ban, the majority on the court interpreted the US Constitution as saying that it gives corporations the same right to free speech that individual citizens have.

In effect, the Supreme Court legalized the corrupting influence of money from powerful interests in US elections. In fact, it invites more collusion between moneyed interests and elected officials. The voice of ordinary citizens doesn't stand a chance amid the chorus of money changers in the nation's capital.

· *12* ·

Government by Default

$\mathcal{H}$ow much is a trillion dollars? If you spent $1 million a day since the day Jesus Christ was born, you would not have spent a trillion dollars.

America has dug itself into a big financial hole. In 2011 the federal government spent about $1.5 trillion more than it received in revenue, its deficit for the year. The total debt it owed, accumulated from all prior years' deficits, was $14.3 trillion.

The United States has two choices to curb the national debt that threatens to sink the country into bankruptcy. Congress and the White House can act swiftly and decisively. If not, someone else will have to do it.

How did the country get in this mess? Democrats and Republicans share the blame. The wars in Iraq and Afghanistan have drained federal coffers. Instead of building power stations and roads in faraway places, money should have been spent at home to fix collapsing bridges and crumbling schools. Closer to home, visitors to the Lincoln Memorial on the National Mall in Washington, DC, witnessed the disrepair of one of the most majestic memorials in the city. The memorial itself was crumbling, and the grounds surrounding it were in a shambles. It has since been repaired.

President George W. Bush's tax cuts took away the revenue needed to pay the military-industrial complex for the wars. The Medicare prescription drug benefit is another unduly expensive burden from the Bush years that future generations will bear. During his presidency, debt levels mushroomed. Fiscal hawks were rightly apoplectic, but they didn't stop the financial bleeding.

Democrats inherited a devastated economy in 2008 and had to clean up an economic mess. At the same time, it was their turn to favor constituents who had been waiting for the Bush era to end. Every party and its special interests take a crack at grabbing an ever larger share of the country's fiscal pie. Avarice knows no bounds.

How close is the federal government to falling over the financial cliff? The federal government borrows more than forty cents of every dollar it spends. If, and when, terrorists strike the New York subway or the Washington, DC, metro, the government doesn't have money in the bank to pay for repairs to the infrastructure. It will have to borrow from China and other lenders.

The cost of Medicare and Medicaid is the largest contributor. Cutting the debt requires cutting health care. This is not a Democrat or Republican interpretation of the numbers. Nor is it a political statement for or against health care reform. It is simple math.

Cutting the federal debt is a tough job. No elected official wants to do it. It is much better to give than to take away. Congress will have to say no to health care industry special interests. Accusations of rationing will fill the airwaves and the blogosphere. If Congress had the wisdom to prune the waste, people who rely on Medicare and Medicaid will be better off, not worse, as we have noted earlier. The special interests who will lose from a reduction in waste will stoke unwarranted fear among the public.

If past performance is an indicator of future performance, we don't believe that Washington politicians can make these tough choices. We hope they prove us wrong, but the political gridlock is so entrenched, and policy making so dysfunctional, that hard decisions will be postponed until it is too late.

THE SUMMER OF DISCONTENT

The debate over raising the federal debt ceiling in Washington in the summer of 2011 shook the nation's confidence. An increase in the federal borrowing limit was necessary to pay the government's debts and keep Social Security checks, military pay, and all other government spending flowing.

Republicans in the House of Representative who came to Washington after the 2010 midterm elections vowed to cut unsustainable government spending. Raising the debt ceiling, they thought, would allow Washington to continue its bad habits. For the same reason, they didn't want to increase taxes and give more blank checks in the never-ending spiral of government spending. Meanwhile, conservatives wanted to preserve their favored programs—primarily, defense spending and lucrative subsidies for oil companies and agriculture. On the other side of the aisle, Democrats wanted to preserve Medicare, Medicaid, and Social Security while raising taxes on people with higher incomes.

Americans had never witnessed such a height of dysfunctional politics in Washington. The country's leadership needed to work together at full throttle but couldn't. The full faith and credit of the United States was on the brink of becoming meaningless. The country's financial standing was eroding, and the entire world was watching Americans battle among themselves in political warfare. The paralysis in Washington casts doubts on the ability of the government to govern.

At the last minute, Congress voted to raise the debt ceiling so the government would not default and could send out Social Security checks and Medicare hospital and doctor payments, among everything else it pays for.

The battle that Americans watched with despair, anger, and resignation is a harbinger of the future. Congress made only a small down payment on the debt. Meanwhile, spending for health care will continue to be uncontrolled and add to the debt. The toughest decisions have been postponed as Congress and the president kicked the can down the road, the inevitable price to pay for Washington-style dithering.

A year earlier, Democrats and Republicans could not even agree on why the 2008 financial meltdown occurred. A Financial Crisis Inquiry Commission, composed of former elected officials and political appointees, was divided in its assessment. The report reads like a "Tale of Two Crises." Democrats say Wall Street greed, corporate incompetence, and regulatory failures were the reason for the near collapse. Republicans blamed government housing policies that encouraged home ownership and broader economic forces.

THE LAST RESORT

When Washington teeters on the brink of default and its usual lenders won't come to its rescue, the lender of last resort is the International Monetary Fund (IMF). Here's how it works.

The IMF provides financial assistance to countries that have serious financial and economic difficulties. It loans money that its 187 member countries deposit with it. The United States is a member of the IMF and can request a loan to fill a gap. In return, countries are required to abide by conditions dictated by the IMF bureaucrats, which typically require draconian spending cuts and tax increases.

The IMF had its beginning in 1944 when President Franklin Roosevelt invited representatives of forty-five countries to meet in the small town of Bretton Woods, New Hampshire, near Mount Washington to agree on economic cooperation and stability after World War II. Countries were eager to avoid a repeat of the disastrous economic policies that led to the Great Depression in the 1930s. The IMF came into formal existence in 1945, when its first twenty-nine countries became members.

When the IMF lends money to a government, it comes with strings attached—or rather ropes. A borrower has little bargaining power. The IMF sets the targets for budget slashing and tax increases. It monitors compliance, and money is released only if the targets are met. The international bureaucrats are technocrats and immune to lobbying. They deal directly with the US Treasury Department. Special interests have no access to them.

When Greece teetered on the verge of default on the debt it owed to creditors, the IMF and the European Union lent the government money. The Greek government agreed to severe conditions required by the IMF. Public-sector employees' wages were cut, as were payments to retirees and low-income families. Sales taxes and taxes on gasoline were raised. Greeks protested in the streets against the draconian cuts and a government that had failed to prudently manage its financial affairs.

Ireland followed in Greece's footsteps. The Celtic Tiger had spent so much money bailing out its banks that government coffers teetered on empty. The markets lost faith in the government's efforts to deal with its ballooning debt. Ireland was compelled to take the bailout to restore confidence in the markets. It was a moment of humiliation.

Portugal was next. The governing party proposed austerity measures that included spending cuts and tax increases, but opposition parties thought the cuts in welfare and increases in public transportation costs were too severe. Investors who lend money to the government demanded higher interest rates for a country whose creditworthiness was becoming more precarious. Higher interest rates made it too costly for the government to pay its debts. This is what triggered Portugal to require a bailout.

The IMF is keeping a finger on the pulse of the US fiscal situation. Every year it conducts reviews of member countries' economies. The IMF is calling on the United States to stabilize the size of its public debt and recommends specific steps, including cuts in tax deductions, higher taxes on energy, and a national consumption tax or a financial activities tax. The IMF suggests that the United States reform entitlement programs such as Medicare and develop a clear plan for stabilizing debt over the coming years, while making a down payment on debt reduction.

The IMF is tracking health care reform and its impact on US debt. It acknowledges the law's cost-control measures but is skeptical that substantial savings will occur. It says that the Medicare Independent Payment Advisory Board has the potential to rein in excess cost growth, but any savings are not imminent. If the payment advisory board is not successful, the IMF recommends that the United States reduce tax exemptions for employer health insurance contributions.

While the IMF's report is understated and diplomatic, as is usual for these reports, the unspoken word in international circles is that the United States is basically bankrupt.

International watchers are vigilant about US debt because there's a saying, "When the United States sneezes, everyone else gets a cold." Because the US economy looms so large in the affairs of other nations, they are deeply affected by US actions.

The financial meltdown that began in the United States in 2008 triggered global chaos. Many countries and people around the world suffered because of America's mistakes. A default by the US government would drive the global economy into a tailspin far worse than the Great Recession.

If the United States cannot get its own financial house in order, lenders will increase interest rates and eventually tear up the country's credit cards. With too little cash and no credit, the federal government's buying power will be dramatically curtailed. It will have no choice but to ask the IMF to bail it out.

Enter the IMF, lender of last resort. The United States will fumble away its sovereignty. The country will cease to be a master of its own internal affairs. The humiliation will be of epic proportions, never seen in the country's history. Outsiders will tell the US government how to cut its budget and raise taxes. The United States will have to comply. It will join the ranks of low-income developing countries who are the majority of borrowers from the IMF because they are unable to manage their own affairs. Political and economic rivals of the United States will uncork champagne bottles and cheer as the United States falls to its knees.

Americans may say that the IMF has no business meddling in the country's domestic affairs. If the United States cannot act on its own, it will have no choice but for the IMF to meddle.

TRIPLE-A RATINGS ARE NOT FOREVER

The United States can step back from the brink of bankruptcy if it increases its national income by rebuilding its manufacturing base. Without a sustained surge in investment in manufacturing, the only option is to slash spending and raise taxes to levels that will be exceedingly painful.

The United States is not at the point of default, but lenders around the world question the political will of Congress and the White House to pare back the national debt. The gridlock that nearly triggered a government default in the summer of 2011 did not build confidence in the minds of investors. When they become skeptical, the United States will pay higher interest rates, similar to how credit card holders pay higher interest rates when they don't pay their bills on time.

The United States is already on track to pay higher interest rates. In April 2011 Standard & Poor's issued a negative outlook for the United States and said there is a one-in-three chance that it will lower the government's credit rating from the cherished triple-A rating to a double-A rating. Three months later, it ratcheted down the government's credit rating and rattled investors around the globe. Americans watched in somber disbelief as the country continued to unravel.

"No triple-A rating is forever," said Carol Sirou, a Standard & Poor's executive, three months before the ratings agency lowered its outlook. The jobless nature of the US recovery is one of the biggest threats to economic well-being, as is a nearly universal lack of confidence that Congress can get the country back on a firmer fiscal footing.

Japan lost its triple-A rating in January 2011, two months before the earthquake and tsunami. Its sovereign debt rating was lowered from extremely strong to very strong, a double-A rating it now shares with China. Europe's debt crisis threatens the sovereign credit rating of governments in the European Union. The possibility of multiple governments defaulting on their debt is real. This is a preview of what the United States can expect if it does not reduce spending.

HOW TO DEAL TOUGHLY WITH YOUR BANKER

China is American's largest foreign lender. This makes it hard for President Obama, Treasury Secretary Timothy Geithner, and Secretary of State Hillary Clinton to negotiate from a position of advantage when its lender is sitting across the table.

When WikiLeaks released US embassy cables, one of them included notes of a meeting between Clinton and then Australian prime minster Kevin Rudd in which China was discussed. Clinton asked, "How do you deal toughly with your banker?"

The truth is that the United States negotiates from a position of disadvantage. It owes $800 billion to China and pays $50 billion a year in interest. China has the United States by the tail.

Meanwhile, China monitors US health care reform because it is carefully watching how the US government spends the money it lends. In 2011 the Chinese rating agency, Dagong Global Credit Rating Company, downgraded US creditworthiness from A+ to A with a negative outlook.

HEALTH CARE IN AN AGE OF AUSTERITY

The National Commission on Fiscal Responsibility and Reform proposed a plan in December 2010 called "The Moment of Truth." It recommended a $4 trillion reduction in the national debt before 2020. Co-chair Alan Simpson, former senator from Wyoming, spoke about the commission's work. "If we're not Americans first instead of Republicans and Democrats, we won't get out of this hole."

The Commission proposed drastic Medicare changes, far more than the spending reductions in the health care overhaul.

The proposals were draconian because the fiscal outlook is dire. According to the White House commission, federal government revenue in 2025 will finance only interest payments, Medicare, Medicaid, and Social Security. Interest on the debt could increase to $1 trillion by 2020. Every other federal government activity—from national defense and homeland security to education, food stamps, and welfare—will have to be paid for with borrowed money. The amount of debt the federal government owes will be greater than the value of all the goods and services the country produces. By 2035 the federal government's debt will be as much as 185 percent of GDP. In sum, the money is running out.

With this dire situation, eleven members of the eighteen-member commission voted to forward the recommendations to the president and Congress, which was not enough to meet the required fourteen votes. The recommendations were put aside.

SO WHAT IF THE FEDERAL GOVERNMENT DEFAULTS?

Bankruptcy does not have the same stigma in the United States that it once did. In fact, more Americans are declaring bankruptcy. Struggling with too much debt and not enough money to pay it back, 1.5 million consumers filed for bankruptcy in 2010. This number keeps rising even though the Bankruptcy Abuse Prevention and Consumer Protection Act of 2005 made it harder for consumers to declare bankruptcy.

The federal government is headed down the same road with too much debt and not enough money to pay it back. Does it matter if the government defaults?

For a preview, the United States can look at the United Kingdom. It didn't default on its debt but stepped back from the brink. It launched the largest reduction in government spending in living memory, prompted by the fear that investors may no longer lend it money. Nearly 500,000 government jobs were cut. Tuition at the country's public universities was increased 300 percent. The budget of the famed British Broadcasting Corporation, the BBC, was slashed 25 percent.

Violence erupted as the pie shrank. Protestors attacked the Bentley in which Prince Charles and the Duchess of Cornwall were riding. An angry mob broke into the headquarters of the Conservative Party.

If the United States defaults, here is what will happen. In 2011 Treasury Secretary Timothy Geithner laid out the consequences in a letter to every member of Congress. Here are the commitments that would be discontinued, limited, or adversely affected if the federal government defaulted:

- US military salaries and retirement benefits
- Social Security and Medicare benefits
- veterans' benefits
- federal civil service salaries and retirement benefits
- individual and corporate tax refunds
- unemployment benefits to states
- defense vendor payments
- interest and principal payments on Treasury bonds and other securities
- student loan payments
- Medicaid payments to states
- payments necessary to keep government facilities open

Geithner wrote,

> If the federal government defaulted, it would cause catastrophic damage to the economy, potentially much more harmful than the effects of the financial crisis of 2008 and 2009. Interest rates for state and local government, corporate and consumer borrowing, including home mortgage interest, would all rise sharply. Equity prices and home values would decline, reducing retirement savings and hurting the economic security of all Americans, leading to reductions in spending and investment, which would cause job losses and business failures on a significant scale.
>
> Default would have prolonged and far-reaching negative consequences on the safe-haven status of Treasuries and the dollar's dominant role in the international financial system, causing further increases in interest rates and reducing the willingness of investors here and around the world to invest in the United States.

For these reasons, any default on the legal debt obligations of the United States is unthinkable and must be avoided. Throughout our history, that confidence has made U.S. government bonds among the best and safest investments available and has allowed us to borrow at very low rates.

By raising the debt ceiling in 2011, Congress and the White House allowed the federal government to borrow more money. This temporary fix is equivalent to a doctor placing a Band-aid on a metastatic cancer.

SHOVING HEALTH CARE COSTS
TO FUTURE GENERATIONS

Beginning January 1, 2011, the first baby boomers began to receive their Medicare cards. They have paid into Medicare for all their working lives and deserve their benefits. The truth is they will receive far more than what they have paid for, according to an analysis by the Urban Institute.

A couple that earns $89,000 a year and retires in 2011 will have paid $114,000 in Medicare payroll taxes during their working life. They will receive benefits worth three times as much, about $355,000.

Workers' payroll taxes don't go into a trust fund and build up over a lifetime. Instead, payroll taxes are used to pay for the medical care of current retirees. As baby boomers join Medicare's ranks, the program's financial solvency will crack. The number of workers who will be paying taxes to support the boomers will drop from 3.5 for each person receiving benefits now to 2.3 workers. This means there will be one less worker putting money into Medicare. Coupled with nonstop health care cost increases, these are the reasons that drastic measures are needed to fix Medicare. The program has been "shoving all those costs to future generations," said Eugene Steuerle, who developed the estimates.

Many boomers are not counting on Medicare and fear they will outlive it. Forty-three percent of boomers say they don't expect Medicare to be around forever, 37 percent are uncertain, and only 20 percent of boomers believe they can depend on the program for their health care, according to an Associated Press–GfK poll.

Social Security is in better financial shape. When the same couple retires, they will have paid $614,000 in Social Security payroll taxes during the years they worked and can expect to receive $555,000 in benefits.

"WE'RE STILL DANCING"

A year before the financial meltdown, Charles Prince, the former CEO of Citigroup, remarked, "We're still dancing. When the music stops . . . things will be complicated. But as long as the music is playing, you've got to get up and dance."

Prince was referring to the fears about loose lending standards in the subprime mortgage market. Knowing that an abrupt downturn would inevitably occur, the bankers didn't care as long as money was still flowing.

When the music stops, Americans will be unprepared financially and psychologically for the turmoil. Whether rich or poor, young or old, the day of reckoning is coming. People from all walks of life will be helpless in a maelstrom that even their government will be unable to control.

Abrupt cuts in federal spending and tax increases in the middle of a crisis will cause far more disruption and pain than occurred during the Great Recession. A federal stimulus will be impossible because the government will be broke. The rich will seek refuge behind their gated communities.

Years ago, America managed its money wisely. It could afford to do just about anything. The economy was growing. The United States was the dominant economic powerhouse. It was a lender to the rest of the world. Now it must borrow.

Governments must make choices, just as individuals and families make tradeoffs for how they spend their money. Wise governments borrow money to invest in the future, not to spend for today. They build mass transit systems to increase productivity and invest in new sources of sustainable energy to create energy independence that will benefit future generations.

Borrowing money from China and other countries to pay today's Medicare and Medicaid hospital and doctor bills is bad public policy. Adam Smith said that public debt "has gradually enfeebled every state which has adopted it." To use a medical analogy, America won't be felled by a massive heart attack. Instead, America will become frail from congestive heart failure. The heart of the country that once made it great will be weakened to the point that it cannot pump enough life through itself to allow the nation to breathe and prosper.

During the health care reform debate, Nancy Pelosi, then Speaker of the House, was adamant that the health care law won't add a dime to the deficit. As health care industry lobbyists work to repeal provisions that require it to pay fees to cover the cost of insurance for the uninsured, the reform law will add to the deficit. The United States was on a fiscal collision course before the health care overhaul and still is.

When government intervenes to advance a worthy social goal, it has an obligation to ensure the sustainable use of public resources. Without cost control, the vicious cycle will repeat itself.

As costs continue to climb, even more expensive health insurance coverage will be needed. More employers will drop insurance because the cost will be impossible to afford. More people will qualify for federal subsidies. If the federal subsidies do not continue to increase, individuals and families will need to spend more of their own money. Medical bankruptcies will rise once again.

THE FISCAL ICEBERGS

The story of the *Titanic*, the largest and most luxurious passenger vessel of its time, is a metaphor for life.

According to historical accounts, the ship had received warnings from other ships on April 14, 1912, about icebergs and their locations in the North Atlantic. The ship's captain failed to steer the ship to avoid a collision and the possibility of disaster. The *Titanic* was moving toward a vast belt of ice stretching nearly eighty miles across its path. The warnings went unheeded.

That night a crewman who was peering out into the darkness from the crow's nest saw a menacing black shape five hundred yards away. An iceberg was moving closer by the second. Eyewitnesses on the ship said it looked like the Rock of Gibraltar. The ship could not stop in time. At the last moment, the crew tried to steer the ship to avoid a direct hit. This created an even larger gash in the hull that accelerated the sinking of the unsinkable.

A hundred years later, the fiscal icebergs are visible on the horizon. With health care reform, more people will board the ship of state to seek refuge from the cold waters and harsh conditions. As the country moves toward the fiscal icebergs, everyone will be on board—executives of the medical-industrial complex, the newly insured, the young and the old, the sick and the healthy.

Part 5

PRIVATIZE THE GAINS,
PRIVATIZE THE LOSSES

In chapter 13 we tackle the perennial problem of medical malpractice. We explore the root cause of much of the malpractice that occurs and examine the work of leading doctors and hospitals that have made health care safer and dramatically reduced lawsuits. Meanwhile, the health care industry continues to lobby for a quick fix, namely tort reform to prevent people from suing when they are harmed. We show how tort reform is not a solution.

In chapter 14 we highlight the Obama administration's efforts to crack down on health care fraud, which has reached epidemic levels. We examine estimates of fraud from the US Department of Justice and conclude that the amount of fraudulent expenditures is enough to pay the entire annual cost of health care for thirty-two million newly insured Americans. The sheer magnitude, coupled with unsustainable fiscal deficits, has prompted proposed legislation that would require unprecedented transparency and public access to information about how much money individual hospitals, doctors, and other providers and suppliers receive from Medicare. The media has joined the fray and sees abundant opportunity to open up well-kept secrets about where money spent on health care is really going. The welcome surfeit of scrutiny by the media will finally open the black box of big money.

In the final chapter we highlight ten steps that Washington policy makers can take to bend the cost curve and protect the public from higher costs and eroding benefits. These ideas will not be politically popular with the medical-industrial complex, but they are in the public's best interests. They need to be in the spotlight so the public is aware of alternatives to slashing benefits and raising premiums.

· 13 ·

The Real Medical Malpractice Fix

$\mathcal{T}$he health care reform law includes a medical malpractice fix that is refreshingly different from the usual approach coming out of Washington.

In the current system, Americans who are harmed by medical malpractice can file civil lawsuits against doctors, hospitals, and other providers for alleged torts, or wrongful actions that result in harm. The intent is to compensate people for injuries, lost wages, and pain and suffering that occur because of health care harm. There is no evidence, though, that medical malpractice lawsuits make care safer.

The AMA and other health care industry groups have long sought nationwide limits on medical malpractice lawsuits. The usual approach is to place caps on awards for noneconomic damages such as pain and suffering. One-third of states already have caps on noneconomic damages. Proponents also seek limits on the amounts awarded for punitive damages.

The health care law provides $50 million for states to experiment with alternative approaches to resolve cases of patient harm. To be eligible, states must ensure that hospitals and doctors tell patients when they have been harmed and redesign their care to prevent the errors from happening again. States cannot impose limits on an injured patient's right to file a medical malpractice claim. In a pivotal step, patient advocates must be included in developing alternative approaches along with health care providers, medical malpractice insurers, and patient safety experts.

At the health care summit at Blair House a month before the health care bill was signed into law, Senator John McCain didn't agree with this approach. He said, "I don't think we have to experiment around." He wanted limits, or caps, on noneconomic damages.

Senator Dick Durbin, a Democrat from Illinois, stated an opposing view. "I worked in a courtroom," he said. "For years I defended doctors and hospitals, and for years I sued them on behalf of people who were victims of medical malpractice. So I've sat at both tables in a courtroom." He said that tort reform takes away accountability for the preventable harm that doctors and hospitals cause.

Durbin cited a case in a Chicago hospital where a woman had surgery to remove a mole from her face. A fire occurred in the operating room and her face was burned. She had repeated surgeries, scars, and deformity. "Her life will never be the same. . . . And you are saying that this innocent woman is only entitled to $250,000 in pain and suffering? I don't think that's fair."

Republicans pressed ahead. Less than a year after the reform law was enacted, the Republican-led House Judiciary Committee voted along party lines to approve a bill to curb patients' right to sue hospitals and doctors. The Help Efficient, Accessible, Low-Cost, Timely Healthcare (HEALTH) Act was introduced by representatives Phil Gingrey, a Republican from Georgia, and David Scott, a Democrat from Georgia, along with chief cosponsor Republican Lamar Smith of Texas in early January 2011. The bill would impose a $250,000 cap on noneconomic damages and a $250,000 limit on punitive damages or twice the economic damages, whichever is greater.

Older Americans and children are especially disadvantaged by restrictions on lawsuits. They are less likely to be employed and earn money, which means they have little economic value from the perspective of the courts. They can recoup little, if anything, even in cases where they become disabled because of preventable health care harm. Lawyers will be unwilling to take their cases because the compensation will be insufficient to cover the often costly process to pursue a medical malpractice case, especially when injured patients are up against the substantial legal resources of lawyers who represent doctors and hospitals.

Limits on medical malpractice typically require that people sue within a specified period—say, three years—of when they were harmed. When people are seriously injured, their first priority is to regain their health. It may take months and years to muster the time and energy to navigate the legal system. In fact, it may take that long for them to realize that the harm they suffered occurred because of medical malpractice.

The battle lines are drawn between the doctors and the health care industry on one side and trial lawyers on the other. The doctors blame the trial lawyers and the trial lawyers blame the doctors. The public is caught in the crossfire. They are invisible in Washington because they have no money to hire lobbyists to represent them. As the saying goes in Washington, if you aren't at the table, you're on the menu.

Limiting patients' ability to seek redress when they have been harmed is a distraction from a deep-seated and widespread problem of poor quality medical care. Dr. Donald Berwick, the administrator of the Centers for Medicare and Medicaid Services appointed by President Obama in a recess appointment, to the annoyance of Republicans in Congress, has been candid about the extent of poor quality health care. He told a group of physician and nursing leaders at a meeting in Washington that when he was teaching students at Harvard Medical School, he offered a case of wine to anyone who could find a patient who had not been harmed in the hospital. He said he never lost a wager.

Before the health care reform law was enacted, the Obama administration announced a $25 million Patient Safety and Medical Liability Initiative. The aim is to reduce lawsuits by making care safe. The administration outlined four commonsense principles: put patient safety first and work to reduce preventable injuries; enable better communication between doctors and their patients; ensure that patients are compensated in a fair and timely manner for medical injuries while reducing lawsuits that have no merit; and reduce liability premiums.

This approach serves the public's interest. Consider Richard Flagg, a Vietnam veteran who worked in special operations during the war. Decades later when he was in his late fifties, he had a benign tumor on his left lung and went to the hospital to have it removed. When he woke up in the recovery room, he realized that surgery had been performed on the other side of his chest. When he asked the surgeon what happened, the surgeon told him that the tumor on the other lung was much worse and required surgery.

Mr. Flagg requested a copy of the pathology report. It showed that the lung tissue that had been removed had no evidence of a tumor. The surgeon had performed the operation on the wrong lung but didn't tell his patient. The New Jersey state medical board, which regulates medical practice and issues medical licenses, found that the surgeon deliberately altered the medical record to try to cover up his mistake.

Mr. Flagg had very little lung function remaining because a large part of his healthy lung had been removed. He could no longer work, was confined to a wheelchair, and needed oxygen twenty-four hours a day. He lost his job-related health insurance. Mr. Flagg required medical care and financial resources to pay his living expenses and medical bills. The only way to stop hospitals and doctors from sending medical bills is to file a lawsuit. Mr. Flagg sued. Even though the doctor made a mistake, the doctor's lawyers fought the lawsuit.

Lawyers for health care providers advise their clients to deny and defend, an approach that increases the ire of patients and families. It also keeps lawyers in business in perpetuity.

Mr. Flagg died before the case was resolved. The doctor's license was suspended by the New Jersey medical board and eventually reinstated.

Most patients are treated badly when harm occurs. Lawyers who represent hospitals and doctors may deliberately prolong a case because it is less expensive to pay damages for a person who has died than for a person who lives with a disability.

Filing a malpractice suit is not for the faint of heart. The process is brutal. Patients encounter a phalanx of lawyers from malpractice insurance companies, hospitals, and doctors who have seemingly unlimited resources to spend on a case and who wear down their less well-financed opponents. People who have been seriously injured by health care harm may not have the physical and emotional stamina to withstand the trauma. This is a reason that only a small percentage of people who are seriously harmed file a medical malpractice lawsuit.

In the aftermath of harm, people want to be told the truth about what happened and why. They don't want to be abandoned by the hospital or doctor or bear the financial burden of follow-up medical care, or have the mistake happen to another person. We talk about patient and family wishes in the aftermath of preventable harm in our book *Wall of Silence*.

If the AMA and the health care industry continue to succeed in limiting patients' rights to sue, it will be harder, if not impossible, for people such as Richard Flagg to seek redress in the courts and hold hospitals and doctors accountable for the preventable harm they cause.

Tort reform merely shifts the financial cost of mistakes to the people least able to afford it—individuals, families, and taxpayers. It is another example of privatized gain and socialized losses. People who have been harmed bear the cost, and some become impoverished and rely on government health insurance and public assistance as a last resort.

A seasoned obstetrician at a busy inner-city hospital on the east coast said one night at a private dinner, "The reason we have a malpractice crisis is because there's so much malpractice." He takes care of women with high-risk pregnancies and is dismayed at the poor quality care he has seen women receive from other doctors.

The AMA disagrees and says that medical malpractice problems occur because patients file frivolous lawsuits. While it makes for a good sound bite, it belittles the seriousness of the problem. Trust in the AMA would increase exponentially if it sought solutions that serve the interests of both the public and doctors.

A constructive approach is needed more than ever. Many doctors do not have long-standing relationships with their patients. Misunderstandings are more likely to occur when a trusting relationship does not exist. Patients may have unrealistic expectations about the outcomes they should expect. Conscientious doctors may have legitimate fears of being sued.

The solution is not to close the door on those who are seriously harmed. The real solution is to identify the root causes of poor medical care and engineer defects out of the system.

A BETTER WAY

If hospitals and doctors want people to stop suing them, they can follow the example of anesthesiologists, who have transformed anesthesia care nationwide to make it safer. Here is what they did and how they did it.

The ABC television program *20/20* aired a segment, "The Deep Sleep: 6,000 Will Die or Suffer Brain Damage." The program began with a voice-over saying, "If you are going to go into anesthesia, you are going on a long trip and you should not do it, if you can avoid it in any way. General anesthesia is safe most of the time, but there are dangers from human error, carelessness and a critical shortage of anesthesiologists. This year, 6,000 patients will die or suffer brain damage."

The program reported that people who had experienced anesthesia mistakes died or were severely brain damaged. In one instance, a person remained in a coma after the anesthesiologist mistakenly turned off the life-sustaining oxygen when he meant to turn off the nitrous oxide.

The program host said, "The people you have just seen are tragic victims of a danger they never knew existed—mistakes in administering anesthesia."

Later in the program, an unidentified spokesperson said to the reporter, "There is a hospital in New York City where there are two anesthesia people covering five operating rooms." The reporter asked, "How do they do it?" The spokesperson replied, "Well, they run quickly and pray a lot."

The program aired thirty years ago on April 22, 1982. Anesthesiologists didn't write letters to the television network to criticize the program for stoking fear among the public or for making doctors look bad. Nor did they raise millions of dollars to lobby members of Congress to prevent patients from suing doctors. The anesthesiologists said they avoided "the urge to fixate on tort reform."

At the time, a malpractice crisis was occurring that reduced the incomes of anesthesiologists, many of whom wanted to lobby Congress to limit lawsuits. With the leadership of the president of the American Society of Anesthesiologists, Dr. Ellison Pierce Jr., anesthesiologists took an unprecedented step and focused on reducing the harm that was causing exorbitant malpractice awards. In 1985 Pierce and his colleagues created the Anesthesia Patient Safety Foundation "to ensure that no patient is harmed by anesthesia."

There was a lot of work to do. In the 1950s death from anesthesia was recognized as a major public health problem. As was noted at the time, "You members of the medical profession, gentlemen, are in a favored position—the world acclaims your successes and flowers cover your failures."

In the 1970s the mortality rate from anesthesia during surgery was very high. One to two people died per ten thousand anesthetics administered. In the 1980s anesthesiologists were only 3 percent of physicians, but they accounted for a disproportionate share—12 percent—of medical malpractice payments.

Dr. Pierce said, "When a patient did not survive, the families were simply told that 'old Joe' just didn't tolerate the anesthesia—'too bad.'"

Doctors and engineers studied why harm occurred so they could learn from their mistakes. In fact, no study had ever been conducted to examine the reasons for so many bad outcomes. A pioneering bioengineer from Harvard, Jeffrey Cooper, used critical-incident analysis, a technique used in aviation in World War II, to understand the causes of errors. He interviewed doctors and nurses to identify the causes and circumstances, as well as the procedures and devices involved.

Patterns emerged about the causes of harm. Solutions were identified. Doctors worked with manufacturers of equipment used in operating rooms to develop new technology that provided real-time information to anesthesiologists to ensure that patients were receiving oxygen. The pulse oximeter was developed, which is a clip placed on a person's finger that detects the percentage of oxygen saturation in the blood. It allows anesthesiologists to know whether a patient is receiving enough oxygen.

A device to measure carbon dioxide in a patient's exhalation was developed, which helped doctors ensure that breathing tubes had been properly placed. Also, machines in the operating room were reengineered so that doctors would not accidentally shut off oxygen flowing to the patient.

The American Society of Anesthesiologists took another forward-thinking approach and reviewed thousands of closed malpractice claims to study the causes of harm that led people to file lawsuits. Now it has nearly nine thousand closed claims, a treasure trove of information for learning and improvement.

Anesthesiologists pioneered the use of realistic patient simulators, or mannequins, that are operated by a computer to mimic lifelike situations. Young doctors in training can hone their skills on a mannequin rather than a real patient. Seasoned doctors can sharpen their skills. Training in team work during critical events is simulated just as airline pilots train in simulators to handle rare events.

The number of deaths per anesthesia administration plummeted from one in ten thousand anesthetics in the mid-1980s to one in nearly two hundred thousand today.

Anesthesiologists' medical malpractice insurance premiums have declined dramatically. In the 1980s anesthesiologists paid $35,000 to $50,000 a year for premiums, among the highest rates for all doctors. In 2006 average annual premiums were $19,558.

Jeffrey Cooper, now the director of biomedical engineering at Partners HealthCare System in Boston and associate professor of anesthesia at Harvard Medical School, says, "I see no reason that every medical specialty organization should not be achieving the same results, either alone or in partnership with others."

Other medical specialties have not followed the example of the anesthesiologists. Dr. Lucian Leape, a nationally recognized leader in patient safety and adjunct professor at the Harvard School of Public Health, says that unlike other medical specialties, anesthesiologists work in an operating room environment that they can control. Technical fixes were developed to yield dramatic improvements in safety. Still, he says, other specialties "don't see a burning need" for safety improvements and there is "a lack of real leadership" for safety. As a former pediatric surgeon, he is particularly struck by the lack of surgical leadership on the use of checklists that can eliminate wrong-site surgery and surgery performed on the wrong patient.

Recently, one of us visited a teaching hospital to give a presentation to doctors and medical students about patient safety. Doctors at the hospital had just begun to examine their closed malpractice claims. They noticed a pattern: young doctors in training were involved in a significant share of lawsuits because they had not been properly supervised by senior doctors. This is a familiar problem to anyone who works in a teaching hospital. Remarkably, the senior doctors had never looked at closed claims before to understand patterns of harm and the circumstances in which it occurred so they could prevent the harm from happening again.

THE RIGHT WAY

If doctors and hospitals want people to stop suing them and prevent future lawsuits, they can follow the example of two hospitals in the Midwest that help people who are harmed and have reduced medical malpractice lawsuits and premiums.

The University of Michigan Health System is one of those hospitals. It wanted to try a different approach than the usual "defend and deny" strategy that lawyers have typically advised hospitals to take when patients have been harmed. It did something radical in health care: it began to tell patients the truth when they were injured.

The hospital agreed on a set of commonsense principles. When harm occurs through unreasonable care, the organization must make it right. When the care that staff members provide is reasonable under the circumstances, they need to be supported even when something goes wrong. A commitment to learning from medical errors helps the organization continually improve its quality.

According to the chief risk officer for the hospital, Rick Boothman, the policy of honesty was initially a way for the hospital to save money. If the hospital made a mistake, it made sense to admit it and compensate the family rather than spend hundreds of thousands of dollars defending the indefensible.

Boothman began to see that the culture of disclosure created unprecedented opportunities to improve care and prevent harm. "The culture of deny and defend prevents us from improving," Boothman says. "Being open with patients starts with being honest with ourselves about our failings—that is a necessary prerequisite to any real improvement."

The hospital has had fewer medical malpractice claims and lawsuits. In the beginning, 39 lawsuits a year were filed; six years later 17 were filed. The hospital spent 61 percent less on lawyers to defend itself. The amount of money the hospital sets aside to pay claims has been reduced and the time to resolve cases has been cut by about one-third.

The University of Illinois Medical Center at Chicago (UIC) was inspired by the Michigan experience and developed a more comprehensive approach to respond to adverse events. At first the hospital's own lawyers were the biggest barrier to telling patients the truth when harm occurred. "We had one horrendous sentinel event and I pushed for full disclosure," said Dr. Tim McDonald, chief patient safety and risk officer. "We'd done a wrong site surgery in a neurosurgery case. [We said,] 'Isn't this a case where we should just tell the family we made a mistake and settle it instead of letting it become a lawsuit?'" The hospital would not tell the truth because it had no institution-wide policy to disclose an error. So they created one.

Hospital staff meet with the patient, apologize, and provide a remedy, whether patients want to file a claim or not. They waive fees for hospital and physician services and prescription drugs. The hospital puts a hold on bills that would otherwise be mailed to the patient's home.

In the first two years, the policy of open and honest communication resulted in more than four thousand incident reports annually, prompted more than two hundred investigations to analyze the cause of the incidents, and led to nearly two hundred system improvements. Nearly three hundred conversations occurred with patients and families, and fifty more in-depth disclosures took place when inappropriate or unreasonable care caused harm to a patient. A substantial decline in lawsuits and associated legal costs ensued, according to Dr. McDonald.

The hospital hired new lawyers. It also interviewed sixteen law firms and asked them how they would handle a case of wrong-site surgery. Twelve of the firms said they would defend the hospital, which meant they would knowingly lie to a patient who had been harmed. Four firms said they would help the hospital tell the truth. The hospital took a bold step and contracted with the four law firms.

Malpractice premiums plummeted after hospital staff began to tell the truth to patients. So far only one patient has filed a lawsuit. The hospital is located in Cook County, which is considered by some observers to be a haven for trial lawyers.

The hospital pays for follow-up medical care to restore the person to health and apportions the cost to the departments responsible for the harm, a tactic that is unusual. Doctors in the departments whose premiums have increased are becoming more interested in learning about patient safety.

In one case, a young man donated his kidney to his brother. During the surgery performed on the kidney donor, the surgeon made an error that resulted in the young man's death. The hospital was honest and forthright with his family. The case was settled within three months. The family did not file a lawsuit. The hospital's legal costs and the cost of the settlement were dramatically less than if the hospital had fought against the family. The best outcome is that the young man's family continues to receive care at the hospital because they can trust the hospital to act in an ethical and honorable way.

Transparency and honesty has allowed the hospital to understand why mistakes occur and take steps to prevent them from happening over and over again. It has learned that the best risk-management strategy is patient safety.

Patients who are harmed and their family members are asked about the events that led up to the error because they may have valuable information that can help the hospital uncover the root cause.

A committee at UIC examines errors that would have otherwise vanished into lawyers' files under lock and key. Advocates for patients attend the meetings where cases of patient harm are reviewed. They may make observations that doctors and nurses may be thinking but cannot say because it is politically incorrect to do so among their colleagues.

Dr. McDonald, who is also a lawyer, says, "The way we're going to successfully manage the medical malpractice crisis is through safer care, not tort reform."

If hospitals develop a reputation in their communities for handling errors in an ethical and forthright manner, lawyers who file meritless lawsuits will have more difficulty convincing a jury.

It is not easy for hospitals and doctors to acknowledge a serious mistake. Unintentional harm is devastating to conscientious doctors, nurses, pharmacists, and other health care professionals. Mistakes often occur because hospitals are so chaotic that even the best doctors and nurses cannot stop them from happening.

Nor is it easy to convince hospitals to adopt this approach. Many doctors are afraid of being honest with their patients when they hurt them. They are fearful of lawsuits and how their colleagues may perceive them. Honest and full disclosure is contrary to the culture in which most doctors have trained and practiced.

Rick Boothman helps doctors overcome fear by reminding them that full disclosure serves their best interests. "But," he says, "this is an intellectual argument that has to overcome the emotional reticence of doing this. You've got to be able to say to a doctor, 'I serve you best by helping you avoid litigation. And if we made a mistake, the best way to avoid litigation is to make it right, right now.'" In fact, he has learned that a commitment to a principled approach to dealing with harm to a patient eviscerates legal concerns.

Lawyers are among the biggest opponents of this commonsense solution. Lawyers for patients and lawyers who defend hospitals and doctors will lose business if honesty was the norm. In fact, one of us met an official at a hospital on the east coast who worked in the risk-management department. He expressed concern that fewer cases of health care harm could mean that he could lose his job.

Instead of lobbying Congress to curb lawsuits, the AMA would perform a great public service by helping their members learn why mistakes occur and how to reengineer health care to make mistakes as rare as possible.

This approach is needed more than ever. Many hospitals and clinics will have more patients, and doctors, nurses, and other health professionals will be even more pressed for time and have less opportunity to build a relationship and trust with patients, which increases the chance for more mistakes, miscommunication, and lawsuits.

STOP LAWSUITS OR STOP MEDICAL MALPRACTICE?

Proponents of tort reform say it will reduce health care costs. Medical malpractice lawsuits do increase legal costs and defensive medicine. According to the Congressional Budget Office, when the right to sue is limited, fewer lawsuits will occur and medical liability insurance premiums paid by hospitals and doctors would decline by about 10 percent. Health care spending would decline by one-fifth of 1 percent, or about $5 billion a year.

These savings are illusory. The costs of harm are merely shifted to patients, family members, insurers, and taxpayers. Consider an Oregon family whose husband acquired three infections while hospitalized. He fell off his roof while cleaning his gutters and broke his leg and hurt his back. His doctors expected he would be hospitalized for a few days. He was hospitalized for several months because of the infections he acquired owing to poor care. He suffered brain damage and can no longer work. The family filed for bankruptcy because they could not afford to pay the tens of thousands of dollars of hospital, doctor, and home health care bills.

Some families are forced into poverty because of medical mistakes. They become eligible for public programs for financial support and health insurance whose costs are borne by taxpayers.

The largest savings will come from preventing harm, not stopping lawsuits. By making care safe, fewer people are harmed, costs for medical care decline, and lawsuits decrease. This is the real solution and smart public policy.

PRIVATIZE THE LOSSES

While browsing in a bookstore one day, we found a book titled *Reform That Makes Sense* that recommended federal legislation to limit medical malpractice lawsuits. The author was the chief executive of the company that owned the two California hospitals that Medicare officials sought to terminate from the program because of substandard care. In fact, the book was published in 2009, the same year that the hospitals received letters from Medicare stating its concerns about their care. When Toyota's stuck accelerators were headline news, federal regulators from the National Highway Transportation Safety Administration scrutinized the company's actions. If Toyota's CEO wrote a new book that recommended a federal law to make it harder for customers to sue his company, it would have created a public relations nightmare for the company. The public rightly expects that Toyota should not be shielded from lawsuits and should pay the injured for its failures. Privatized gain with privatized losses places the cost where it belongs. Companies have the incentive to ensure safety. The same is true for hospitals and doctors. When they bear the cost of harm, they have more incentive to make care safe.

THE OSTRICH AND THE GOLDEN EGG

Dr. Ernest A. Codman was a Boston orthopedic surgeon who believed in an idea that was radical in the early 1900s when he practiced medicine. He said that every hospital "should follow every patient it treats long enough to determine whether or not the treatment has been successful, and then to inquire, 'If not, why not?' with a view to preventing similar failures in the future." It is remarkable that his commonsense idea remains radical in twenty-first-century American health care.

Codman practiced what he preached. He documented good outcomes and bad outcomes. He kept track of mistakes and their impact on patients. He searched for the cause of errors so he could learn from them.

While at Massachusetts General Hospital, Codman was unhappy with its lack of attentiveness to outcomes. He resigned and established his own hospital where he kept track of every patient. During a five-year period, three hundred and thirty-seven people had been in his hospital. He recorded one hundred and twenty-three errors, one for every three patients. The causes ranged from lack of knowledge and skill to poor surgical judgment and a lack of care or equipment.

Codman sent copies of his annual reports to major hospitals around the country to challenge them to document their outcomes. None did.

He made his reports available to the public because he believed that patients should know the outcomes of care so they could judge hospitals for themselves.

One night Codman chaired a meeting of his local medical society. Frustrated at his colleagues' lack of interest in knowing whether their patients were actually better, he drew a cartoon and displayed it. It showed an ostrich with its head in the sand, kicking up sand behind him, all the while digging up golden eggs. Codman explained that the ostrich represented surgeons and hospital administrators who had their heads in the sand and never studied the outcomes of the care they provided to patients. They were content, he said, as long as they produced the "golden eggs." That night, he was asked to resign from the society.

Although Codman showed doctors a way to improve the care they provided to their patients, they disparaged and ostracized him. They stopped referring patients to him. He died penniless. In fact, he didn't even have enough money to buy a headstone for his grave in Mount Auburn Cemetery in Massachusetts.

If doctors had followed Codman's simple yet profound practice, health care in the United States would be markedly different than it is today. Doctors would have had more than a hundred years to continuously study the outcomes of the care they provide to their patients. Advances in medical science would have occurred far more rapidly because doctors would have studied what works and what doesn't and applied that knowledge for the benefit of their patients. The public would have confidence that the medical profession is working for their benefit.

The medical profession has paid a steep price for ignoring the commonsense approach that Codman offered them. Instead of owning the outcomes of the care they provide to patients, too many doctors pay little attention. They seek the assistance of lawyers to defend them in cases that are indefensible and cede the moral and ethical responsibility they have to their patients. They follow the advice of their lawyers to fight the patients they harm. Lawyers for patients take advantage of the abundant opportunity to find fault with American medicine. There's a better way, and it's never too late to begin anew.

· 14 ·

Health Care Fraud: Follow the Money

$\mathcal{T}$he health care reform law ramps up the fight against health care fraud. It provides an additional $350 million over ten years to combat the leakage from fraud, and it gives federal authorities new powers to deter and prosecute perpetrators. These changes cannot come soon enough.

The amount of money lost to health care fraud each year is almost enough to pay the entire annual cost of care for thirty-two million newly insured Americans. Here is how we came to this remarkable fact.

The Federal Bureau of Investigation reports that 3 to 10 percent of all health care spending is fraudulent. The federal government's watchdog group, the Government Accountability Office, says that 10 percent of all state Medicaid payments are improper. If 10 percent of all health care spending is lost to fraud, $250 billion a year is forgone that could be used to pay for health care for the uninsured.

About $8,000 is spent per person per year on health care. With thirty-two million more people expected to be insured, the total cost of care for the uninsured is about $256 billion a year, roughly the same as the leakage to fraud, give or take a few billion.

The federal government recoups only a tiny fraction of its loss—$3 billion in the first six months of 2010. Private health insurance companies have their own antifraud swat teams but are silent about how much is stolen and the portion they recoup.

PAY AND CHASE

Why is health care littered with fraud? When the foundation was laid for health care in the 1950s and 1960s, members of Congress deferred to doctors to determine how public money should be spent. In those days, the country was riding high on the discovery of the polio vaccine, a triumph in the annals of science. A grateful nation had faith, trust, and respect for those who brought the benefits of medical research to people.

In 1965 when President Lyndon Johnson signed Medicare and Medicaid into law, the two health care programs were designed based on trust. Hospitals and doctors submitted bills for services and the government paid them. No one imagined that health care would become the business it is today.

Unlike the framers of the Constitution, who established a system of checks and balances among the three branches of government, health care architects did not design a system with a countervailing force to restrain human impulses. This was naive.

The government's approach to fraud has been to "pay and chase." Medicare pays the bills that hospitals and doctors send to it, and officials chase after criminals if the claims are fraudulent. This approach is equivalent to opening the door to Fort Knox, the country's gold depository, and chasing after those who loot the bullion stockpile.

Veteran fraud investigators say that criminal gangs engaged in illegal drug activity have shifted their business to health care fraud because it is more lucrative and the sanctions are virtually nonexistent.

As fraud escalated, Congress failed to act. Federal agencies lacked funding and authority to protect taxpayers. When President George W. Bush requested Congress to provide nearly $600 million to combat fraud, Congress refused, saying the money would be better spent curing cancer. This is surprising because the return on investment in fraud prevention is lucrative. For every dollar spent, taxpayers receive $17 in return.

FORTUNE 500 FRAUD

The Obama administration has scaled up enforcement and prevention. In 2011 the Office of Inspector General (OIG) of the US Department of Health and Human Services launched its most-wanted fugitives list for health care fraud, the first-ever list of individuals sought by authorities on charges of fraud and abuse. The list includes photos and profiles of each featured fugitive.

The first ten individuals on the list allegedly cost taxpayers more than $124 million in fraud. In all, more than 170 fugitives are being sought.

Federal officials are beginning to use the same technology that banks use to scan credit card charges so they can spot a sudden shopping spree at high-end stores. Secretary Sebelius said, "This is the same type of predictive modeling tools that banks and insurance companies use to identify potential fraud before it occurs. . . . And it's about time we put that same technology to use in the public system when it comes to protecting our health care."

During the health care reform debate, Senator Bernie Sanders of Vermont reminded his colleagues that Fortune 500 companies are among the biggest perpetrators of health care fraud. Sanders said that government investigators found that 80 percent of insurance companies participating in the Medicare prescription drug benefit overcharged subscribers and taxpayers by an estimated $4.4 billion.

"What we have seen for many years is the systemic fraud perpetrated by private insurance companies, private drug companies, and private for-profit hospitals ripping off the American people and the taxpayers of this country to the tune of many billions of dollars," he said.

The government's list of most wanted individuals does not include executives of the firms that have defrauded Medicare.

Sanders proposed an amendment to the health care reform law to double the penalties under the False Claims Act for fraudulently billing new health exchanges created by the reform bill. "What we have to tell these big multinational corporations is that if they are going to engage in fraud, they're going to pay for it dearly," Sanders said.

Fines have proven to be an inadequate deterrent against the blockbuster scale of criminal enterprise that has infiltrated health care. A former federal prosecutor said stronger measures are needed—namely, "heads on sticks."

FEET TO THE FIRE

The health care reform law provides the government with authority to crack down on relatively small-time corruption, but it needs different tools to deal with billion-dollar corporations and executives who are hard to prosecute because lower-level employees carry out the illegal activity.

In a welcome move, the federal government is tightening the vise on health care executives whose companies violate the law. The latest weapon in the battle over health care fraud is prosecution of culpable executives of drug and device companies. When that isn't feasible, the government is seeking the authority to exclude them from receiving Medicare and other federal funds.

In May 2007 Purdue Frederick, a subsidiary of Purdue Pharma, pleaded guilty in federal court in Virginia to illegally marketing to doctors a powerful narcotic, Oxycontin, without telling them about its dangers and the high risk of drug addiction and abuse. Deep in the coal country of southwest Virginia, more than two hundred deaths were attributed to the drug.

The convicted company was automatically prevented from receiving payment from Medicare, Medicaid, and other federal government programs. The parent company avoided criminal charges by striking a nonprosecution agreement and paying $634.5 million in penalties. It was not excluded from receiving federal money.

Three executives of Purdue Frederick were found guilty of a criminal misdemeanor whereby responsible corporate officers can be held liable for failing to prevent, detect, or correct federal drug violations even though there is no proof that they engaged in any misconduct. The drug company executives paid fines of $34.5 million and avoided prison. The former president and CEO, Michael Friedman, paid $19 million; chief medical officer Paul Goldenheim paid $7.5 million; and general counsel Howard Udell paid $8 million.

After they were convicted, they were banned by the US Department of Health and Human Services from participation in Medicare and all other federal programs for twenty years. Legal maneuvering by the executives reduced the exclusion to twelve years.

To add muscle to the exclusion, if any of them formed their own company or worked for another firm, the entire company could be excluded from doing business with any taxpayer-funded federal health care programs for twelve years.

The former executives challenged the ban in US District Court in Washington. In December 2010, US District Judge Ellen Huvelle upheld the ban, saying that the government acted within its authority. She noted that the Purdue Frederick executives admitted they had responsibility to prevent or correct the inappropriate marketing of the drug. "It strains credulity to argue that, despite this admission, they 'were not accused of committing any unlawful acts themselves,'" she wrote.

A Washington, DC, law firm warned its health industry clients about the stronger tactics, saying, "The focus of governmental enforcement activity against manufacturers has expanded to include individual officers, employees, and counsel."

The ruling begins to close the gap in disparate treatment meted out in cases of corporate fraud and smaller-scale crime. "We are going to see more CEOs lose their seats and be excluded from working in any management position in a company that does business with the federal government," says Patrick Burns of Taxpayers Against Fraud, a nonprofit that supports whistleblower lawsuits. "If fraud is a disease, then exclusion of CEOs and corporate officers who ignore fraud, is surely the cure." It's the next best thing to prosecution, he says, because "companies that are too big to fail are too big to jail."

To tighten the vise on fraud, Congressmen Wally Herger, a Republican from California, and Pete Stark, a Democrat from California, introduced the Strengthening Medicare Anti-Fraud Measures Act of 2011 to plug two loopholes.

Executives from companies that are convicted of fraud can be excluded from Medicare under current law. However, if the executive has left the company by the time of conviction, he or she cannot be barred from federal health programs. These executives are able to move from one company to another and continue to defraud Medicare, older Americans, and taxpayers. The bill would give the federal government the authority to ban these executives from doing business with Medicare.

Companies that engage in fraud often set up shell companies to insulate themselves from liability. Criminal settlement negotiations can result in the dissolution of these shell organizations with no real penalty to the parent company. The bill gives the government the authority to exclude the parent companies from the Medicare program.

Congressman Stark said, "This legislation gives the Office of Inspector General the authority to go after crooked executives and corporations that continue to bilk Medicare."

The bill responds to the federal government's request for more authority. Says the OIG's Lewis Morris at a hearing chaired by Congressman Stark,

> We think that one of the challenges we need to address is having executives understand that they will be held personally accountable for schemes that are then hatched and pushed downstream. . . . There are challenges to building a criminal case against a high-level executive—there's a lot of plausible deniability built into these large companies—it's an area where we and our partners at the Department of Justice are focusing on, because we recognize that the way we are going to change corporate cultures is by focusing on individuals. . . . Fortune 500 companies (need to) understand that they will be treated the same way as anyone else who abuses our program.

AARP, the powerful lobby group, supports the measure and says it increases the long-term sustainability of the Medicare program by ensuring that funds go to services that people need.

FROM COMPANY FRAUD TO POLITICAL CAMPAIGNS

As the 2010 midterm congressional elections unfolded and led to Republicans gaining control of the House of Representatives, another story was playing out in Florida. Rick Scott, a former hospital CEO, campaigned for governor and won.

In 1997 Scott was CEO of Columbia/Hospital Corporation of America (HCA), a for-profit hospital chain that was the target of the largest multiagency investigation of a health care provider ever undertaken at the time by the US Justice Department.

Scott helped to found the Columbia Hospital Corporation in 1987, which merged with HCA in 1989 to become the largest for-profit hospital group in the country.

The company was accused of billing for lab tests that were not medically necessary, assigning false diagnoses to patient records to increase reimbursement, disguising marketing and advertising costs as community education and charging taxpayers for them, paying kickbacks to doctors to have them refer Medicare and Medicaid patients to its facilities, and billing for home health visits for patients that never took place.

In two federal settlements in 2000 and another in 2002, Columbia/HCA agreed to pay $1.7 billion in fines and also agreed to plead guilty to fourteen felonies in five states for bilking Medicare, Medicaid, and Tricare, the health insurance program for the military. The Justice Department said the Columbia/HCA settlement was, at that time, the largest government fraud case settled in US history.

Scott resigned in 1997 in the middle of the investigation but left with a platinum parachute worth $10 million in severance and $300 million in stock options. Later, he started another company, Solantic Corporation, which operates urgent care centers in Florida that provide treatment to people on a walk-in basis. They post their prices on menu boards like those in McDonald's.

Scott says he didn't know about the fraud that occurred in his company. On his campaign website, he said, "I've made mistakes in my life. And mistakes were certainly made at Columbia/HCA. I was the CEO of the company and as CEO I accept responsibility for what happened on my watch. I learned very hard lessons from what happened and those lessons have helped me become a better businessman and leader."

When Scott resurfaced and ran for governor of Florida, his campaign website heralded Columbia/HCA as one of the most admired companies in America when he was at the helm. It quotes *Time* magazine praising Columbia in 1997: "Scott's credo is a classic: quality care doesn't have to come at a premium price. But it's the way Scott is accomplishing that goal that is transforming how American hospitals do business. In an industry notorious for waste and inefficiency, Scott aggressively consolidates operations and imposes cost controls."

During the campaign, Scott's opponents used the Justice Department's prosecution of Columbia/HCA against him in attack ads. One of his opponents was Bill McCollum, who was a member of Congress during the investigation of Columbia/HCA. He sponsored the Health Care Claims Guidance Act, which tried to curb the government's authority to crack down on fraud, an unusual position for someone who later became Florida's state attorney general.

CORRALING WHITE-COAT CRIME

Federal officials and prosecutors concede that holding company executives accountable is not sufficient to stop illegal activity by drug and device companies. Morris, the OIG counsel, says, "What we need to do is make examples of a couple of doctors so that their colleagues see that this isn't worth it. Somehow physicians think they're different from the rest of us. But money works on them just like everybody else."

Many doctors run afoul of the law. Dr. Julie Taitsman, the chief doctor in the fraud office at the US Department of Health and Human Services, says that aggressive drug and device sales representatives offer inducements that are too lucrative for some doctors to pass up. A common come-on might be, "How would you like to earn more money without working harder?"

Dr. Taitsman described in the *New England Journal of Medicine* how a manufacturer for a prostate-cancer drug encouraged urologists to bill Medicare for the free samples they provided to patients. In return, the drug company reps offered the urologists extra free samples if the doctors bought more of the drug. Federal law prohibits doctors from billing for free samples and accepting money in return for prescribing a company's product. Several urologists paid tens of thousands of dollars in penalties for bilking government programs.

Another doctor paid a $107,000 penalty for charging Medicare beneficiaries an annual "concierge" fee to cover an annual physical exam, same-day or next-day appointments, around-the-clock physician availability, prescription facilitation, expedited and coordinated referrals, and other amenities. Physicians who participate in Medicare cannot charge for some of the services already covered by Medicare. The doctor was charged with double billing.

These cases are not the most egregious. More than five thousand physicians have been excluded from participation in the federal health care programs because they have accepted kickbacks, up-coded bills, or provided inappropriate and unnecessary surgery, among other violations of the law. Many physicians have served prison terms, paid hefty fines, or faced other civil, criminal, and administrative penalties.

In April 2010 the OIG surveyed all medical school deans and designated officials for institutions that sponsor residency and fellowship programs to determine whether their institutions provide education about fraud, waste, and abuse to ensure that future doctors know the rules and steer clear of fraud.

Medical school deans were more likely to respond to the survey and reported that their students receive some training. Forty-one percent of the academic teaching hospitals, where students and residents are trained in patient care, didn't complete the survey.

THE *WALL STREET JOURNAL* VS. THE AMA

Intrepid *Wall Street Journal* reporters, together with the nonprofit Center for Public Integrity, obtained limited access to a large government database with Medicare records that contain information about how much individual doctors and other providers bill Medicare.

The government imposed restrictions on how the reporters could use the information. For example, they were not given the names of the doctors and other providers. Despite the restrictions, *Journal* reporters uncovered a treasure trove. They cobbled together information from other sources to identify the doctors and other providers who had patterns of filing potentially inappropriate and costly Medicare claims. Among the cases they uncovered are the following:

A family-practice doctor in the New York City area who, government records suggest, pocketed more than $2 million in 2008 from Medicare for performing sophisticated tests that are unusual for a family practice doctor to perform. Twenty-five other doctors were identified across the country who performed many of the same sophisticated tests. Six of the doctors have been either linked to fraud, sued for improper billings, or disciplined by a state medical board for misconduct. The doctors, who were contacted by the reporters, denied wrongdoing or declined to answer questions.

In another case, an Oregon neurosurgeon who performed an enormously high volume of back surgeries showed up as an outlier in the Medicare database. He performed six back surgeries on one patient in two years and planned to perform another surgery. The patient declined and said that none of the other operations helped him. After an article appeared in the *Wall Street Journal*, the hospital where the doctor performed the surgeries fired him.

Information on how much individual doctors bill Medicare is kept secret. Thirty years ago, the AMA sued the government to keep it that way and won. The judge who issued the 1979 injunction that keeps the information secret ruled that physicians' privacy trumped the public's interest in knowing how tax dollars are spent. He relied on a privacy pro-vision in the Freedom of Information Act, or FOIA. The AMA defends the secrecy of the Medicare information. Cecil B. Wilson, the AMA president, said, "Physicians, like all Americans, have the right to privacy and due process, and should not suffer the consequences of having false or misleading conclusions drawn from complex Medicare data that has significant limitations."

In a welcome move in early 2011, Dow Jones & Company, publisher of the *Wall Street Journal*, filed a lawsuit to overturn the AMA-instigated 1979 court order.

The AMA has successfully defended the injunction from recent chal-lenges, including a case when the US Court of Appeals for the District of Columbia ruled in 2009 against a Washington, DC–based organization, the Center for the Study of Services, which publishes *Consumers' Check-book*, a publication that helps consumers make smart choices when buying services in the marketplace. The court ruled that physicians' privacy out-weighed the public interest in knowing how much doctors were receiving from Medicare.

The Dow Jones company thinks differently. "It's time to overturn an injunction that, for decades, has allowed some doctors to defraud Medicare free from public scrutiny," says Mark Jackson, general counsel for Dow Jones.

Pressure to open the information is coming from all sides. In a jointly authored opinion editorial published in the *Washington Post*, Michael O. Leavitt, former secretary of the US Department of Health and Human Services under President George W. Bush, and Robert Krughoff, president of the Center for the Study of Services, asked Congress to make Medicare information available to the public. "The focus should [be] . . . how our society can get the most value for the dollars it spends on health care," Leavitt and Krughoff wrote.

As with all trade associations, the AMA protects its members rather than the public's interest. By protecting the bad apples in an era of trans-parency when every dollar counts, the AMA is out of step.

The pressure to open up Medicare information increased with the Medicare Data Access for Transparency and Accountability Act, or DATA Act, which was introduced by Senators Ron Wyden, a Democrat from Oregon, and Charles Grassley, a Republican from Iowa, in the spring of 2011. The legislation would require the US Department of Health and Human Services to make information available at no cost about how much individual doctors bill Medicare. Patient identities would remain confidential.

In Senate floor remarks, Senator Grassley said the act might deter some wasteful practices and overbilling. Senator Wyden took the stance that "hiding" the data was "indefensible in a free society."

IT'S NOT JUST THE FRAUD THAT HURTS

One of the doctors who may have appeared as an outlier in the Medicare data is a Maryland cardiologist, Dr. Mark Midei. A US Senate Committee on Finance investigation delved into the relationship between cardiac stent maker Abbott Labs and Dr. Midei, who allegedly implanted cardiac stents in five hundred eighty-five people who didn't need them at St. Joseph Medical Center in Towson, Maryland.

A hospital committee that reviewed the case found that, "Dr. Midei's practice of placing stents in patients where not clinically indicated has resulted in the substantial likelihood of harm to his patients." The hospital sent letters to all five hundred eighty-five patients to tell them they may have had an unnecessary procedure. It entered into a $22 million settlement with the US Justice Department for billing federal programs unnecessarily. The hospital did not admit liability.

The state medical board opened an investigation into Midei's use of cardiac stents. The board identified patients who reportedly had stents implanted but didn't have heart disease that warranted the procedures. The medical board revoked the doctor's license for falsifying patient records to justify unnecessary and expensive cardiac stent procedures that exposed his patients to the risk of harm.

A stent is placed during a cardiac catheterization when a thin plastic tube called a catheter is inserted into an artery, usually in the groin, and guided up a blood vessel to the arteries that surround the heart. A stent, or tiny mesh tube, is placed in the artery to prop it open. The risks of the procedure include heart attack, stroke, blood clots, and penetration of the artery wall.

Abbott officials lauded the sales of its stents. In emails subpoenaed by the Senate Committee, Abbott congratulated one of its sales representatives for cultivating extraordinary personal relationships with Midei and other cardiologists:

> As you prepare to complete another year in the top five in rankings, I want to again congratulate you on this remarkable feat. Moreover, the relationships you have formed at accounts like St. Joe's, Union, and Hopkins are hallmarks of what every rep strives for in their accounts. In my fifteen years of being in this business, I have never seen personal relationships as strong as the ones you have developed with Dr. Mark Midei. . . . Outstanding job. . . . I recommend you take some time over the holidays to reflect on your accomplishments.

An email from Abbott to Midei hailed him as a hero for being one of its top users. "I heard thru the grapevine that you had a truly outstanding day . . . in the labs on Friday, possibly setting the single day implant record." Midei reportedly implanted thirty stents that day.

Two days after Midei achieved this milestone, Abbott paid $2,000 for a pig roast in the doctor's backyard as a token of appreciation.

Midei lost his privileges to practice at St. Joseph because of the allegations. Abbott helped its loyal customer by arranging a consulting gig in Saudi Arabia. Company emails obtained by the Committee on Finance revealed that the company believed, "It's the right thing to do because he helped us so many times over the years." Midei sued the hospital for informing patients that they probably had unnecessary stents implanted.

Abbott expressed no concern about the people who were exposed to unnecessary risks from the inappropriate use of its product. Yet the company was miffed about the bad publicity it received in articles about the scandal in the *Baltimore Sun*. The vice president of global marketing for Abbott Vascular wrote an email about *Baltimore Sun* reporter Jay Hancock, to a company vice president: "Don't you have connections in Baltimore????? Someone needs to take this writer outside and kick his ass! Do I need to send the Philly mob?"

The company was right to be worried about the bad publicity. A company email revealed that the volume of stent procedures declined in the entire Baltimore region after the allegations against Dr. Midei became public.

The overuse of cardiac stents is rampant around the country. Few doctors are prosecuted. One exception is a Lafayette, Louisiana, cardiologist who was convicted for implanting unnecessary cardiac stents and performing other unnecessary procedures. In Salisbury, Maryland, a cardiologist was indicted by a grand jury for performing more than two hundred unnecessary cardiac stent procedures and later convicted.

Cardiac stents are just one of many devices and drugs that are pushed into the health care cockpit. Unsuspecting patients have no clue that their well-being does not appear on the radar of powerful corporate interests.

Here's what an Abbott official wrote to the Baltimore-area sales rep: "We will have to work as hard in maintaining and looking for growth as we ever did. . . . The expectations will not decline but only grow. But you are the person for the job. I am proud to have you on my team."

After the dust settles from the Midei case, Abbott and other companies will continue to push their products into the health care cockpit whether or not people need them.

THE SUNSHINE LAW

The health care reform law includes a provision that will shine a light on any gifts or payments that drug companies and device makers give to doctors and teaching hospitals. If they receive more than one hundred dollars from a company in any one year, all payments and gifts must be reported.

The information will be published on a searchable public website beginning in September 2013. It will include the name, address, and specialty of the doctor who receives the money, the date the money was received, the reason the payment was made, and the product related to the payment.

Companies are already trying to persuade the public that their payments will bring innovation and better care to people. Here is a preview of how the companies will make the payments appear as if they benefit society.

When device maker Medtronic was found to have paid bribes to doctors in return for using the company's devices and was required to publicly name the doctors, Bill Hawkins, the chairman and chief executive, said, "Through greater transparency about the nature of these relationships, we will help people better understand how important they are to developing life-saving and enhancing products for patients who need them."

You don't need to wait to find out if your doctor is receiving any of the billions of dollars that companies pay doctors. You can find out now by searching the website Dollars for Docs created by ProPublica, a remarkably effective public-interest journalism project based in New York City. It compiles existing information on companies' websites.

We predict that the sunshine provisions will have unintended consequences. Payments to doctors will become normalized and more deeply embedded in the culture of medicine. More doctors will be tempted to follow the herd and allow themselves to be used as salespersons for companies' products. When they do, they put their interests and the companies' interests ahead of their patients' interests.

Just as public reporting of political campaign contributions does not stop special interests from buying elected officials in return for special favors, public reporting of the financial ties between doctors and the companies will not stop doctors from being bought. Nothing short of a ban on payments of any kind to doctors will stop the corruption of medicine and its threat to the public's health.

• 15 •

Ten Steps to More Affordable Health Care

$\mathcal{I}$t is possible to have affordable health care without slashing essential benefits or driving the country into bankruptcy. The solution is to reduce the health care industry's culture of dependency on the blind generosity of the public. Taking the blinders off, here are ten steps that Washington policy makers can take to help make health care affordable. They will not be politically popular with the health care industry. Nonetheless, we make these recommendations so the public can see how health care *can* be affordable.

1. DON'T TURN OFF THE CIRCUIT BREAKER

The Independent Payment Advisory Board is the only meaningful part of health care reform to directly rein in Medicare spending. Like a circuit breaker, it triggers cuts if spending increases too much. If you think that Congress is capable of reining in the health care industry, ignore this recommendation and let the board be scuttled. If you think past performance by Congress is a predictor of its future performance, then the board should be allowed to do its job.

2. DIVORCE THE AMA

The American Medical Association should no longer determine the relative value of primary care and specialist physician services. It has a

183

massive conflict of interest that serves its benefit, not the public's. The AMA overvalues costly high-tech medical procedures at the expense of keeping people healthy. This recommendation should be a condition imposed by Congress when it makes a necessary fix to the formula for how Medicare reimburses doctors. Primary care needs a primary place in the nation's health care system. The greatest threat to the health of older Americans is the lack of trained primary-care doctors and nurse practitioners who specialize in the care of an aging body. Since the Medicare program's responsibility is to the people it insures, this recommendation should be high on the to-do list in Washington.

3. EXPAND AMERICA'S MOST WANTED LIST

As we have shown, the amount of money wasted on health care fraud each year is enough to pay for health care for the thirty-two million people who are uninsured without spending a penny more. The health care reform law provided a needed boost to antifraud measures with an extra $35 million a year. That's not enough. About 10 percent of all health care spending, about $250 billion, is lost to fraud annually. A much larger investment is needed to plug the leakage. Also, a legal loophole allows executives of companies convicted of health care fraud to find work at other firms that receive funding from the federal government. This loophole needs to be closed. The law should ban their employment in any company that does business with the government. Holding individuals accountable is a powerful deterrent to curb corporate health care fraud.

4. PRIVATIZE THE GAINS, PRIVATIZE THE LOSSES

During the near collapse of the banking industry, the public came to understand how banks privatize financial gains but socialize, or spread, their losses. Taxpayers were called upon to bail out the banks and pay for their mistakes. In health care, medical mistakes, hospital-acquired infections, medical device defects, and marketing of unapproved drugs are examples of how the health care industry spreads the cost of its failures among patients, health insurance policyholders, and taxpayers. Public-policy makers have taken initial steps to privatize the losses—that is, to have the industry own its losses and pay for them. This is good public policy. It instills market discipline that has been absent in the health care sector. It should continue.

5. OPEN UP MEDICARE DATA AND PUBLICLY REPORT HIGH-VOLUME PROVIDERS

The federal government should make Medicare data on doctors and other health care providers available to the public. Transparency will give investigative reporters the information they need to shine a light on fraud and inappropriate use of health care services. It will accelerate the government's effort to curb fraud and abuse, which the government cannot do alone.

6. ESTABLISH A HARVARD SCHOOL OF REGULATION

The United States lacks a robust and sophisticated regulatory infrastructure to curb the unfettered market in health care and many other sectors of the economy. In health care, with 10 percent of deaths in the United States occurring because of preventable medical harm, the need for a regulatory apparatus similar to aviation and highway safety is urgent. The reservoir of talent for regulation of a complex market is scarce. Business schools train future corporate executives, but no specialized entity trains people to regulate the marketplace. A Harvard School of Regulation or similar high-profile entity is needed that draws on the best talent inside and outside of the health care sector. Its first task should be to develop a regulatory strategy to hold health care providers accountable for safer patient care.

7. START A HEALTH CARE CORPS OF ENGINEERS AND RECYCLE THE WASTE

The health care reform law includes incentives to hospitals and other health care providers to become more efficient. They can become efficient only if they know *how* to do so. Foundations and other philanthropic organizations should provide funding to interprofessional teams of engineers, doctors, nurses, pharmacists, and health care administrators in leading universities who are prepared to train the next generation of health care professionals in state-of-the-art management science. The aim is to develop a cadre of experts with clinical and engineering knowledge and skills to reduce monumental inefficiencies that plague day-to-day operations of hospitals and other health care facilities. Billions of dollars could be saved by applying tools of management science that are used routinely in other industries but rarely in health care. Even better, health care will be a lot safer.

8. FOLLOW THE MONEY: PUBLICLY REPORT INSURANCE COMPANY CONTRACTS WITH HOSPITALS

In the health care reform law, there is no authority granted to the federal government or states to curb the growth of private health insurance premiums. To find out where all that money is going, every state should examine the contracts between private insurers and hospitals for price variations that are explained by excessive market clout rather than differences in the quality of care provided. The information should be publicly reported similar to how the Massachusetts attorney general's office publicly reported its analysis of contracts between insurers and hospitals in the state. Transparency alone will not make health care affordable, but at least the public and employers will be able to follow the money. Foundations and other philanthropic organizations could fund this work.

9. START A *CONSUMER REPORTS* FOR MEDICAL DEVICES

Millions of Americans have medical devices such as stents, defibrillators, and joint replacements in their bodies. The public should have access to information from the Food and Drug Administration (FDA) about defects and recalls of these products. The public should be informed if devices have been recalled, if safety alerts have been issued, or if they are associated with high rates of infection. An independent *Consumer Reports*–type publication for common medical devices should be available to the public to hold manufacturers and the FDA accountable for the safety of these devices.

10. NEGOTIATE PRICES

The time is long past due for the federal government to have the authority to be a prudent buyer of drugs similar to how governments in other countries purchase drugs. Here is why it is desperately needed. While we were writing this book, a colleague who works in an influential position in health care sent an email about a company's profiteering. Women at risk of giving birth prematurely are given a drug that has been proven to prevent preterm births. It costs about three hundred dollars for treatment throughout a woman's pregnancy. About 139,000 women receive it every year, and it is safe. The manufacturer tweaked the drug and added a preservative. The change required no research or development. In early 2011, after the FDA approved it for sale, the manufacturer increased the price to $29,000 per pregnancy. The total annual cost will jump from $41 million to $4 billion without any material improvement. Pressure from doctors and nurse-midwives forced the company to reduce the price, but it remains much higher than the original low price. Uncontrolled profiteering requires negotiated prices based on drug prices paid in other Western countries.

To address drug company concerns that lower, negotiated prices will reduce their ability to develop the next generation of drugs, an explicit subsidy from the federal government should be made to the companies. This approach will allow elected officials to place a dollar value on the research-and-development activities of the drug industry, rather than have the costs buried in the price of drugs. The public can determine if it is getting its money's worth.

Looking ahead, the future of health care in America depends on policy makers making care affordable. We hope this book informs and whets the appetite for more ways to do that. The stakes are higher than they have ever been. We hope the country can do it right—and do it soon—for the sake of the health and well-being of Americans and the nation's future.

Notes

CHAPTER 1

9 "With 116,000 pages of documents . . ." House Committee on Energy and Commerce, Subcommittee on Oversight and Investigations, "Memorandum on Supplemental Information Regarding the Individual Health Insurance Market," June 16, 2009, 9–10, http://democrats.energycommerce.house .gov/Press_111/20090616/rescission_supplemental.pdf, accessed December 28, 2010.

10 "Seventy-five percent of people . . ." Drew Armstrong and Alex Nussbaum, "WellPoint, UnitedHealth Stock Buyback Focus Concerns Investors," *Bloomberg*, October 12, 2010, http://www.bloomberg.com/news/2010-10-12/ wellpoint-unitedhealth-stock-buyback-focus-concerns-investors.html, accessed March 25, 2011.

10 "I don't think we ought . . ." Howard Dean, interview on MSNBC, August 17, 2009, http://www.msnbc.msn.com/id/32446157/ns/politics-white _house/, accessed December 27, 2010.

11 "Or you can try . . ." Howard Dean, "Public Option is Key to Healthcare Reform," July 23, 2009, http://www.youtube.com/watch?v=8SKfW2dUnow, accessed March 25, 2011.

11 "John Boehner . . ." Glen Thrush, "Boehner Hasn't Met 'Anyone' Who Backs Public Option," *Politico*, October 1, 2009, http://www.politico.com/ blogs/glennthrush/1009/Boehner_searching_for_first_public_option_backer .html?showall, accessed April 19, 2011.

11 "The insurance industry orchestrated . . ." Vanessa Fuhrmans and Avery Johnson, "Insurers' Employees Counter Criticism," *Wall Street Journal,* August 24,

2009, http://online.wsj.com/article/SB125107323271252625.html, accessed May 23, 2011.

11 "At the same time, Karen Ignagni . . ." Karen Ignagni, letter to the editor, *Washington Post*, October 20, 2009, http://www.washingtonpost.com/wp -dyn/content/article/2009/10/19/AR2009101902936.html, accessed January 17, 2011.

11 "Instead, it included a requirement . . ." "The President's Proposal," February 22, 010, http://www.whitehouse.gov/sites/default/files/summary-presidents -proposal.pdf, accessed March 25, 2011.

12 "There are a number of Republicans . . ." White House Health Care Summit, February 25, 2010, http://www.c-span.org/Events/White-House -Health-Care-Summit-with-Congressional-Leaders/16350-2/, accessed March 10, 2011.

12 "After the November 2008 election . . ." America's Health Insurance Plans, "Now Is the Time for Health Care Reform: A Proposal to Achieve Universal Coverage, Affordability, Quality Improvement and Market Reform," December 2008, http://www.americanhealthsolution.org/assets/Uploads/health carereformproposal.pdf, accessed December 7, 2010.

12 "Achieving this objective . . ." Ibid., 6.

14 "For me, it is hard to distinguish . . ." Keith Martin, "Virginia First State in Nation to Pass Anti-Mandate Health Reform Bill," *Insurance and Financial Advisor*, March 12, 2010, http://ifawebnews.com/2010/03/11/virginia-first-state -in-nation-to-pass-anti-mandate-health-reform-bill/, accessed March 25, 2011.

15 "The health care market . . ." US District Court, Eastern District of Michigan, Southern Division, *Thomas More Law Center vs. Barack Hussein Obama*, October 7, 2010, 16–17, http://www.mied.uscourts.gov/News/Docs/09714485866.pdf, accessed March 25, 2011.

15 "I hold that there is a rational basis . . ." US District Court, Western District of Virginia, *Liberty University vs. Timothy Geithner*, November 30, 2010, 27, http://www.vawd.uscourts.gov/opinions/moon/libertyuniversityvgeithner.pdf, accessed March 25, 2011.

16 "Neither the Supreme Court . . ." US District Court, Eastern District of Virginia, *Commonwealth of Virginia vs. Kathleen Sebelius*, December 13, 2010, 24, 37, http://www.scribd.com/doc/45232409/Mandatory-Health-Insurance -Unconstitutional-U-S-District-Court-Case-Commonwealth-v-Sebelius-Final -Judgment, accessed March 25, 2011.

16 "A lot of people . . ." Melissa Nelson, "20 States Ask Judge to Throw Out Obama Health Law," *Orlando Sentinel*, December 16, 2010, http://articles .orlandosentinel.com/2010-12-16/news/os-health-care-overhaul-suit-pensa col20101216_1_health-insurance-health-care-vinson, accessed March 25, 2011.

16 "In his ruling, Vinson . . ." US District Court, Northern District of Florida, *State of Florida et al. vs. U.S. Department of Health and Human Services,* January 31, 2011, http://bloximages.chicago2.vip.townnews.com/heraldextra.com/content/ tncms/assets/editorial/2/02/198/202198a2-2e2d-11e0-bf9b-001cc4c002e0 -revisions/4d484a3d49c4a.pdf.pdf, accessed March 25, 2011.

18 "There will be zero tolerance . . ." Letter from Kathleen Sebelius to Karen Ignagni, September 9, 2010, http://www.hhs.gov/news/press/2010pres/09/20100909a .html, accessed December 5, 2010.

18 "The Obama administration came out . . ." Nancy-Ann DeParle, "Health Insurance Premium Hike Rejected," December 6, 2010, http://www.white house.gov/blog/2010/12/06/health-insurance-premium-hike-rejected, ac- cessed December 6, 2010.

18 "Less than a year after . . ." "Carmen Balber on the Need for States to Rein in Excessive Rate Hikes," *ABC Nightly News,* January 7, 2011, http://www .consumerwatchdog.org/video/abc-nightly-news-carmen-balber-need-states -rein-excessive-rate-hikes#, accessed January 16, 2011.

18 "The federal government has been helping . . ." US Department of Health and Human Services, "New Affordable Care Act Rules Shed Light on High Health Insurance Rate Hikes," December 21, 2010, http://www.hhs.gov/ news/press/2010pres/12/20101221a.html, accessed December 29, 2010.

18 "Nonetheless, when Secretary Sebelius . . ." "Carmen Balber on the Need for States to Rein in Excessive Rate Hikes," *ABC Nightly News,* January 7, 2011, http://www.consumerwatchdog.org/video/abc-nightly-news-carmen -balber-need-states-rein-excessive-rate-hikes#, accessed January 16, 2011.

19 "We're clearly understanding the risks . . ." Sarah Kliff, "Investors See Health Reform's Potential," *Politico,* January 13, 2011, http://www.politico.com/ news/stories/0111/47534.html#ixzz1AvZODREB, accessed January 13, 2011.

CHAPTER 2

21 "We'll allow the safe reimportation . . ." See "Healthcare Flashbacks," *Huff- ington Post,* http://www.huffingtonpost.com/2009/08/09/flashback-obama -promises_n_254833.html, accessed December 28, 2010.

21 "You know I don't want to learn . . ." See http://www.youtube.com/watch ?v=NCRO0g9CfAw&feature=player_embedded, accessed December 27, 2010.

22 "A portion of the money . . ." Timothy Burger, "Obama Campaign Ad Firms Signed On to Push Health-Care Overhaul," *Bloomberg,* August 15, 2009, http://www.bloomberg.com/apps/news?pid=newsarchive&sid=aV3dLt 6wmZH4, accessed December 27, 2010.

22 "The AKPD website . . ." AKPD Media, http://akpdmedia.com, accessed April 18, 2011.

22 "Axelrod sold his interest . . ." Burger, "Obama Campaign Ad Firms Signed On."

22 "This plan . . . to better insure . . ." Billy Tauzin, interview on CNBC, March 4, 2009, http://www.theatlantic.com/business/archive/2009/03/big -pharmas-top-lobbyist-said-what/1284/, accessed December 18, 2010.

23 "If you come in first . . ." David Kirkpatrick and Duff Wilson, "Tauzin Resigns from PhRMA," *New York Times*, February 11, 2010. Accessed February 7, 2011. http://www.nytimes.com/2010/02/12/health/policy/12pharma.html.

23 "A terse email . . ." David Kirkpatrick, "White House Affirms Deal on Drug Cost," *New York Times*, August 5, 2009, http://www.nytimes.com/2009/08/06/ health/policy/06insure.html, accessed March 25, 2011.

23 "U.S. consumers are charged . . ." Jeffrey Young, "FDA Opposes Senate Drug Importation Amendment Offered to Healthcare Bill," *The Hill*, December 8, 2009, http://thehill.com/homenews/senate/71307-fda-opposes-senate -drug-importation-amendmen, accessed April 18, 2011.

23 "The average prices for patented drugs . . ." Congressional Budget Office, "Would Prescription Drug Importation Reduce U.S. Drug Spending?" April 29, 2004, http://www.cbo.gov/doc.cfm?index=5406&type=0, accessed January 4, 2011.

23 "I expected this." Young, "FDA Opposes Senate Drug Importation Amendment."

24 "Also, through both Pfizer . . ." Pfizer Corporation, "Notice of Annual Meeting and Proxy Statement," 49–50, http://www.sec.gov/Archives/edgar/ data/78003/000119312510046029/dpre14a.htm#tx64512_13, accessed December 20, 2010.

24 "According to the consumer watchdog group . . ." Public Citizen, "Rapidly Increasing Criminal and Civil Monetary Penalties Against the Pharmaceutical Industry: 1991 to 2010," December 16, 2010, http://www.citizen .org/documents/rapidlyincreasingcriminalandcivilpenalties.pdf, accessed December 18, 2010.

24 "The company also agreed to pay . . ." Federal Bureau of Investigation, Press Release, "Court Imposes Record Fine and Forfeiture of $1.3 billion for Pharmacia & Upjohn Company's Fraudulent Marketing of Bextra," October 16, 2009, http://www.fbi.gov/boston/press-releases/2009/bs101609.htm, accessed July 1, 2011. See also http://www.stopmedicarefraud.gov/pfizerfact sheet.html, accessed July 20, 2011.

24 "The size and seriousness . . ." US Department of Justice, Press Release, "Justice Department Announces Largest Health Care Fraud Settlement in

Its History," September 2, 2009, http://www.justice.gov/opa/pr/2009/September/09-civ-900.html, accessed March 25, 2011.

24 "Federal prosecutors had especially harsh words . . ." US Department of Justice, Press Release, "Warner-Lambert to Pay $430 Million to Resolve Criminal & Civil Health Care Liability Relating to Off-Label Promotion," May 13, 2004, http://www.justice.gov/opa/pr/2004/May/04_civ_322.htm, accessed January 9, 2011.

25 "Today's enormous fine . . ." US Department of Justice, "Justice Department Announces Largest Health Care Fraud Settlement."

27 "Eli Lilly writes on its blog . . ." Amy O'Connor, "IPAB in Spotlight After Elections," *Lillypad Blog*, November 4, 2010, http://lillypad.lilly.com/public-policy/ipab-in-spotlight-after-elections, accessed December 27, 2010.

27 "The promotion of drugs for unapproved uses . . ." US Department of Justice, "Eli Lilly and Company Agrees to Pay $1.415 Billion to Resolve Allegations of Off-label Promotion of Zyprexa: $515 Million Criminal Fine Is Largest Individual Corporate Criminal Fine in History; Civil Settlement up to $800 Million," January 15, 2009, http://www.justice.gov/opa/pr/2009/January/09-civ-038.html, accessed July 21, 2011.

27 "I personally challenge each of you . . ." US District Court, Eastern District of Pennsylvania, *United States of America vs. Eli Lilly*, January 15, 2009, 12, http://www.justice.gov/usao/pae/News/2009/jan/lillygovtmementrypleasent.pdf, accessed July 21, 2011.

28 "If we succeed, Zyprexa will be . . ." Ibid.

CHAPTER 3

29 "Vice President Joe Biden . . ." Jesse Lee, "The Consensus Grows: Hospitals for Health Reform," *The White House Blog*, July 8, 2009, http://www.whitehouse.gov/blog/The-Consensus-Grows-Hospitals-for-Health-Reform/, accessed March 26, 2011.

30 "That's been going on now . . ." Richard Umbdenstock, interview on National Public Radio, June 9, 2009, http://www.npr.org/templates/story/story.php?storyId=105490018, accessed January 12, 2011.

30 "They say it 'threatens the long-time . . .'" American Hospital Association, "AHA Voices Support for IPAB Repeal Bill," October 26, 2010, http://www.ahanews.com/ahanews/2010/101026-ms-ipab.html, accessed March 26, 2011.

30 "They said that no one provider group . . ." "Strengthening the Independent Medicare Advisory Board: Amendment Proposed by Senators Rockefeller, Lieberman, and Whitehouse to the Patient Protection and Affordable

Care Act (H.R. 3590)," http://rockefeller.senate.gov/press/FINALRocke
feller-Lieberman-WhitehouseIMABAmendmentSummary121509.doc, accessed January 4, 2011.

30 "It is time to take the special interests . . ." Jay Rockefeller, "Floor Statement
on IMAB Amendment to the Patient Protection and Affordable Care Act as
Prepared for Delivery," December 17, 2009, http://rockefeller.senate.gov/
press/record.cfm?id=321047, accessed January 4, 2011.

31 "He said, 'We support health reform . . .' Leigh Page, "10 Trends for Hospitals in 2011 from Chip Kahn of the Federation of American Hospitals,"
Becker's Hospital Review, November 18, 2010, http://www.beckershospital
review.com/hospital-financial-and-business-news/10-trends-for-hospitals-in
-2011-from-chip-kahn-of-the-federation-of-american-hospitals.html#, accessed March 28, 2011.

31 "Its president, J. James Rohack . . ." Jennifer Lubell, "AMA Backs Healthcare Reform Bill," *ModernHealthcare.com*, March 19, 2010, http://www
.modernhealthcare.com/article/20100319/NEWS/303199956, accessed January 10, 2011.

31 "It's a pretty big bullfrog . . ." Robert Lowes, "AMA Supports Latest Healthcare Reform Legislation with Reservations," *Medscape*, March 19, 2010, http://
www.medscape.com/viewarticle/718909, accessed March 28, 2011.

32 "It was disappointed that the reform measure . . ." American College of
Surgeons, letter to Nancy Pelosi, March 19, 2010, http://www.facs.org/hcr/
acsopposes3590.pdf, accessed July 21, 2011.

33 "And so he's a corporate Democrat . . ." Glenn Greenwald, "Bill Moyers on
the Health Care Debate, Democrats, and Afghanistan," *Salon*, August 29, 2009,
http://www.salon.com/news/opinion/glenn_greenwald/2009/08/29/moyers,
accessed December 4, 2010.

33 "In the 2008 presidential race . . ." Center for Responsive Politics,
"Top Industries, Barack Obama," http://www.opensecrets.org/pres08/indus
.php?cycle=2008&cid=n00009638, accessed March 28, 2011.

33 "In a more measured way, former senator Tom Daschle . . ." Thomas Daschle
and David Nather, *Getting It Done* (New York: Thomas Dunne, 2010), 157.

34 "About 30 percent of the $2.5 trillion . . ." Pierre Yong, LeighAnne Ol-
sen, Roundtable on Evidence-Based Medicine, Institute of Medicine, "The
Healthcare Imperative: Lowering Costs and Improving Outcomes," February
24, 2011, http://www.nap.edu/catalog.php?record_id=12750, accessed July
20, 2011.

34 "It has been said . . ." Dr. Paul Batalden is credited with this statement.

35 "President Ronald Reagan said . . ." Ronald Reagan, "Inaugural Address, January 20, 1981," http://www.reagan.utexas.edu/archives/speeches/1981/12081a.htm, accessed March 28, 2011.

35 "When the health care overhaul was passed . . ." Joanne Lublin, "The Year's Top 10 Highest Paid CEOs," *Wall Street Journal*, November 14, 2010, http://online.wsj.com/article/SB10001424052748704393604575614852198144276.html, accessed December 6, 2010.

36 "In 2010, the year that the reform was signed . . ." "The Wall Street Journal Survey of CEO Compensation," November 14, 2010, http://graphicsweb.wsj.com/php/CEOPAY10.html, accessed December 6, 2010.

36 "Among health insurers, the CEO . . ." Ibid.

36 "In 2010 the CEO of Community Health Systems . . ." Vince Galloro, "Subsidized Then Scrutinized: Reform Will Bring Billions of Dollars to the Industry, but It Could Also Deliver Added Examination of Executive Pay," *Modern Healthcare*, August 16, 2010, http://www.modernhealthcare.com/article/20100816/MAGAZINE/100819944/1138&template=mobile, accessed January 4, 2011.

36 "The CEO of University Health Systems . . ." Jim Bispo, "UHS CEO Made $9,139,727 in 2009," *Beaufort Observer*, November 21, 2010, http://www.beaufortobserver.net/Articles-c-2010-11-22-248906.112112-UHS-CEO-made-9139727-in-2009.html, accessed March 28, 2011.

37 "In the councils of government . . ." Dwight Eisenhower, "Farewell Address, January 17, 1961," http://www.americanrhetoric.com/speeches/dwightdeisenhowerfarewell.html, accessed March 28, 2011.

38 "We want democracy to survive . . ." Ibid.

39 "We have many uninsured Oklahomans . . ." Dan Boren, "Why I Voted to Repeal Health Reform," *Politico*, March 16, 2011, http://www.politico.com/news/stories/0311/51343.html, accessed March 16, 2011.

39 "It's more like a starter home . . ." Tom Harkin, "In Iowa's Interest: Health Reform Law Turns One," March 17, 2011, http://harkin.senate.gov/press/column.cfm?i=332021, accessed March 18, 2011.

39 "Consider the story of an older gentleman . . ." Author conversation with Kate O'Malley, resident fellow, Institute of Medicine, January 16, 2011.

CHAPTER 4

44 "According to the Tax Foundation . . ." Patrick Fleenor and Gerald Prante, "Health Care Reform: How Much Does It Redistribute Income?" Tax

Foundation, April 15, 2010, http://www.taxfoundation.org/publications/show/26200.html, accessed December 6, 2010.

45 "The Congressional Budget Office . . ." Letter from Douglas Elmendorf to Congressman Paul Ryan, November 4, 2010, http://www.cbo.gov/ftpdocs/116xx/doc11674/11-04-Drug_Pricing.pdf, accessed March 28, 2011.

46 "Even with slower growth in payments . . ." Congressional Budget Office, "Medicare Fact Sheet," http://www.cbo.gov/budget/factsheets/2009b/medicare.pdf, accessed January 4, 2011.

47 "An independent commission that advises Congress . . ." Letter from Glenn Hackbarth to Dr. Donald Berwick, January 6, 2011, http://www.medpac.gov/documents/01062011_MA_COMMENT.pdf, accessed January 11, 2011.

47 "The extra bonuses reduce . . ." Brian Biles and Grace Arnold of George Washington University analyzed the data and estimate much higher figures. See Steve Pizer, "Obama's Quiet $49 Billion Gift to America's Health Insurance Plans," *The Incidental Economist*, http://theincidentaleconomist.com/wordpress/obama-ahip-gift/, accessed March 28, 2011.

47 "An equity analyst . . ." Fran Matso Lysiak, "Medicare Advantage Plans Could Soften Payment Cuts with Rating Program," *InsuranceNewsNet.com*, December 20, 2010, http://insurancenewsnet.com/article.aspx?id=240707&type=lawregulation, accessed December 29, 2010.

47 "While it is impossible to predict . . ." Henry J. Kaiser Family Foundation, "Health Reform Subsidy Calculator," http://healthreform.kff.org/SubsidyCalculator.aspx, accessed March 25, 2011. The estimates are based on an analysis by the Congressional Budget Office of premium costs for 2016. See http://www.cbo.gov/ftpdocs/107xx/doc10781/11-30-Premiums.pdf. Actual premiums may vary depending on the health status and age of the people who enroll.

48 "Undocumented immigrants are not permitted . . ." Congressional Budget Office, "Payments of Penalties for Being Uninsured Under the Patient and Protection and Affordable Care Act," April 30, 2010, http://www.cbo.gov/ftpdocs/113xx/doc11379/Individual_Mandate_Penalties-04-30.pdf, accessed March 25, 2011.

49 "Health care spending in the year 2030 . . ." Peter Orszag and Ezekiel Emanuel, "Health Care Reform and Cost Control," *New England Journal of Medicine*, June 16, 2010, http://healthpolicyandreform.nejm.org/?p=3564, accessed October 27, 2010.

CHAPTER 5

54 "It says the AMA . . ." Government Accountability Office, "Medicare Physician Payments," report number GAO-09-647, July 2009, http://www.gao.gov/new.items/d09647.pdf, accessed November 15, 2010.

54 "We are letting 'the fox decide . . .'" Representative Jim McDermott, House Ways and Means Subcommittee on Health Hearing, March 18, 2011, http://careand cost.com/2011/03/18/rep-jim-mcdermott-questions-medpac-chair-glen-hack barth-about-the-rvs-update-committee-ruc/, accessed July 21, 2011.

54 "An opinion editorial . . ." Richard Hannon, "How Medicare Killed the Family Doctor," *Wall Street Journal*, November 8, 2010, http://online.wsj.com/article/SB 10001424052748704353504575596140752021042.html#articleTabs%3Darticle, accessed January 17, 2011.

54 "The AMA touts its influence . . ." American Medical Association, "The RVS Update Committee," http://www.ama-assn.org/ama/pub/physician-resources/ solutions-managing-your-practice/coding-billing-insurance/medicare/the -resource-based-relative-value-scale/the-rvs-update-committee.page, accessed December 4, 2010.

55 "We were forced to complete . . ." Caroline Poplin, "The End of Internal Medicine as We Know It," *Health Affairs Blog*, January 14, 2011, http://health affairs.org/blog/2011/01/14/the-end-of-internal-medicine-as-we-know-it/, accessed January 18, 2011.

56 "For all the money spent on health care . . ." Central Intelligence Agency, *World Factbook*, https://www.cia.gov/library/publications/the-world-factbook/ rankorder/2102rank.html?countryName=Cuba&countryCode=cu&regionCode =ca&rank=53#cu, accessed January 29, 2011.

57 "It only creates more anxiety . . ." Author conversation with Dr. George Randt, May 4, 2010.

58 "The AMA ranks fourteenth . . ." Center for Responsive Politics, "Heavy Hitters," http://www.opensecrets.org/orgs/list.php, accessed May 13, 2011.

58 "Campaign finance records show . . ." Center for Responsive Politics. "OpenSecrets.org Adds Dozen New 'Heavy Hitters' to Popular Database," August 2, 2010, http://www.opensecrets.org/news/2010/08/opensecretsorg -adds-dozen-new-heavy.html, accessed May 14, 2011.

59 "We have a system that is characterized . . ." National Summit on Health Care, February 25, 2010, transcript, http://www.cnnstudentnews.cnn.com/ TRANSCRIPTS/1002/25/se.06.html, accessed November 24, 2010.

60 "There are more than twice as many registered lobbyists . . ." Karen Tumulty and Michael Scherer, "How Drug-Industry Lobbyists Won on Health-Care," *Time*, October 22, 2009, http://www.time.com/time/politics/ article/0,8599,1931595,00.html#ixzz1I5HxL7Zw, accessed March 30, 2010.

60 "The health care reform overhaul . . ." Centers for Medicare and Medicaid Services, "CMS Introduces New Center for Medicare and Medicaid Innova- tion, Initiatives to Better Coordinate Health Care," press release, November 16, 2010, http://innovations.cms.gov/news/media-center/cms-introduces-new -center-for-medicare-and-medicaid-innovation/, accessed May 15, 2011.

61 "In fiscal year 2008 . . ." Elissa Fuchs, "Overview: Medicare Direct Graduate and Indirect Medical Education Payments," Association of American
Medical Colleges, https://www.aamc.org/newsroom/reporter/feb09/87798/
feb09_payments.html, accessed March 29, 2011.

CHAPTER 6

63 "This is more than the populations . . ." US Census Bureau, "Quick Facts,"
http://quickfacts.census.gov/qfd/index.html, accessed April 18, 2011.

63 "The hospitals' governing board . . ." Letter from Steven Chickering to Dennis
Knox, CEO/Managing Director, Southwest Healthcare System, April 15, 2010,
http://bloximages.chicago2.vip.townnews.com/nctimes.com/content/tncms/
assets/editorial/f/f2/8d0/ff28d060-4913-11df-be2a-001cc4c03286.pdf.pdf, accessed March 31, 2011.

64 "Beginning in 2007 . . ." California Department of Public Health, "Key
Dates/Timeline for Southwest Healthcare System," http://www.cdph.ca.gov/
programs/LnC/Pages/SouthwestTimeline.aspx, accessed March 31, 2011.

64 "The company owes its success . . ." Universal Health Systems, "About
UHS," http://www.uhsinc.com/aboutuhs.php, accessed March 30, 2011.

65 "While two of the company's twenty-five hospitals . . ." Universal Health Services, Inc., "Report to the Securities and Exchange Commission," form 8-K, March 11, 2010, http://www.sec.gov/Archives/edgar/
data/352915/000119312510059584/d8k.htm, accessed March 31, 2011.

65 "A younger executive, the CEO's son . . ." Ibid.

65 "It estimates that in a single year . . ." Office of the Inspector General, "Adverse Events in Hospitals: National Incidence Among Medicare Beneficiaries,"
US Department of Health and Human Services, November 2010, 3, http://
oig.hhs.gov/oei/reports/oei-06-09-00090.pdf, accessed March 30, 2011. The
report states that 15,000 Medicare beneficiaries in October 2008 experienced an
adverse event in a hospital that contributed to their deaths. It further states that
44 percent of the adverse events were preventable, which is 6,600 deaths that
month. In a year, 79,200 people on Medicare die because of preventable harm.

66 "That is why we support . . ." American Hospital Association, "AHA Statement on the HHS' Office of the Inspector General's Report on Adverse
Events in Hospitals," November 16, 2010, http://www.aha.org/aha/press
-release/2010/101116-st-adverse-events.html, accessed November 17, 2010.

66 "'I know that our recalls . . .'" Peter Whoriskey, "Toyota Issues Public
Apology, Details Plan to Fix Pedals," *Washington Post*, February 2, 2010,

http://www.washingtonpost.com/wp-dyn/content/article/2010/02/01/AR2010020100275.html, accessed May 13, 2011.

66 "The company president . . ." Hiroko Tabuchi, "After Tough Year, Pay Cuts and Forfeited Bonuses for Top Toyota Executives," *New York Times*, June 24, 2010, http://www.nytimes.com/2010/06/25/business/global/25toyota.html, accessed January 22, 2011.

66 "We feel an obligation . . ." Ray LaHood, interview on *ABC News*, February 10, 2010, http://abcnews.go.com/GMA/video/transportation-secretary-ray-lahood-toyota-crisis-9794424, accessed January 22, 2011.

66 "The American public . . ." Linda Kohn, Janet Corrigan, and Molla Donaldson, eds., *To Err Is Human: Building a Safer Health System* (Washington, DC: National Academy Press, Institute of Medicine, 1999).

67 "Former secretary of defense . . ." Donald Rumsfeld, interview on *ABC News*, February 7, 2011, http://abcnews.go.com/WNT/video/abc-news-exclusive-donald-rumsfeld-opens-afghanistan-iraq-war-diane-sawyer-secretary-defense-bush-12861862, accessed March 30, 2011.

67 "While my wife and I . . ." Jane Watrel, "Dennis Quaid Brings His Medical Mistakes Battle to DC," *NBC Washington*, April 12, 2010, http://www.nbcwashington.com/news/health/Dennis-Quaid-Brings-His-Medical-Mistakes-Battle-to-DC-90705994.html, accessed March 30, 2011.

68 "Every data point . . ." Author conversation with Kim Sandstrom, fall 2008.

68 "Researchers at the National Cancer Institute . . ." Amy Berrington de González et al., "Projected Cancer Risks from Computed Tomographic Scans Performed in the United States in 2007," *Archives of Internal Medicine* 169 (2009): 2071–77, http://archinte.ama-assn.org/cgi/content/full/169/22/2071, accessed March 30, 2011.

68 "Unnecessary surgery causes . . ." Barbara Starfield, "Is US Health Really the Best in the World?" *Journal of the American Medical Association* 284 (2000): 483–485. Accessed March 30, 2011. http://jama.ama-assn.org/content/284/4/483.extract.

68 "This is equivalent to . . ." Kenneth D. Kochanek et al., "Deaths: Preliminary Data for 2009," *National Vital Statistics Reports* 59, no. 4 (March 16, 2011): 1–64, http://www.cdc.gov/nchs/data/nvsr/nvsr59/nvsr59_04.pdf, accessed March 30, 2011.

69 "The National Academy of Engineering . . ." National Academy of Engineering and the Institute of Medicine, *Building a Better Delivery System* (Washington, DC: National Academies Press, 2005).

70 "Across the country . . ." Kevin O'Reilly, "Wrong-Patient, Wrong-Site Procedures Persist Despite Safety Protocol," *American Medical News*, November

1, 2010, http://www.ama-assn.org/amednews/2010/11/01/prl21101.htm, accessed May 13, 2011.

71 "Rather than punishing hospitals . . ." Rich Umbdenstock, "Hospitals Take Steps to Improve," *USA Today*, November 18, 2010, http://www.usatoday .com/news/opinion/editorials/2010-11-19-editorial19_ST1_N.htm, accessed January 22, 2011.

72 "Life-threatening infections . . ." Rupak Datta et al., "Environmental Cleaning Intervention and Risk of Acquiring Multidrug-Resistant Organisms from Prior Room Occupants," *Archives of Internal Medicine* 171, no. 6 (2011): 491–94.

74 "The team was called . . ." Letter from the Air Transport Association nominating the Commercial Aviation Safety Team for the Robert J. Collier Trophy, January 31, 2009, http://www.cast-safety.org/pdf/cast_2008_collier_nomi nation_01-30-09.pdf, accessed April 1, 2011.

CHAPTER 7

77 "During the visit . . ." Lindsey Dunn, "10 Best Practices for Increasing Hospital Profitability," *Becker's Hospital Review*, June 17, 2009, http://www.beckers hospitalreview.com/news-analysis/10-best-practices-for-increasing-hospital -profitability.html, accessed January 1, 2011.

79 "Chief health and medical editor . . ." "Lap Band Surgery: Not Only for the Morbidly Obese?" *ABC Nightly News*, December 2, 2010, http://abcnews .go.com/WNT/video/lap-band-surgery-morbidly-obese-expand-requirements -weight-limit-fda-review-12299916, accessed January 23, 2011.

79 "A doctor in Arizona . . ." See http://azlapband.com/blog/you-could-win -a-lapband/, accessed January 3, 2011.

79 "Hurry and Book Now . . ." See http://www.mysurgeryoptions.com/, accessed July 22, 2011.

80 "The hospital said in a statement . . ." John Fauber, "Aurora Fires Milwaukee Heart Doctor," *Milwaukee Journal Sentinel*, January 13, 2011, http://www .jsonline.mobi/features/health/113541984.html?ua=blackberry&dc=smart&c=y, accessed January 16, 2011.

80 "I think behind the scenes . . ." Ibid.

81 "Dr. John Birkmeyer . . ." Peter Waldman and David Armstrong, "Highest-Paid U.S. Doctors Get Rich with Fusion Surgery Debunked by Studies," *Bloomberg*, December 29, 2010, http://www.bloomberg.com/news/2010-12 -30/highest-paid-u-s-doctors-get-rich-with-fusion-surgery-debunked-by -studies.html, accessed April 2, 2011.

81 "Two months after those termination letters . . ." US Department of Health and Human Services and US Department of Justice, "Health Care Fraud and Abuse Control Program Annual Report for Fiscal Year 2010," 33–34, http://oig.hhs.gov/publications/docs/hcfac/hcfacreport2010.pdf, accessed February 2, 2011.

83 "Clinicians and families . . ." Frederick Ryckman et al., "Cincinnati Children's Hospital Medical Center: Redesigning Perioperative Flow Using Operations Management Tools to Improve Access and Safety," in *Managing Patient Flow in Hospitals: Strategies and Solutions*, ed. Eugene Litvak, 97–112 (Oakbrook Terrace, IL: Joint Commission Resources, 2010).

84 "If all hospitals . . ." Eugene Litvak et al., "Managing Variability in Healthcare Delivery," in *The Health Care Imperative: Lowering Costs and Improving Outcomes*, eds. Pierre L. Yong, Robert S. Saunders, and LeighAnne Olsen, 294–301 (Washington, DC: National Academies Press, 2010), 299.

84 "The Institute of Medicine . . ." Quoted in ibid., 297.

85 "Hospitals consume more than 5 percent . . ." Total gross domestic product in the fourth quarter of 2009 was $14.2 trillion. See http://www.bea.gov/newsreleases/national/gdp/2011/pdf/gdp4q10_3rd.pdf, accessed April 18, 2011. Total spending on hospitals in 2009 was $761 billion. See https://www.cms.gov/NationalHealthExpendData/25_NHE_Fact_Sheet.asp#TopOfPage, accessed April 18, 2011.

85 "Lewis died from a perforated ulcer . . ." Rosemary Gibson and Janardan Prasad Singh, *Wall of Silence: The Untold Story of the Medical Mistakes That Kill and Injure Millions of Americans* (Washington, DC: Regnery, 2003).

CHAPTER 8

94 "Just as American families . . ." Congressional Budget Office, "Federal Debt and the Risk of a Fiscal Crisis," July 27, 2010, http://www.cbo.gov/ftpdocs/116xx/doc11659/07-27_Debt_FiscalCrisis_Brief.pdf, accessed January 24, 2011.

95 "We expect doctors to make . . ." US Department of Justice, "Five Companies in Hip and Knee Replacement Industry Avoid Prosecution by Agreeing to Compliance Rules and Monitoring," press release, September 27, 2007, http://www.justice.gov/usao/nj/Press/files/pdffiles/Older/hips0927.rel.pdf, accessed January 23, 2011.

96 "I can't say enough about this . . ." Letter to author from Dr. R. G., August 5, 2010.

96 "President Obama took $20 million . . ." Center for Responsive Politics, "Top Industries," http://www.opensecrets.org/pres08/indus.php?cycle=2008&cid=N00009638, accessed January 23, 2011.

96 "According to American University's . . ." Fred Schulte, "DeParle Profited from Health Care Companies under Scrutiny," *Investigative Reporting Workshop*, American University School of Communication, July 2, 2009, http://investigativereportingworkshop.org/investigations/deparle-portfolio/story/deparle-profited-health-care-companies-under-scrut/, accessed December 19, 2010.

96 "DeParle was also . . ." Ibid. DeParle was paid $680,000.

96 "In all my years in the business . . ." E. Scott Reckard and Jim Puzzanghera, "Countrywide's Angelo Mozilo Is Target of Federal Lawsuit," *Los Angeles Times*, June 5, 2009, http://articles.latimes.com/2009/jun/05/business/fi-mozilo5, accessed January 23, 2011.

97 "Excitement grows about how much . . ." See Natasha Singer, "Medical Papers by Ghostwriters Pushed Therapy," *New York Times*, August 5, 2009, http://d.yimg.com/kq/groups/23272106/1890288972/name/Ghostwriters+Paid+by+Wyeth+....pdf, accessed April 18, 2011.

97 "Cancer rates drop . . ." See Gina Kolata, "Sharp Drop in Rates of Breast Cancer Holds," *New York Times* April 19, 2007, http://query.nytimes.com/gst/fullpage.html?res=9a03e6d91e3ff93aa25757c0a9619c8b63; National Institutes of Health, "Decrease in Breast Cancer Rates Related to Reduction in Use of Hormone Replacement Therapy," April 18, 2007, http://www.nih.gov/news/pr/apr2007/nci-18a.htm; Gina Kolata, "Reversing Trend, Big Drop Is Seen in Breast Cancer," *New York Times*, December 15, 2006, http://query.nytimes.com/gst/fullpage.html?res=9F04E5DA1231F936A25751C1A9609C8B63&scp=1&sq=kolata%2C+breast+cancer%2C+hormones%2C+initiative%2C+berry&st=cse&pagewanted=print.

97 "A few years later, another study . . ." Michael Smith, "ASCO: Combined Hormone Therapy Linked to Lung Cancer Mortality," *MedPage Today*, May 31, 2009, http://www.medpagetoday.com/MeetingCoverage/ASCO/14459.

100 "I take no pleasure in this conclusion . . ." Marcia Angell, "Drug Companies and Doctors: A Story of Corruption," *New York Review of Books*, January 15, 2009, http://www.nybooks.com/articles/archives/2009/jan/15/drug-companies-doctorsa-story-of-corruption/?page=2, accessed July 22, 2011.

100 "The banks could not have done . . ." Elliot Blair Smith, "Bringing Down Wall Street as Ratings Let Loose Subprime Scourge," *Bloomberg*, September 24, 2008, http://www.bloomberg.com/apps/news?pid=newsarchive&sid=ah839IWTLP9s, accessed May 13, 2011.

101 "The courts were unwilling . . ." US District Court, Eastern District of Pennsylvania, *United States of America vs. Eli Lilly*, January 15, 2009, 31, http://www.justice.gov/usao/pae/News/2009/jan/lillygovtmementrypleasent.pdf, accessed July 22, 2011.

102 "In the *Wealth of Nations* . . ." Adam Smith, *An Inquiry into the Nature and Causes of the Wealth of Nations* (Edinburgh: Thomas Nelson and Peter Brown, 1827), 54.

102 "Another insurer, Harvard Pilgrim . . ." Massachusetts Attorney General, "Examination of Health Care Cost Trends and Cost Drivers," March 16, 2010, http://www.mass.gov/Cago/docs/healthcare/final_report_w_cover_appendices_glossary.pdf, accessed April 10, 2011.

102 "In some instances, hospitals . . ." Massachusetts Attorney General, "Attorney General Coakley Testifies and Releases Report Regarding Health Care Cost Drivers at DHCFP Hearing," press release, March 16, 2010, http://www.mass.gov/?pageID=cagopressrelease&L=1&L0=Home&sid=Cago&b=pressrelease&f=2010_03_16_ag_testimony_dhcfp_hearing&csid=Cago, accessed October 27, 2010.

103 "In California, hospitals with clout . . ." Jordan Rau, "California Hospitals: Prices Rising Rapidly, But Quality Varies," *Kaiser Health News*, October 18, 2010, http://www.kaiserhealthnews.org/Stories/2010/October/17/california-hospital-costs.aspx, accessed October 27, 2010.

103 "A few months after . . ." In the video, a bespectacled health care executive is seeking advice from a woman who is obviously some kind of expert consultant. He admits, however, that he's been too busy to read the new bill.

104 "Two days before the global . . ." See Frederic S. Mishkin et al., *The Squam Lake Report: Fixing the Financial System* (Princeton, NJ: Princeton University Press, 2010).

105 "People are no longer sure . . ." Nitin Nohria, "Remarks by Nitin Nohria to the Harvard Business School Community," May 4, 2010, http://www.hbs.edu/dean/about-dean-nohria/remarks.html, accessed April 18, 2011.

105 "Bogle observes that . . ." John Bogle, *The Battle for the Soul of Capitalism* (New Haven, CT: Yale University Press, 2006), 98.

106 "Then [when that] isn't enough . . ." Ibid., 15.

106 "Bogle says that America has become . . ." Ibid., 3.

107 "Board members received . . ." Eli Lilly Proxy Statement 2009, 19, http://files.shareholder.com/downloads/LLY/1100865836x0x357090/99D528C9-E7DF-48E2-99B0-8D4FA2403BE8/English.PDF, accessed April 18, 2011.

CHAPTER 9

109 "At Johns Hopkins Hospital . . ." Liz Kowalczyk, "Patient Alarms Often Unheard, Unheeded," *Boston Globe*, February 13, 2011, http://www.boston.com/lifestyle/health/articles/2011/02/13/patient_alarms_often_unheard_unheeded/, accessed April 3, 2011.

110 "A former hospital chief nursing officer . . ." Author communication with Bonnie Jennings, December 16, 2010.

111 "The aggressive timeline . . ." Dean Sittig and David Classen, "Safe Electronic Health Record Use Requires a Comprehensive Monitoring and Evaluation Framework," *Journal of the American Medical Association* 303 (2010): 450–51, http://jama.ama-assn.org/cgi/content/short/303/5/450, accessed November 28, 2010.

112 "A study in the . . ." Ross Koppel et al., "Workarounds to Barcode Medication Administration Systems: Their Occurrences, Causes, and Threats to Patient Safety," *Journal of the American Medical Informatics Association* 15 (2008): 408–23, http://jamia.bmj.com/content/15/4/408.abstract, accessed April 6, 2011.

113 "Six hundred fires . . ." Anesthesia Patient Safety Foundation, fire safety video, http://www.apsf.org/resources_video.php, accessed March 5, 2011.

114 "As the hospital investigated . . ." Diane Suchetka, "Cleveland Clinic Reports Six Operating Room Fires in the Past Year, Three Patients Injured," *Cleveland Plain Dealer*, May 1, 2010, http://blog.cleveland.com/metro/2010/05/clinic_reports_six_operating_r.html, accessed November 28, 2010.

115 From 2005 to 2009 . . ." US Food and Drug Administration, "FDA Issues Statement on Baxter's Recall of Colleague Infusion Pumps," press release, May 3, 2010, https://www.ecri.org/Forms/Documents/FDA_Statement_Baxter_Recall.pdf, accessed April 6, 2011.

116 "In fiscal year 2006 . . ." US Food and Drug Administration, Center for Devices and Radiological Health, "CDRH FY 2006 Highlights," www.fda.gov/downloads/AboutFDA/CentersOffices/CDRH/CDRHReports/ucm129258.pdf, accessed July 22, 2011.

117 "More than three-fourths . . ." Diana Zuckerman, Paul Brown, and Steven Nissen, "Medical Device Recalls and the FDA Approval Process," *Archives of Internal Medicine* 171 (2011): 1006–11, http://archinte.ama-assn.org/cgi/content/abstract/archinternmed.2011.30, accessed February 20, 2011.

CHAPTER 10

121 "A *Washington Post* . . ." "*Washington Post*–ABC News Poll," January 28, 2011, http://www.washingtonpost.com/wp-srv/politics/polls/post poll_01172011.html, accessed January 29, 2011.

121 "A year later . . ." Paul Fronstin, "Sources of Health Insurance and Characteristics of the Uninsured: Analysis of the March 2010 Current Population Survey," *Issue Brief*, no. 347 (September 2010), http://www.ebri.org/pdf/briefs pdf/EBRI_IB_09-2010_No347_Uninsured1.pdf, accessed April 11, 2011.

122 "More than twenty years earlier . . ." Olivia Mitchell, "Benefits for an Older Workforce," (paper prepared for the AARP/Wharton Impact Conference, November 10, 2004), http://assets.aarp.org/www.aarp.org_/articles/international/ MitchellPresentation.pdf, accessed December 31, 2010.

122 "Wages and salaries . . ." See Kaiser Family Foundation and Health Research and Educational Trust, "Employer Health Benefits 2011 Annual Survey," September 2010, http://ehbs.kff.org/, accessed November 24, 2010.

122 "For example, AT&T. . ." Jennifer Haberkorn, "Firms Mulled Dropping Insurance Plan," *Politico*, May 7, 2010, http://dyn.politico.com/printstory .cfm?uuid=72E4D136-18FE-70B2-A8EEC0B227313A08, accessed April 11, 2011.

122 "Governor Philip Bredesen . . ." Philip Bredesen, "ObamaCare's Incentive to Drop Insurance," *Wall Street Journal*, October 21, 2010, http://online.wsj.com/ article/SB10001424052702304510704575562643804015252.html?mod=WSJ _Opinion_LEADTop#printMode, accessed November 24, 2010.

122 "Twenty percent of them say . . ." Mercer Consulting, "Few Employers Planning to Drop Health Plans after Reform Is in Place, Survey Finds," November 9, 2010, http://www.mercer.com/press-releases/1399495, accessed November 15, 2010.

122 "In 2010, 59 percent . . ." Kaiser Family Foundation and Health Research and Educational Trust, "Employer Health Benefits," 5.

122 "Beginning in 2014 . . ." Henry J. Kaiser Family Foundation, "How Are Small Businesses Affected by Health Care Reform?" http://healthreform.kff .org/Faq/How-are-small-businesses-affected-by-health-reform.aspx, accessed July 22, 2011.

123 "By 2007 . . ." Employee Benefit Research Institute, "New Research from EBRI: Downturn Cut Median Retirement Account Balances by at Least 15

Percent," press release, August 4, 2010, http://www.prnewswire.com/news
-releases/new-research-from-ebri-downturn-cut-median-retirement-account
-balances-by-at-least-15-percent-62136627.html, accessed December 31, 2010.

123 "A traditional employee benefit . . ." Mark Merlis, "Health Policy Brief: Early Retiree Insurance," *Health Affairs,* November 23, 2010, 1, http://www.healthaffairs.org/healthpolicybriefs/brief_pdfs/healthpolicybrief_32.pdf?source=newonline, accessed April 10, 2011. See the following for 2010 estimate: Kaiser Family Foundation and Health Research and Educational Trust, "Employer Health Benefits," 5.

123 "The golden age . . ." Mitchell, "Benefits for an Older Workforce."

124 "The Fortune 500 list . . ." Matthew J. Slaughter, "How U.S. Multinational Companies Strengthen the U.S. Economy," Spring 2009, 3, http://www.uscib.org/docs/foundation_multinationals.pdf, accessed January 4, 2011.

125 "More worrying, 39 percent . . ." European Union Chamber of Commerce in China, "European Business in China Position Paper, 2010/2011," http://www.europeanchamber.com.cn/images/documents/marketing_department/beijing/publications/2010/executive_summary.pdf, accessed January 2, 2011.

125 "This strategy makes it hard . . ." U.S.-China Economic and Security Review Commission, *2010 Report to Congress* (Washington, DC: US Government Printing Office, 2010), 59, http://www.uscc.gov/annual_report/2010/annual_report_full_10.pdf, accessed April 11, 2011.

125 "Firms are folding parts . . ." Shai Oster, Norihiko Shirouzu, and Paul Glader, "China Squeezes Foreigners for Share of Global Riches," *Wall Street Journal*, December 28, 2010, http://online.wsj.com/article/SB10001424052970203731004576045684068308042.html, accessed April 11, 2011.

126 "I am not sure . . ." Guy Dinmore and Geoff Dyer, "Immelt Hits Out at China and Obama," *Financial Times*, July 1, 2010, http://www.ft.com/cms/s/0/ed654fac-8518-11df-adfa-00144feabdc0.html#axzz1CSn6ZzXh, accessed January 29, 2011.

126 "The negotiating, the ability to find . . ." Jeffrey Immelt, speech to the American Chamber of Commerce in Shanghai, June 2, 2010, http://www.amcham-shanghai.org/NR/rdonlyres/981258CC-4A05-4AFD-B204-6C95D63194E2/12590/JeffImmeltSpeech_AmChamShanghaieventatUSAP_2JUNE20.pdf, accessed January 29, 2011.

126 "By comparison, the US pace . . ." National Science Foundation, "Science and Engineering Indicators Report, 2010," http://www.nsf.gov/statistics/seind10/c4/c4h.htm, accessed April 11, 2011.

127 "In 10 years. . ." "Remarks by CEO Jim Owens on Policy Implications for Global Competitiveness," *Business Roundtable*, September 10, 2010, http://

businessroundtable.org/news-center/remarks-by-ceo-jim-owens-on-policy
-implications-for-global-competitive/, accessed January 10, 2011.

127 "The United States had a record . . ." US-China Economic and Security
Review Commission, "China's Industrial Policy and Its Impact on U.S. Companies, Workers and the American Economy," March 24, 2009, http://www
.uscc.gov/hearings/2009hearings/transcripts/09_03_24_trans/09_03_24_trans
.pdf, accessed December 29, 2010.

128 "Jobs—and health insurance benefits . . ." See Slaughter, "How U.S. Multinational Companies Strengthen the U.S. Economy."

128 "During the same period . . ." Don Lee, "Outsourcing U.S. Jobs: U.S.
Jobs Continue to Flow Overseas," *Los Angeles Times*, October 6, 2010,
http://articles.latimes.com/print/2010/oct/06/business/la-fi-jobs-offshoring
-20101006, accessed January 3, 2011.

128 "So I guess we can add . . ." "Are Too Many American Jobs Still Being
Outsourced?" *Los Angeles Times*, October 6, 2010, http://latimesblogs.latimes
.com/comments_blog/2010/10/american-jobs-outsourced-offshoring-.html,
accessed January 2, 2011.

CHAPTER 11

131 "He axed $2.85 billion . . ." Nicholas Confessore and Thomas Kaplan,
"With Cuts, Cuomo Offers Shrunken Budget," *New York Times*, February 1, 2011, http://www.nytimes.com/2011/02/02/nyregion/02budget
.html?pagewanted=all, accessed July 22, 2011.

132 "States can generally change . . ." Letter from Kathleen Sebelius to Governors,
February 3, 2011, http://www.hhs.gov/news/press/2011pres/01/20110203c
.html, accessed February 21, 2011.

132 "State officials estimate . . ." George Skelton, "California Could Take Big
Hit from Healthcare Overhaul," *Los Angeles Times*, March 24, 2010, http://
articles.latimes.com/2010/mar/24/local/la-me-cap25-2010mar25, accessed
April 11, 2011.

132 "It makes little sense . . ." Ibid.

133 "The state medical society . . ." Massachusetts Medical Society, "Massachu-
setts Health Reform: Fact Sheet," June 2010, http://www.massmed.org/AM/
Template.cfm?Section=Health_Care_Reform2&TEMPLATE=/CM/Content
Display.cfm&CONTENTID=35254, accessed July 5, 2011.

133 "Health care spending in the state . . ." RAND Corporation, "Controlling Health Care Spending in Massachusetts," *Policy Brief*, 2009, http://www

.rand.org/pubs/research_briefs/RB9464-1/index1.html, accessed November 24, 2010.

134 "In California, the head of the . . ." Sara Murray, "State Finance Directors Warn of More Trouble Ahead," *Wall Street Journal*, November 13, 2009, http://online.wsj.com/article/SB125814283469047497.html, accessed December 2, 2010.

134 "Altogether, the states have . . ." Pew Center on the States, "Pew Study Finds States Face $1 Trillion Shortfall in Retiree Benefits," February 18, 2010, http://www.pewcenteronthestates.org/news_room_detail.aspx?id=57334, accessed April 11, 2011.

135 "In other words, for the past twenty years . . ." Susan Weston, "State Spending for Selected Years," unpublished graphs prepared for the Kentucky Prichard Committee on Academic Excellence, June 1, 2010.

135 "Republicans Jeb Bush . . ." Jeb Bush and Newt Gingrich, "Better Off Bankrupt," *Los Angeles Times*, January 27, 2011, http://articles.latimes.com/2011/jan/27/opinion/la-oe-gingrich-bankruptcy-20110127, accessed February 24, 2011.

136 "States spend more of . . ." National Association of State Budget Officers, "State Expenditure Report, Fiscal Year 2009," fall 2010, http://nasbo.org/LinkClick.aspx?fileticket=w7RqO74llEw%3d&tabid=38, accessed July 22, 2011.

136 "By 2030 nine million Americans . . ." US Census Bureau, "Projections of the Population by Selected Age Groups," http://www.census.gov/population/www/projections/files/nation/summary/np2008-t2.xls, accessed March 19, 2011.

136 "Ryan says, 'Americans . . .'" Paul Ryan, *The Roadmap Plan*, http://www.roadmap.republicans.budget.house.gov/Plan/, accessed April 18, 2011.

137 "There is no justification . . ." Pete Welch, "Welch Introduces Prescription Drug Negotiation Bill," press conference, March 3, 2010, http://www.youtube.com/watch?v=xY59BG4h2pw, accessed March 18, 2011.

CHAPTER 12

140 "The cost of Medicare . . ." National Commission on Fiscal Responsibility and Reform, "The Moment of Truth," December 2010, 31, http://www.c-span.org/pdf/debtCmsn120110.pdf, accessed April 11, 2011.

143 "The IMF is calling on . . ." International Monetary Fund, "U.S. Economy Recovering, Debt and Unemployment Next Challenges," July 8, 2010, http://www.imf.org/external/pubs/ft/survey/so/2010/new070810b.htm, accessed December 30, 2010.

143 "It acknowledges the law's . . ." International Monetary Fund, "United States of America—Concluding Statement of the 2010 Article IV Mission," June 21, 2010, http://www.imf.org/external/np/ms/2010/070810.htm, accessed December 30, 2010.

144 "No triple-A rating is forever . . ." Mark Gongloff, Mark Brown, and Nathalie Boschat, "S&P, Moody's Warn on U.S. Credit Rating," *Wall Street Journal,* January 14, 2011, http://online.wsj.com/article/SB1000142405274870 3583404576079311379009904.html?mod=WSJ_hp_LEFTWhatsNewsCollecti on#articleTabs%3Darticle, accessed January 13, 2011.

145 "Clinton asked . . ." "U.S. Embassy Cables: Hillary Clinton Ponders U.S. Relationship with Its Chinese 'Banker,'" *Guardian,* December 4, 2010, http://www.guardian.co.uk/world/us-embassy-cables-documents/199393, accessed January 20, 2011.

145 "If we're not Americans first . . ." Josh Loftin, "Obama Debt Commission Co-Chair Speaks in Utah," *Bloomberg BusinessWeek,* April 15, 2011, http://www.businessweek.com/ap/financialnews/D9MKCFK00.htm, accessed April 19, 2011.

148 "Throughout our history . . ." Letter from Timothy Geithner to Senator Harry Reid, January 11, 2011.

148 "The program has been 'shoving . . .'" Ricardo Alonso-Zaldivar, "Your Medicare Taxes Won't Cover What You'll Cost," *Associated Press,* December 31, 2010, http://finance.yahoo.com/news/Your-Medicare-taxes-wont -apf-3563455708.html?x=0, accessed July 5, 2011.

148 "Forty-three percent of boomers . . ." "Poll: Baby Boomers Fear Outliving Medicare," *CBS News,* December 29, 2010, http://www.cbsnews.com/stories/2010/12/29/national/main7195298.shtml, accessed April 10, 2011.

149 "But as long as the music is playing . . ." Michiyo Nakamoto and David Wighton, "Citigroup Chief Stays Bullish on Buy-outs," *Financial Times,* July 9, 2007, http://www.ft.com/intl/cms/s/0/80e2987a-2e50-11dc-821c-0000779fd2ac .html#axzz1ZpshST21, accessed April 11, 2011.

149 "Adam Smith said that public debt . . ." Adam Smith, *An Inquiry into the Nature and Causes of the Wealth of Nations* (Edinburgh: Thomas Nelson and Peter Brown, 1827), 395.

CHAPTER 13

155 "One-third of states . . ." Congressional Budget Office, letter to Senator Orrin Hatch, October 9, 2009, 2, http://www.cbo.gov/ftpdocs/106xx/ doc10641/10-09-Tort_Reform.pdf, accessed March 11, 2011.

155 "The health care law . . ." *Patient Protection and Affordable Care Act*, Public Law 111-148, *U.S. Statutes at Large* 124 (March 23, 2010): 119–1025, http://www.gpo.gov/fdsys/pkg/PLAW-111publ148/pdf/PLAW-111publ148.pdf, accessed March 28, 2011. See Section 10607, "State Demonstration Programs to Evaluate Alternatives to Current Medical Tort Litigation."

156 "He said, 'I don't think . . .'" "White House Health Care Summit with Congressional Leaders," *C-SPAN*, February 25, 2010, http://www.c-span.org/Events/White-House-Health-Care-Summit-with-Congressional-Leaders/16350-2/, accessed March 8, 2011.

156 "He said that tort reform . . ." "Remarks by the President in Discussion of the Deficit at Bipartisan Meeting on Health Care Reform," February 25, 2010, http://www.whitehouse.gov/the-press-office/remarks-president-discussion-deficit-bipartisan-meeting-health-care-reform, accessed March 16, 2011.

156 "I don't think that's fair . . ." Ibid.

156 "The Help Efficient . . ." Memorandum to the House Judiciary Committee from Lamar Smith, February 4, 2011, http://judiciary.house.gov/hearings/pdf/Memo282011.pdf, accessed March 16, 2011.

157 "The administration outlined four . . ." Agency for Health Care Research and Quality, "HHS Announces Patient Safety and Medical Liability Demonstration Projects," press release, June 11, 2010, http://www.hhs.gov/news/press/2010pres/06/20100611a.html, accessed March 8, 2011.

157 "When he asked the surgeon . . ." Center for Justice and Democracy, "In Memoriam: Richard Flagg," http://www.centerjd.org/archives/malpractice/stories/Flagg%20Obit.php, accessed March 10, 2011.

158 "The New Jersey state medical board . . ." New Jersey State Board of Medical Examiners, "In the Matter of Santusht Perera," December 4, 2008, 2, http://www.nj.gov/lps/ca/bme/orders/20081204_PERERAS.pdf, accessed March 10, 2011.

158 "We talk about patient and family wishes . . ." Rosemary Gibson and Janardan Prasad Singh, *Wall of Silence: The Untold Story of the Medical Mistakes That Kill and Injure Millions of Americans* (Washington, DC: Regnery), 2003.

159 "The ABC television program . . ." "The Deep Sleep: 6,000 Will Die or Suffer Brain Damage," *ABC News 20/20*, April 22, 1982.

159 "This year, 6,000 patients will die . . ." Quoted in Ellison Pierce Jr., "The 34th Rovenstine Lecture: 40 Years Behind the Mask: Safety Revisited," *Anesthesiology* 84, no. 4 (April 1996): 965–75, http://journals.lww.com/anesthesiology/fulltext/1996/04000/the_34th_rovenstine_lecture__40_years_behind_the.25.aspx, accessed March 5, 2011.

160 "Well, they run quickly . . ." Ibid.

160 "The anesthesiologists said . . ." Anesthesia Patient Safety Foundation, "Foundation History," http://www.apsf.org/about_history.php, accessed March 5, 2011.

160 "At the time, a malpractice crisis . . ." Jeffrey Cooper, "Getting Into Patient Safety: A Personal Story," Agency for Health Care Research and Quality, August 2006, http://www.webmm.ahrq.gov/perspective.aspx?perspectiveID=29, accessed March 10, 2011.

160 "In 1985 Pierce and his colleagues . . ." Anesthesia Patient Safety Foundation, "Foundation History."

160 "You members of the medical profession . . ." O. C. Philips and L. S. Capizzi, "Anesthesia Mortality," in *Public Health Aspects of Critical Care Medicine and Anesthesiology*, ed. Peter Safar, 220–39 (Philadelphia: FA Davis, 1974); cited in Pierce, "The 34th Rovenstine Lecture: 40 Years Behind the Mask."

160 "Dr. Pierce said . . ." Pierce, "The 34th Rovenstine Lecture: 40 Years Behind the Mask."

161 "In 2006 average annual premiums . . ." K. B. Domino, "Malpractice Insurance Premiums: Greater Stability for Most Anesthesiologists," *American Society of Anesthesiologists Newsletter* 70, no. 6 (2006): 6–7, http://depts.washington.edu/asaccp/prof/asa70_6_6_7.shtml, accessed March 8, 2011.

162 "Jeffrey Cooper, now the director . . ." Cooper, "Getting Into Patient Safety."

162 "As a former pediatric surgeon . . ." Author communication with Lucian Leape, March 14, 2011.

163 "Being open with patients . . ." Rick Boothman, presentation at Telluride Summer Symposium on Medical Error Disclosure, July 12, 2010.

163 "In August 2001 . . ." Allen Kachalia et al., "Liability Claims and Costs Before and After Implementation of a Medical Error Disclosure Program," *Annals of Internal Medicine* 115 (2010): 213–221.

163 "[We said,] 'Isn't this a case . . .'" Eve Shapiro, "Disclosing Medical Errors: Best Practices from the 'Leading Edge,'" (paper based on "Disclosure: What's Morally Right Is Organizationally Right," a presentation at the 18th Annual Institute for Healthcare Improvement National Forum on Quality Improvement in Health Care, Orlando, Florida, December 10–13, 2006), 4, http://www.nhpatientvoices.org/downloads/DisclosingMedicalErrors.pdf, accessed March 12, 2011.

164 "A substantial decline in lawsuits . . ." Author communication with Dr. Timothy McDonald, September 28, 2010.

165 "Dr. McDonald, who is also a lawyer . . ." Timothy McDonald, Telluride Summer Symposium on Medical Error Disclosure, July 12, 2010.

165 "And if we make a mistake . . ." Shapiro, "Disclosure of Medical Errors," 14.

166 "Health care spending would decline . . ." Congressional Budget Office, letter to Senator Orrin Hatch, October 9, 2009, 2–3, http://www.cbo.gov/ftpdocs/106xx/doc10641/10-09-Tort_Reform.pdf, accessed March 11, 2011.

166 "Some families are forced into poverty . . ." Author communication with Helen Haskell, March 15, 2011.

166 "While browsing in a bookstore one day . . ." Alan B. Miller, *Reform That Makes Sense: A Detailed Plan to Improve America's Healthcare System, from the Country's Leading Healthcare CEO* (New York: Sterling and Ross, 2009).

167 "He said that every hospital . . ." William J. Mallon, "Codman Considered Father of Evidence-Based Medicine," AAOS *Now*, no. 1 (January–February 2007), http://www.aaos.org/news/bulletin/janfeb07/research1.asp, accessed March 12, 2011.

167 "None did . . ." Duncan Neuhauser, "Ernest Amory Codman MD," *Quality and Safety in Health Care*, 11, no. 1 (2002): 104–5, http://qualitysafety.bmj.com/content/11/1/104.full, accessed March 10, 2011.

168 "They were content, he said . . ." Bill Mallon, "E. Amory Codman Pioneer New England Shoulder Surgeon," New England Shoulder and Elbow Society, http://www.neses.com/news.article.10.3.2009.php, accessed March 11, 2011.

CHAPTER 14

169 "If 10 percent of all health care spending . . ." Centers for Medicare and Medicaid Services, "National Health Expenditures 2009 Highlights," https://www.cms.gov/NationalHealthExpendData/downloads/highlights.pdf, accessed January 11, 2011.

170 "When President George W. Bush requested . . ." John Iglehart, "Finding Money for Health Care Reform—Rooting Out Waste, Fraud, and Abuse," *New England Journal of Medicine* 361 (2009): 229, http://www.nejm.org/doi/pdf/10.1056/NEJMp0904854, accessed May 23, 2011.

170 "In 2011 the Office of the Inspector General . . ." See http://oig.hhs.gov/fraud/fugitives/index.asp.

171 "And it's about time we put . . ." Kathleen Sebelius, "Detroit Fraud Prevention Summit," March 15, 2011, http://www.hhs.gov/secretary/about/speeches/sp20110315.html, accessed May 23, 2011.

171 "What we have seen for many years . . ." "Senate Committee Adds Sanders' Fraud Crackdown to Health Reform Bill," press release, July 13, 2009, http://sanders.senate.gov/newsroom/news/?id=7199664a-d616-4dcb-a5ba-206f28c59e7f, accessed July 25, 2011.

171 "What we have to tell . . ." "Senate Committee Adds Sanders' Fraud Crackdown to Health Reform Bill," http://sanders.senate.gov/newsroom/news/?id=7199664a-d616-4dcb-a5ba-206f28c59e7f, accessed April 18, 2011.

171 "A former federal prosecutor said . . ." Author communication with J. N.

173 "A Washington, DC, law firm . . ." Elizabeth B. Carder-Thompson and Katie Pawlitz, "Pharmaceutical Executives and In-House Counsel Beware: U.S. District Court Affirms Exclusion of Former Purdue Executives Under 'Responsible Corporate Officer' Doctrine," December 2010, http://www.healthindustrywashingtonwatch.com/uploads/file/alert10283(2).pdf, accessed January 31, 2011.

173 "We're going to see more CEOs . . ." Author communication with Patrick Burns, April 20, 2011.

173 "Congressman Stark said . . ." "Stark, Herger Introduce Bipartisan Bill to Fight Medicare Fraud," press release, September 14, 2010, http://www.stark.house.gov/index.php?option=com_content&view=article&id=2034:stark-herger-introduce-bipartisan-bill-to-fight-medicare-fraud&catid=66&Itemid=62, accessed April 17, 2011.

174 "Fortune 500 companies (need to) understand. . ." "Ways and Means Hearing Focuses on Efforts to Combat Waste, Fraud, and Abuse in Medicare," press release, June 15, 2010, http://www.stark.house.gov/index.php?option=com_content&view=article&id=1948:ways-and-means-hearing-focuses-on-efforts-to-combat-fraud-waste-and-abuse-in-medicare&catid=66:2010-press-releases&Itemid=62, accessed April 16, 2011.

174 "The company was accused of . . ." US Department of Justice, "HCA—The Health Care Company and Subsidiaries to Pay $840 Million in Criminal Fines and Civil Damages and Penalties: Largest Government Fraud Settlement in U.S. History," press release, December 14, 2000, http://web.archive.org/web/20030702173234/www.justice.gov/opa/pr/2000/December/696civcrm.htm, accessed January 15, 2011.

175 "I learned very hard lessons . . ." Al Lewis, "Ex-CEO Has Prescription for Politics," *Denver Post*, October 10, 2010, http://www.denverpost.com/allewis/ci_16288222, accessed July 7, 2011.

175 "In an industry notorious for waste . . ." "Governor Scott," Rick Scott for Florida, http://www.rickscottforflorida.com/about/, accessed July 7, 2010.

175 "He sponsored the Health Care Claims . . ." Kathleen Swendiman, "False Claims Act and Health Care Fraud: An Overview," Congressional Research Service, July 10, 1998, http://www.famguardian.org/Subjects/Scams/Reference/98-602.pdf, accessed July 26, 2011.

176 "But money works on them . . ." Gardiner Harris, "Crackdown on Doctors Who Take Kickbacks," *New York Times*, March 3, 2009, www.nytimes.com/2009/03/04/health/policy/04doctors.html, accessed July 28, 2011.

176 "A common come-on might be . . ." Julie Taitsman, "Educating Physicians to Avoid Fraud, Waste, and Abuse," *New England Journal of Medicine* 364 (2011): 102, accessed January 21, 2011. http://www.nejm.org/doi/pdf/10.1056/NEJMp1012609.

177 "The doctors, who were contacted by . . ." Mark Schoofs and Maurice Tamman, "In Medicare's Data Trove, Clues to Curing Cost Crisis," *Wall Street Journal*, October 25, 2010, http://online.wsj.com/article/SB100014240527487046963045755381128566115900.html, accessed January 30, 2011.

178 "It's time to overturn an injunction . . ." Ashby Jones, "How Much Do Doctors Get from Medicare? Dow Jones Sues to Find Out," *Wall Street Journal* blog, January 26, 2011, http://blogs.wsj.com/law/2011/01/26/how-much-do-doctors-get-from-medicare-dow-jones-sues-to-find-out/, accessed April 18, 2011.

178 "The focus should [be] . . ." Michael O. Leavitt and Robert Krughoff, "Release of Medicare Data Could Help Reform Health-Care System," *Washington Post*, March 19, 2010, http://www.washingtonpost.com/wp-dyn/content/article/2010/03/18/AR2010031803637.html, accessed April 17, 2011.

179 "A hospital committee that reviewed the case . . ." US Senate Committee on Finance, *Staff Report on Cardiac Stent Usage at St. Joseph Medical Center*, 111th Cong., 2nd sess., 2010, 5, http://finance.senate.gov/newsroom/chairman/release/?id=ce0c5525-b352-474f-9970-96f5afc140bb, accessed August 4, 2011.

180 "I recommend you take . . ." Ibid., 106.

180 "I heard thru the grapevine . . ." Ibid., 7.

180 "Do I need to send . . ." Ibid., 12.

181 "One exception is . . ." US Department of Justice, "Lafayette, LA Cardiologist Convicted on 51 Counts of Healthcare Fraud," press release, December 31, 2008, http://www.justice.gov/usao/law/news/wdl20081231.pdf, accessed April 18, 2011.

181 "In Salisbury, Maryland, a cardiologist . . ." US Department of Justice, "Salisbury Cardiologist Indicted for Implanting Unnecessary Cardiac Stents," press release, September 1, 2010, http://www.justice.gov/usao/md/Public-Affairs/press_releases/Press10/Salisbury%20Cardiologist%20Indicted%20for%20Implanting%20Unnecessary%20Cardiac%20Stents.pdf, accessed April 18, 2011.

181 "I am proud to have you . . ." Committee on Finance, *Staff Report*, 106.

181 "When device maker Medtronic . . ." "Medtronic to Voluntarily Disclose Payments to U.S. Physicians," press release, February 24, 2009, http://www.medtronic.com/Newsroom/NewsReleaseDetails.do?itemId=1235482300024%26%239001%3B=en_US, accessed April 18, 2011.

CHAPTER 15

187 "The manufacturer tweaked the drug . . ." Joanne Armstrong, "Unintended Consequences—The Cost of Preventing Preterm Births after FDA Approval of a Branded Version of 17OHP," *New England Journal of Medicine* 364 (May 5, 2011): 1689–91, http://healthpolicyandreform.nejm.org/?p=13971, accessed April 18, 2011.

Index

Abbott, 179–81
accountable care organizations (ACOs), 103–104
AKPD Message and Media, 22
Allergan, 78–79
American Academy of Family Physicians, 55
American College of Surgeons, 32
American Hospital Association (AHA), 30, 65, 84
American Medical Association (AMA), 31, 51, 183
American Society of Anesthesiologists, 160–61
American Society of Civil Engineers, 127
America's Health Insurance Plans, 11; health reform lobbying, 12–13; opposition to public option, 11–12
Amazon, 128
Arizona, 131; Medicaid cuts, 131; budget constraints, 131
Assurant Health, 9
AT&T, calculating cost of reform, 122
aviation safety, 73–74
Axelrod, David, 22

Bale, Phillip, 56
bankruptcy, 146; companies, filing for, 101; consumers, filing for, 3, 146,

166; federal government, 3, 139, 144, 183
Baxter infusion pumps, 116
Berwick, Donald, 156
Bextra, 24–25
Biden, Joe, 29, 46
Biomet, 95
Birkmeyer, John, 81
Blackman, Lewis, 85
Blair House summit, 58, 155
Boehner, John, 11
Bogle, John, 105–107
Boothman, Rick, 163–65
Bredesen, Philip, 122
Brown, Jerry, 131
Brown, Scott, 25, 132
Buffet, Warren, 129
bundled payments, 87
Bush, George W., 16–17, 43, 93, 139, 140, 170

Cadillac tax, 44
Center for Public Integrity, 177
Center for Responsive Politics, 60
China: Americans' perception of, 121; competition from, 3, 124; credit rating of, 145; impact on American jobs, 4, 119, 125–28; manufacturing and investment, 121; US federal

government borrowing from, 37, 140, 145, 149
Christie, Christopher, 95
Cincinnati Children's Hospital, 83–85
Codman, Ernest A, 167–68
Columbia/HCA, 174–75
Commercial Aviation Safety Team (CAST), 74
conflict of interest, 89, 94–96, 100, 106, 184
Congressional Budget Office: international drug price comparisons, 23; impact of drug company fees, 45; estimates of savings from Medicare payment innovations, 87; medical malpractice costs, 166
Conrad, Kent, 58–59
Consumer Reports, 53, 115, 186
consumption: use of debt to increase, 93; health care, 93; compared with investment, 126
COPIC, 70
corporate influence, in health care reform law, 2, 8, 26, 33–34, 48
Cuomo, Andrew, 131

Daschle, Tom, 33
Dean, Howard, 10–11
death panels, 39–40
Debt Reduction Commission, 120
default, federal government, 4, 139–44
defined benefits: employers, 123; Medicare, 136
defined contribution: employers, 123; Medicare voucher plan, 136
DeParle, Nancy Ann, 96
DePuy Orthopaedics, 95
donut hole, 59–61
Dorgan, Byron, 23
Dow Jones & Company lawsuit for access to Medicare data, 178
drug importation, Obama's position on, 21–23
drug industry: fraud in, 24; opposition to Independent Payment Advisory

Board, 26; support for health care reform, 22–23
Durbin, Dick, 156

economic security as health care security, 3, 121, 127, 147
Eisenhower, Dwight, 36
Eli Lilly, 26–28, 101–102, 107; repeal of independent payment advisory board, 26–27
Emanuel, Ezekiel, 49
Emanuel, Rahm, 33, 49
employer-provided health insurance: trends, 121–23; impact of global competition on, 127–28; impact of health care reform on providing coverage, 122; impact of increasing health care costs, 150
European Union Chamber of Commerce, 124
excise tax, on medical devices, 45, 48

False Claims Act, 171
Federal Aviation Administration, 70, 74
Feinstein, Dianne, 19
Feldstein, Martin, 107
Financial Crisis Inquiry Committee, 141
Flagg, Richard, 157-58
Food and Drug Administration (FDA), 23–25, 27, 78–79, 97, 115–17

Geithner, Timothy, 145, 147
global competition, 121, 123–24, 127, impact on employer-provided benefits, 119
Government Accountability Office, 54, 100, 169
Great Recession, 1, 3, 121, 128, 133, 143, 149
Greater Boston Interfaith Coalition, 133

Harvard Business School, 105
Harvard School of Regulation, 104–105, 185
Hawkins, Bill, 181

health care executive compensation, 35–36

health care fraud, 169–78; cost of, 169

health care harm, mortality from: estimates for Medicare beneficiaries, 65; hospital-acquired infections, 67; Institute of Medicine, *To Err Is Human*, 66; medical mistakes, 67; overtreatment, 68; response of American Hospital Association to, 65–66

health care reform, impact on federal deficit, 49

health care spending: as a percent of GDP, 146, 149; impact on federal budget, 120

health insurance premiums: cost of insurance with the individual mandate, 47-48; definition of unreasonable increase in, 19; limits on federal authority to control, 18; proposed legislation to limit increases in, 19

highway safety, 72–73

hospital-acquired infections, 63, 67–68, 71–72, 99, 104, 114, 166, 184

hospital readmissions, 86–87

hospital industry: exemption from Independent Payment Advisory Board, 30; hospital-acquired infections and, 71–72; opposition to Medicare penalties for poor quality care, 71; support for health care reform, 29–30

House Ways and Means Committee, 54

Hudson, Henry, 16

Ignagni, Karen, 11, 70

Immelt, Jeffrey, 125–26, 128

income redistribution from health reform, 44

Independent Payment Advisory Board: AMA position on, 31; description, 19, 26; health care industry position on, 26; hospital exemption, 30; International Monetary Fund and, 143; recommendation to keep, 120, 183; repeal, 26–27, 30

individual mandate: constitutionality, 15–16; cost of, 47–48; Massachusetts, 133; Obama's position, 12; penalties to enforce, 29; voting on, 14

Inland Valley Regional Medical Center, 63

Institute of Medicine, 34, 52, 66, 69, 84

insurance coverage, expansion under health care reform, 29

International Monetary Fund, 4, 120, 141–44

Jassie, Larry, 53–54

Johns Hopkins Hospital, 90, 109

Johnson & Johnson, 95

Kahn, Charles "Chip," 31

Kennedy, Anthony, 17

Kennedy, Ted, 25

Kessler, Gladys, 15–16

Kindler, Jeff, 23–24

lap-band surgery, 78–79

Lieberman, Joseph, 30

Lincoln, Abraham, 5

Litvak, Eugene, 82–85

Loucks, Mike, 24

Massachusetts: health care reform, 132–33; analysis of contracts between insurance companies and hospitals, 102–103, 186

McAllen, Texas, 81

McDermott, Jim, 54

McDonald, Timothy, 163–65

McDonnell, Bob, 14

Medicaid: expansion under health reform, 20, 132; cuts in spending, 130–31; Sebelius letter to governors, 131

medical homes, 60

medical-industrial complex, 2, 37, 40, 60–61, 80, 88, 94–95, 136 medical malpractice: improved safety prevents, 161, 165; tort reform, 155–59; wrong-site surgery, 70

Medicare: donut hole closed, 60–61; drug price discounts in health reform, 22; estimates of patient harm, 65; Independent Payment Advisory Board, 19, 26; negotiating drug prices, 21; physician reimbursement, 32–33; prescription drug benefit, 38; Ryan voucher plan, 136–37; spending cuts in health care reform, 29

Medicare Advantage plans, bonuses paid to, 46–47

Medicare Payment Advisory Commission, 47

Medtronic, 181

Messina, Jim, 23

McCain, John, 11, 107, 155

Midei, Mark, 179–80

Mozilo, Angelo, 96

Moon, Norman, 15

Morris, Lewis, 174–75

Moyers, Bill, 33

Nader, Ralph, 72

National Academy of Engineering, 52, 60

Neurontin, 24

Obama, Barack: campaign pledges on health care, 21; drug importation, 23; signing the health care reform law, 1

oligopolies, health care firms as, 104–105

operating room fires, 113–14

Orszag, Peter, 49

overuse of medical care, 3, 53, 63, 181

Owens, Jim, 127

pathological mutation, 105-107, 117

Patient-Centered Outcomes Research Institute, 87

Patient Protection and Affordable Care Act: affordability, 35; signed into law, 8

payroll taxes, 43, 148–49

Pelosi, Nancy, 19, 32, 127, 137, 150

penalties, for not buying insurance, 13, 16, 17, 29, 45, 48, 122

Pfizer: accountability of, 102; criminal prosecution of, 24–25; health reform negotiation, 23–24; Prempro, 97–99; proxy statement on payment to Kindler, 24

Pharmaceutical Research and Manufacturers of America (PhRMA): health care reform, 21–22; repeal of payment board, 26

Prempro, 97–99

price bubbles, 89, 92–94, 106

primary care doctors: impact of RUC, 54–55, 183; increased payment for in health reform law, 32, 58–59; medical homes, 60; reasons for shortage, 51, 53–56; shortage of doctors, 32, 184

Prince, Charles, 149

Public Citizen, 24

public option, 10–12, 29

Quaid, Dennis, 67

Rancho Springs Medical Center, 63

recommendation for Harvard School of Regulation, 104–105

regulation: authority to regulate health insurance premiums, 18–19; of health care for safety, 185; of the marketplace, 104–105

Reid, Harry, 38

Relative-Value Scale Update Committee (RUC), 54, 183

Rockefeller, Jay, 30

Rohack, J. James, 31

Romney, Mitt, 132

Roosevelt, Franklin, 2, 142

Rumsfeld, Donald, 67

Ryan, Paul, 136–37

Sanders, Bernie, 171

Schakowsky, Jan, 19

Scott, Rick, 174–75

Sebelius, Kathleen: health care fraud, 171; hospital-acquired infections, 71; letter to governors on cutting Medicaid spending, 131; letter to Karen Ignagni, 17; response to insurance premium increases, 18

Securities and Exchange Commission, 65, 96, 104

Simpson, Alan, 145

Smith, Adam, 35, 102, 149

Smith and Nephew, 95

socialized losses, 4, 70, 98–99, 116, 159, 184

Standard & Poor's, 1, 100, 144

Steeh, George, 115

Stiglitz, Joseph, 28, 100

Stryker, 95

subsidy for purchase of health insurance: amount, 48–49; eligibility, 47; in Massachusetts, 133

suntan tax, 46

Sutter Health, 103

Tauzin, Billy, 22–23, 25

tax increases in health reform, 43–45

The Treatment Trap, 94, 53

The Joint Commission, 100–101

Titanic, 150

too big to fail, 3, 33, 89, 91–107, 136, 173

toxic assets, 3, 89, 92, 96–99, 106

trillion dollars, how much is, 139

triple-A rating, US loss of, 144–45

Umbdenstock, Richard, 30, 71

UnitedHealth Group, 9, 11

Universal Health Services (UHS), 64–65, 81

unnecessary surgery, 68, 176

US-China Economic Security Review Commission, 125

US Chamber of Commerce, 11

US Department of Justice, 27, 81, 97, 153, 174–75, 179

US Supreme Court: *Citizens United v. Federal Election Commission*, 137; health care reform, 17;

Vinson, Roger, 16

Virginia legislature, vote on individual mandate, 14

Wall of Silence, 158

Wall Street fever, 3, 16, 89

Waxman, Henry, 9

Welch, Pete, 137

WellPoint, 9, 11, 18

White House Commission on Debt Reduction, 145

Whitehouse, Sheldon, 30

WikiLeaks, 145

wrong-site surgery, 70

Zimmer, 95

Zyprexa, 27, 28

About the Authors

Rosemary Gibson is a distinguished leader in US health care. At the Robert Wood Johnson Foundation, she designed and led national initiatives to improve health care. She was vice president of the Economic and Social Research Institute and served as senior associate at the American Enterprise Institute. She is principal author of *Wall of Silence* and *The Treatment Trap*. She serves as an editor for the Archives of Internal Medicine series, *Less Is More*.

Janardan Prasad Singh is an economist at the World Bank. He has been a member of the International Advisory Council for several prime ministers of India. He worked on economic policy at the American Enterprise Institute and on foreign policy at the United Nations. He has also written extensively on health care, social policy, and economic development, and was a member of the Board of Contributors of the *Wall Street Journal*. He is coauthor of *Wall of Silence* and *The Treatment Trap*.